Palgrave Philosophy Today

Series Editor: **Vittorio Bufacchi**, Unive

CW00548451

The *Palgrave Philosophy Today* series [
major areas of philosophy currently being taught in philosophy departments
around the world. Each book gives a state-of-the-art informed assessment of a key
area of philosophical study. In addition, each title in the series offers a distinct
interpretation from an outstanding scholar who is closely involved with current
work in the field. Books in the series provide students and teachers with not only
a succinct introduction to the topic, with the essential information necessary
to understand it and the literature being discussed, but also a demanding and
engaging entry into the subject.

Titles include:

Helen Beebee
FREE WILL
An Introduction

Shaun Gallagher
PHENOMENOLOGY

Simon Kirchin
METAETHICS

Duncan Pritchard
KNOWLEDGE

Mathias Risse
GLOBAL POLITICAL PHILOSOPHY

Joel Walmsley
MIND AND MACHINE

Forthcoming Titles:

Pascal Engel
PHILOSOPHY OF PSYCHOLOGY

James Robert Brown
PHILOSOPHY OF SCIENCE

Neil Manson
ENVIRONMENTAL PHILOSOPHY

Chad Meister
PHILOSOPHY OF RELIGION

Lilian O'Brien
PHILOSOPHY OF ACTION

Don Ross
PHILOSOPHY OF ECONOMICS

Nancy Tuana
FEMINISM AND PHILOSOPHY

Palgrave Philosophy Today
Series Standing Order ISBN 978–0–230–00232–6 (hardcover)
Series Standing Order ISBN 978–0–230–00233–3 (paperback)
(*outside North America only*)

You can receive future titles in this series as they are published by placing a standing order. Please contact your bookseller or, in case of difficulty, write to us at the address below with your name and address, the title of the series and the ISBN quoted above.

Customer Services Department, Macmillan Distribution Ltd, Houndmills, Basingstoke, Hampshire RG21 6XS, England

Also by Helen Beebee

HUME ON CAUSATION

METAPHYSICS: The Key Concepts (*with Nikk Effingham and Philip Goff*)

THE OXFORD HANDBOOK OF CAUSATION (*co-edited with Christopher Hitchcock and Peter Menzies*)

READING METAPHYSICS (*co-edited/authored with Julian Dodd*)

THE SEMANTICS AND METAPHYSICS OF NATURAL KINDS (*co-edited with Nigel Sabbarton-Leary*)

TRUTHMAKERS: The Contemporary Debate (*co-edited with Julian Dodd*)

Free Will

An Introduction

Helen Beebee
Samuel Hall Professor of Philosophy, University of Manchester, UK

First published 2013 by
PALGRAVE MACMILLAN

Palgrave Macmillan in the UK is an imprint of Macmillan Publishers Limited,
registered in England, company number 785998, of Houndmills, Basingstoke,
Hampshire RG21 6XS.

Palgrave Macmillan in the US is a division of St Martin's Press LLC,
175 Fifth Avenue, New York, NY 10010.

Palgrave Macmillan is the global academic imprint of the above companies
and has companies and representatives throughout the world.

Palgrave® and Macmillan® are registered trademarks in the United States,
the United Kingdom, Europe and other countries

ISBN: 978–0–230–23292–1   (hardback)
ISBN: 978–0–230–23293–8   (paperback)

This book is printed on paper suitable for recycling and made from fully
managed and sustained forest sources. Logging, pulping and manufacturing
processes are expected to conform to the environmental regulations of the
country of origin.

A catalogue record for this book is available from the British Library.

A catalog record for this book is available from the Library of Congress.

Contents

Series Editor's Preface

It is not easy being a student of philosophy these days. All the different areas of philosophy are reaching ever increasing levels of complexity and sophistication, a fact which is reflected in the specialised literature and readership each branch of philosophy enjoys. And yet, anyone who studies philosophy is expected to have a solid grasp of the most current issues being debated in most, if not all, the other areas of philosophy. It is an understatement to say that students of philosophy today are faced with a Herculean task.

The books in this new series by Palgrave are meant to help all philosophers, established and aspiring, to understand, appreciate and engage with the intricacies which characterise the many faces of philosophy. They are also ideal teaching tools as textbooks for more advanced students. These books may not be meant primarily for those who have yet to read their first book of philosophy, but all students with a basic knowledge of philosophy will benefit greatly from reading these exciting and original works, which will enable anyone to engage with all the defining issues in contemporary philosophy.

There are three main aspects that make the *Palgrave Philosophy Today* series distinctive and attractive. First, each book is relatively short. Second, the books are commissioned from some of the best-known, established and upcoming international scholars in each area of philosophy. Third, while the primary purpose is to offer an informed assessment of opinion on a key area of philosophical study, each title presents a distinct interpretation from someone who is closely involved with current work in the field.

In recent years Helen Beebee has established herself as an international authority in metaphysics, arguably the oldest and most eminent of all branches of philosophy. Now she tackles one of the most enduring questions in metaphysics, the nature of free will. More specifically, in this book Beebee sets out to answer the question: what are the conditions under which people have free will?

The problem of free will is at the crossroads of many concerns in philosophy, so much so that it is virtually impossible to make sense of the human condition without, at some point, venturing into issues of free will. It is also widely recognised as one of the most difficult questions in philosophy; anecdotal evidence suggests that the problem of free will is to blame for more unfinished PhD theses than any other philosophical problem. Rescue is finally here! Beebee has written the perfect book: readers will understand this philosophical puzzle (perhaps for the first time), appreciate its complexity, and even have a laugh along the way, and all this in less than 200 pages. This is a book that will delight both novices and experts. For those uninitiated to the problem of free will, mysterious concepts such as determinism, indeterminism, compatibilism, incompatibilism, and libertarianism will be comprehensively explained, while experts in the field will be challenged by Beebee's own original views on the matter.

Finally, as Beebee takes us through this philosophical maze, the related issue of moral responsibility looms large at every turn; this is one reason why moral philosophers will benefit from reading this book as much as metaphysicians.

Vittorio Bufacchi
University College Cork, Ireland

Preface

This book tackles one of the great questions of metaphysics: Do we have free will? In fact, quite a lot of the book is taken up with a slightly different question: What are the *conditions* under which people have free will? That is, how do we, or the world around us, or both, have to be, in order for it to be true that we act freely at least some of the time? This is because we can't, unfortunately, answer the first question unless we have an answer to the second question. If I asked you whether there are any *blurgs*, you wouldn't be able to answer the question unless you already knew what a *blurg* is – that is, what it *takes* for something to be a *blurg*. If by 'blurg' I just mean 'elephant', then of course there are blurgs. If, on the other hand, I mean 'elephant bigger than my house', then there aren't. Similarly, we need to figure out what we *mean* when we say that someone has free will before we can figure out whether any of us actually has it.

The debate about whether or not we have free will has raged long and hard, and it shows no sign of abating. This book offers no decisive answers. I express my own views at various points, and sometimes I even argue for them, but I'm not naïve enough to think that those views are unimpeachable; philosophical views never are. You might think that this is a reason to think that there is really no fact of the matter about whether or not we have free will – maybe it's a question that just can't be answered, or one that doesn't even make sense. I think this would be a mistake. Philosophical questions are hard – not because you have to be really clever to answer them (though doubtless being really clever is going to help), but, at least in part, because philosophers have so few concrete, definitive, uncontestable facts to appeal to – the kinds of data that can settle answers to other kinds of question. If I claim that there's an elephant outside the window, you can verify – or, more likely, refute – this claim by taking a look. (Or so we ordinarily suppose. Of course, it's conceivable that you're hallucinating, or that there's an elephant squeezed into the bus parked outside, or whatever – so maybe you can't *absolutely conclusively* verify the presence or absence of an elephant. But now we've moved onto philosophical territory.)

Similarly, if I claim to be making a cup of tea, you can verify this claim by looking at what I'm doing, at least if you're in the same room. If I tell you I'm *freely* making a cup of tea, however, observing my behaviour clearly isn't going to be enough to verify my claim. So, what else would you need to know? That's the million-dollar question. Would knowing enough about my current state of mind be enough? Would you need to know whether my current state of mind was *determined* to be the way it is by facts about my genetic make-up, upbringing, and so on? These are the kinds of question that this book aims to shed some light on.

Having started out by saying that whether we have free will is one of the great questions of metaphysics, it's perhaps worth saying something about what metaphysics *is*. This is an extremely difficult thing to do in the abstract – and, needless to say, philosophers cannot agree amongst themselves what metaphysics is. Perhaps the best way to describe metaphysics is to contrast it with other areas of philosophy. For example, *epistemology* is the study of *knowledge*: epistemologists worry about what makes a belief count as knowledge, the circumstances in which a belief is and isn't justified, and so on. The philosophy of language, unsurprisingly, concerns the nature of language, so philosophers of language ask, for example, what it is for a linguistic expression to have *meaning*, or to mean the same thing as some other expression; what it is for a sentence or proposition to be *true*; and so on. Metaphysics is the study of, well, the nature of *reality*: what is the *world* (including us inhabitants of the world) like?

You might think that this is a question for scientists rather than philosophers. Of course, scientists do study the nature of reality. But it certainly doesn't look as though *all* the questions we want to ask about the nature of reality are susceptible to scientific investigation. Take, for example, the question of whether God exists. This is certainly a question about the nature of reality, but it is very implausible to think that it's one that can be answered by looking to the sciences. God, if he exists, has no spatio-temporal location (or perhaps occupies *all* spatio-temporal locations, since he is omnipresent). There are no scientific instruments that can detect his presence. So how on earth could a scientist go about *searching* for this elusive entity? On the other hand, there are plenty of *philosophical* considerations we can bring to bear on the question of God's existence. Is the existence of evil incompatible with the existence of God? Does the amazing complexity and organisation of the Universe imply that it has a designer? And so on.

The question about the existence of free will, as we'll see, isn't in quite the same boat as the question about the existence of God. For – once we've figured out what *conditions* are required for acting freely – it *may* turn out that it *is* discoverable by broadly empirical methods whether or not anyone ever satisfies those definitions. Nonetheless, whether or not this is so is itself a philosophical – indeed, a metaphysical – question. And, again as we'll see, how best to answer the question about the existence of free will itself depends at various points on how we answer various *other* metaphysical questions. These include questions about the laws of nature, modality (that is, the notions of necessity and possibility), determinism and causation.

Having contrasted metaphysics with various other branches of enquiry, it's worth noting that the concept of *moral responsibility* looms extremely large in this book. This being so, you might wonder why I'm characterising it as a book about metaphysics rather than moral philosophy. The short answer is this: The reason why questions about free will and questions about moral responsibility are intimately related is that acting freely is generally (though not without exception) taken to be a *precondition* for moral responsibility. So, one way of 'testing' (without using any scientific instruments, obviously) whether or not it's plausible to think that someone has acted freely is to think about whether or not it's plausible to think that they were culpable for what they did.

Nonetheless, freedom of the will and moral responsibility are distinct. After all, most of the acts we perform as we go about our daily lives are ones for which questions of culpability simply don't arise. If you were to ask whether I was morally responsible for making a cup of tea just now, I'd think you were asking a very odd question indeed (unless, of course, I was doing it in order to annoy you, or in the circumstances it was an exceptionally generous thing for me to do, or I did it knowing full well that doing it was likely to blow up the entire street somehow; but I can assure you that I was not in any of these situations). So, if we want to know whether I just made the tea *freely* – or indeed whether anyone, ever, does anything freely – we'll have to do some metaphysics.

A few words are in order about whom this book is aimed at. It presupposes no prior knowledge of philosophy at all: I have tried to explain all the concepts and issues you need to know about as I go along. On the other hand, parts of the book are pretty challenging. If you're a philosophical novice, you may find those parts heavy going – but not, I hope, impossible, if you approach them with an open mind, a willingness to think hard, and a supply of strong coffee. If you make it all the way to the end, you really will know quite a lot about the contemporary free will debate. More importantly, you'll have the resources you need for trying to figure out for yourself whether reading the book was something you did of your own free will.

Finally, I owe sincere thanks to Matthew Elton, Ben Matheson and Al Mele, who all provided me with incredibly helpful comments on an earlier draft of the book. Thanks also to Brendan George and Priyanka Gibbons at Palgrave and Vittorio Bufacchi, the series editor, for their patience and encouragement.

1
Free Will: The Basics

1.1 Introduction

Are we morally responsible for what we do? Ordinarily, we take it for granted that we are. You might feel guilty about forgetting your mother's birthday, or declining a friend's party invitation when you knew they really wanted you to go. If your mother forgets *your* birthday, or your friend declines your invitation, you might resent them for it, and you might (or might not) forgive them later; whereas, if a friend does something kind for you, you might be grateful to them. These emotional responses are central to our lives, and they are part and parcel of our conception of ourselves and others as bearers of moral responsibility. If we were to think that we are not really morally responsible for what we and others do, it would be inappropriate to feel guilty when we harm others, or resentful or grateful when other people do things that harm or benefit us.

So, what are the conditions under which someone is truly morally responsible for what they do? That's a big question, and this book focuses on just one aspect of it, namely *freedom of the will*. Our starting point is that one requirement that must be satisfied if someone is to be morally responsible for a given act, such as doing a favour for a friend, is that one perform the act *freely*.

It's easy to see why acting freely looks like a plausible requirement on moral responsibility. Imagine, for example, that it turns out that the reason your friend declined your invitation was that she was coerced into doing it: some deranged enemy of yours, hell-bent on ensuring that your party is a failure, had made it clear that if she were to accept, there would be terrible repercussions for her and all her family. In that case, it would certainly be inappropriate for you to resent her for declining the invitation, and it would be inappropriate because she didn't decline freely. We might put this in other words by saying that she didn't really have a *choice* about whether to decline.

Another kind of situation that seems to remove or diminish moral responsibility concerns one's mental state at the time of the action. Consider 'crimes of passion', where the perpetrator is so overwhelmed by their emotional state – anger, say – that they lose their ability to control their actions. A woman who has been subjected to domestic abuse over a long period of time finally cracks and – without premeditation – stabs her husband to death. Or perhaps she discovers him in the throes of passion with another woman, and – again without premeditation – kills them both. Such cases are legal and moral minefields, but insofar as we take the perpetrators of such acts to lack or have a lower degree of responsibility for their action, we do so because we judge that they were not fully in *control* of what they were doing. And, again, we might put this by saying that they were not acting *freely*, or *of their own free will*.

A third kind of case concerns the personal history of the person whose action we're evaluating. Imagine that your car is stolen. You very much resent the perpetrator of this crime – let's call her Carly. When Carly is apprehended, however, you discover a lot of facts about her life history. She was born into a family of car thieves, was taught to break into cars at a very young age and was expected to assist her parents in their nightly car-thieving rounds, and was generally lacking in any kind of moral education: she was praised for doing some things (stealing cars, for example) and punished for others, but was never taught or encouraged to think about the reasons why some acts are apparently praiseworthy and others merit punishment. Having learned all of this, you *might* take the view that Carly is not really morally responsible for stealing your car after all: it is really her parents who are to blame for having raised her in the way they did. Carly is disposed to steal cars without even considering whether doing so is right or wrong, but this aspect of her character is one that she was not responsible for forming: it is a result of her upbringing, and she had no control over how that went.

This third kind of case might start to make you feel a little uncomfortable, because, of course, we are all the product of a certain kind of upbringing. Most of us are not brought up to be car thieves – indeed, unlike Carly, we may have been brought up to think carefully about the difference between right and wrong. But that we have that kind of character is just as much a product of our upbringing as Carly's character is a product of *her* upbringing; and – you might start to worry – we are therefore no more morally responsible for our behaviour than Carly is. After all, we had no more choice over who our parents are than she did. Moreover, we are at the mercy not only of the upbringing our parents subjected us to, but also the genes that they endowed us with; and it is entirely possible that many aspects of our character are also influenced by our genetic make-up. And, of course, the same point applies to our parents, too. We might be inclined to blame Carly's parents, rather than Carly, for her car-stealing habit, but they, in turn, were the products of their own upbringing and genetic make-up every bit as much as Carly was. And again, the same point applies to our own parents as well.

The question all of this raises is: Where, if anywhere, does the buck stop – and, if it stops anywhere, *why* does it stop just there? Here's one way you might try to answer that question. Thinking about Carly, you might say: Well, whether or not Carly is morally responsible for stealing my car depends on whether her upbringing and so on *determined* her to steal the car, or whether instead she still had a *choice* about whether to steal it or not. Perhaps her upbringing strongly disposed her towards a life of crime, but perhaps, nonetheless, she was able to *do otherwise* than steal the car. After all, presumably earlier that evening she was sitting down thinking about what she was going to do later on, and after thinking about it, she decided that she would go out car-stealing. But – we might suppose – she didn't *have* to make that decision. She could have decided to stay at home instead, or go to the cinema, or do whatever else she was considering doing. In that case, she really *is* morally responsible for stealing your car. If, on the other hand, her upbringing and so on really did *determine* that there was only one decision she could make in the circumstances – *viz*, to go out car-stealing – then she *isn't* morally responsible for it.

This brings us to what is sometimes known as 'the problem of free will' (although, as we shall see, there is more than one problem of free will), namely, the problem of the apparent incompatibility of free will with *determinism*. The basic idea here is that if someone is *determined* to behave in the way that they do – if Carly, for example, is determined to steal your car by her upbringing, current circumstances and other factors – then it would appear that they do not act *freely*, since there is nothing else they *could* have done. In other words, they *could not have done otherwise* than what they actually did (in Carly's case, stealing your car). If being fully determined to behave in a certain way by one's upbringing (or whatever) deprives one of the ability to do otherwise, and if being able to do otherwise is required for acting freely, then being so determined is incompatible with acting freely. And, finally, if acting freely is required for being morally responsible for that act, then being determined to act is incompatible with moral responsibility.

The argument just rehearsed is known as the 'Consequence Argument', and we'll come back to it in §1.4. Philosophers tend to fall into two broad camps when it comes to the Consequence Argument. Some are in fundamental sympathy with it: they think that determinism and free will just can't be compatible. Such philosophers are known, unsurprisingly, as *incompatibilists*. Other philosophers, on the other hand, think there is something fishy about the Consequence Argument. They think that determinism and free will don't need to be at odds with one another. For obvious reasons, these philosophers are known as *compatibilists*. (Actually, this is oversimplifying the situation. Some incompatibilists are motivated not by the Consequence Argument but by other arguments for the incompatibility of free will and determinism. We'll come back to these other arguments in §1.5.)

The Consequence Argument gets its intuitive pull from the thought that acting freely requires, to use Daniel Dennett's apt phrase, 'elbow room'. If I *freely* decide whether to steal a car or go to my friend's party, surely I *could* have made a different decision: the decision not to steal the car, say, or the decision to go to the party after all. And the claim is that determinism rules such alternative possibilities out; hence, if determinism is true, we never act freely.

We might, however, ask from the outset whether this kind of 'elbow room' really is required. Consider Wally, who finds a wallet lying in the street. He knows that there is a police station around the corner, and, without even considering the option of taking the wallet himself or pocketing the cash it contains, he hands it in to the police station. That's just the kind of person he is: he's the kind of person who doesn't steal other people's money, even when that money has been left carelessly lying around in the street – not ever. (Well, perhaps he would consider taking – or even actually take – the money if he were flat broke and needed the money to buy drugs to save his ailing grandmother, or some such. But let's assume that this is not the situation that Wally is in right now.) In other words, given Wally's character, taking the money simply isn't a possibility that is open to him: it's not something he could do. Now, do we want to say that Wally is praiseworthy for handing in the wallet? Many compatibilist philosophers (myself included) – those who think that free will and determinism are compatible with one another – say 'yes'. No matter if his upstanding character is entirely determined by the moral education he underwent as a child; he was brought up to do the right thing, and here he is, doing the right thing, and for the right reasons. If, instead, we were to take the view that Wally is only morally responsible – and so only praiseworthy – for having handed in the wallet if he was *not* fully determined by his upbringing, via the formation of his character, to do that, then we would have to say that he is not praiseworthy for handing in the wallet. Poor Wally! If only his parents hadn't done such a good job, and had instead left him with some slight inclination to keep the wallet for himself, he'd have deserved a pat on the back for handing in the wallet. As it is, he's just doing what he was determined to do – no pat on the back for him.

You might be inclined to respond to this case by saying that – despite the fact that I've tried to rule this out in the way I set it up – Wally *could* have taken the money for himself, assuming that he is a normal, thoughtful and reflective person (which he is): he was entirely *capable* of acting out of character on this particular occasion. In that case, here's an exercise for you. Try and think of something you really *could not* do. (It doesn't have to be something you couldn't do in *any* circumstances – just something you couldn't do in particular, e.g. normal, circum-stances.) It might be, for example, throwing a kitten off a motorway bridge, pushing a total stranger in front of a bus, unleashing a torrent of expletives at your granny, ... you get the picture. Now ask yourself whether you are morally responsible for refraining from doing whatever it was you just thought of.

If your answer is 'No, I am not morally responsible for refraining from swearing at my granny' (or whatever), then it looks as though you are strongly committed to the 'could have done otherwise' condition being a requirement for moral responsibility. But this commitment may be hard to sustain. Consider, for example, the rather unfortunate dilemma it creates for anyone who is a parent. Parents typically want their chil-dren to grow up to be the kinds of people who don't push people under buses or swear at their grannies. On the other hand, they typically (though admittedly probably not many parents think about this explic-itly) also want their children to grow up to be bearers of moral respon-sibility: people who are the legitimate targets of 'reactive attitudes' such as gratitude and resentment. (Probably they would prefer it if there were a lot more gratitude than resentment.) Given your answer to the above question, that's a lot to ask. In line with the first desire just described, we have to bring our children up so that they are strongly disposed not to swear at their granny or push people under buses. However, we also have to make sure that there is still *some possibility*, on any given occasion, that they will do the wrong thing – otherwise, we will fail to satisfy our second desire, that they grow up to be morally responsible agents. That's a tough call: satisfy the first desire, and you run the risk that you've gone too far and deprived your child of moral responsibility. Satisfy the second desire, on the other hand, and you run the serious risk of your child occasionally behaving in unspeakable ways. After all, if you think you really *could* push someone under the bus when the opportunity arises – which, probably, it frequently does – or, at any given moment, call up your granny and give her an earful of verbal abuse, how come you never, ever actually do those things? It doesn't look like you can consistently say both that you *could* do them and that there is no risk whatsoever that you *will*.

Of course, this might not convince you that we can be morally responsible without having the ability to do otherwise. If so, you will still not be convinced that Wally really is morally responsible (and indeed praiseworthy) for handing in the wallet even though he genuinely could not have done otherwise. The question of whether acting freely requires the ability to do otherwise is one that I'll be discussing in a lot more detail later on.

For now, though, let's return to our question about buck-stopping. Earlier I raised the worry that, supposing that we don't hold Carly responsible for stealing your car, Carly's situation and ours are not relevantly different. You might have a different character to Carly's, thanks to a different upbringing; in particular, you were brought up to pay attention whether your actions are right or wrong, and to act accordingly (though, of course, most of us don't *always* succeed in doing so). But you are just as much a product of your upbringing as Carly is a product of hers, and so if Carly is not responsible for her car-stealing *because* she is not responsible for having the character she has, then perhaps you are also not responsible for what you do, whether it is treating your friends well or badly or remembering your mother's birthday – since, like Carly, you are not responsible for having the character *you* have.

The worry here, then, is not so much that our decisions and actions might be determined by our characters and are unfree *for that reason* (this is a worry you will have if you think that Wally deserves no credit for returning the wallet), but that our character itself might be determined by things that we never had any control over – our upbringing and our genetic inheritance, say. We might (and some philosophers do) take the view that the fact that Wally's character rendered him unable to do otherwise *at the time* does not, in itself, entail that he did not act freely; rather, his action is unfree just if he had no control over the formation of that character – the character that in turn determined that he would return the wallet. So, the worry now is that if our *character* is determined to be the way it is (by our upbringing and so on), then the formation of our character is indeed out of our control. So, determinism threatens free will not because it robs us of 'elbow room' at the time of the relevant decision (Wally could not have done otherwise *at the time*, given his character), but because it entails that the buck *never* stops with us: the chain of determining factors runs right through our own lives, and back through the lives of our parents, and so on. In other words, if determinism is true, *we* cannot be the 'ultimate source' of our actions.

The compatibilist, however, might be inclined to run the argument in the other direction. Rather than saying that you are no more morally responsible for what you do than is Carly, with her unfortunate upbringing, we might start out by saying that manifestly you *are* morally responsible for how you treat your friends or remembering your mother's birthday. Hence Carly is, equally, morally responsible for stealing your car. The circumstances under which people's moral characters develop differ radically. Carly was brought up without any meaningful moral education: she was (we may suppose) discouraged from reflecting on the moral status of car-stealing, or indeed anything else. You (I hope) were not brought up like that: you (let's assume) were brought up to regard the harming of strangers for your own ends as morally unacceptable, and to think carefully about the consequences before making up your mind what to do. It is admittedly a matter of luck – it's out of your control, at least to a large extent – which kind of upbringing you had. Nonetheless, your behaviour stems from the character you actually have, no matter how it was acquired; and, so long as you are not suffering from some psychological compulsion or mental impairment that robs you of the ability to reflect adequately on what you are doing or to consider the consequences of your actions and modify your behaviour accordingly, you and Carly are, equally, morally responsible for that behaviour. That doesn't preclude you from feeling some sympathy for Carly – it is still true, after all, that she is the unlucky victim of an unfortunate upbringing – but that is not the same as thinking that she is not morally responsible, or is less than fully morally responsible, for stealing your car.

One worry about this line of thought is that while it might seem plausible when it comes to Carly, it's unclear whether it's so plausible when it comes to more extreme cases. Imagine, for example, that last week some evil alien neuroscientists rewired your friend Joe's brain while he was asleep. Prior to the rewiring, Joe was a normal, decent person who cared about his friends and would never steal anything unless in extreme circumstances. After the rewiring, Joe cares only about himself and has no qualms at all about stealing, except insofar as he doesn't want to get caught. Joe really likes the look of your new laptop, and so he steals it from you.

Is Joe blameworthy for what he has done? Intuitively – or at least, according to a lot of people's intuitions – he isn't. After all, it's not *his* fault that the evil alien neuroscientists turned him from someone who would never dream of stealing his friend's laptop into someone who just goes ahead and does it. But this sounds a lot like saying that Joe is off the hook because he is not responsible for the formation of his character. And didn't I just suggest that lack of responsibility for *that* is no impediment to acting freely and hence responsibly, and hence, while we might feel sorry for Carly, who had the misfortune of a terrible upbringing, she and we are equally morally responsible for what we do? So, on what basis do we ascribe moral responsibility to Carly – and ourselves – but withhold it from Joe?

Of course, there are major differences between Joe's case and Carly's, but the question is, why should these differences be relevant to the attribution of moral responsibility? If we want to hold Carly (and ourselves) to account but not Joe, we're going to have to explain why exactly the intervention of the evil alien neuroscientists renders Joe non-responsible for stealing the laptop, and that reason cannot simply be that he had no control over the formation of his character, since that claim (we have assumed) is equally true of us. Some incompatibilists claim that argument like this – sometimes known as 'manipulation arguments' – provide a powerful reason to endorse incompatibilism. And the basic idea is simply that, in the end, the manipulation that Joe suffers at the hands of the evil alien neuroscientists is really no different in relevant respects from the 'manipulation' that ordinary agents who are fully determined by their genes, upbringing and circumstances are subject to. Hence if we and Joe are equally determined to behave as we do, and Joe doesn't act freely, then neither do the rest of us. We'll return to manipulation arguments, and a related argument known as the 'zygote argument', in §1.5 and Chapter 4.

Let's sum up where we've got to. We've seen two kinds of worry that threaten the thought that people who are *determined* (e.g. by their upbringing, genes, current circumstances) to act as they do act freely and hence morally responsibly. One is the thought that such agents lack elbow room: we can't *freely* do what we do unless we could have done otherwise. No pat on the back for Wally, then, since his good character prevents him from being able to keep the money for himself; and, indeed, no praise or blame is due to any of us, ever, if we are determined to act as we do by facts that were in place before we were even born. The other is the thought that we cannot act freely if we are not the ultimate *source* of our actions, and that our being determined, since before we were born, to act in the way we do entails that we are not the ultimate source of our actions: the buck needs to stop with us if we are to be accountable, and if we are so determined, then the buck does *not* stop with us. Again, then, no praise or blame is due to any of us, ever, if we are determined to act as we do by facts that were in place before we were born. Most incompatibilists take one or other of these worries to undermine compatibilism.

Compatibilists, by contrast, hold that being determined by our characters, upbringing, or whatever to act as we do is no impediment at all to acting freely. Most compatibilists hold that most of us, most of the time, are morally responsible for what we do, whether or not we are determined to do act in that way. Those who are *not* responsible, or not fully responsible, for what they do – whether it is Joe or Carly or the perpetrator of a crime of passion, or an addict or a kleptomaniac or the victim of coercion or whoever – fail to be responsible not because they are *determined* to act as they do, but because they are determined (if they are determined at all) *in a particular way*. The kleptomaniac, for example, may be *compelled* to steal, but compulsion here does not merely amount to being determined; it's a matter of lacking the kind of *control* over one's actions that normal determined agents have. Of course, compatibilists need to explain exactly what kinds of facts about an agent *do* deliver free will, so that they can explain what it is that's lacking in agents who lack free will (see Chapter 2). The same is true, however – at least to some extent – of incompatibilists, or at least those incompatibilists who hold that actual agents really do act freely at least some of the time. The incompatibilist might, for example, try to maintain that the kleptomaniac is *determined* to steal, while normal people, like Carly perhaps, are *not* determined. But, as we'll see, it's not at all clear that they would be entitled to that claim.

So, who's right – the incompatibilist, who holds that Carly and Wally alike behaved freely and morally responsibly only if they could have done otherwise (either at the time of decision or at some prior relevant point in their lives), or the compatibilist, who holds that the issue of the ability to do otherwise (at least in the sense assumed so far) is irrelevant to freedom and responsibility? Are there any options we haven't yet considered?

A further important question is: What exactly *are* the conditions that are required for acting freely? Compatibilists and incompatibilists disagree about whether or not our not being determined to act as we do is a requirement on acting freely; but even if can resolve that question, it leaves us with a lot of work to do when it comes to giving a positive account of what acting freely requires. As we've just seen, to say, as compatibilists do, that determinism is no bar to acting freely is not yet to say anything about what *is* required. Similarly, no sensible incompatibilist is going to say that our *not* being determined to act as we do is *all* that is required for acting freely. Imagine that Carly has a tiny coin inside her head, so that she'll decide on stealing your car if it lands heads and go to the cinema instead if it lands tails. Would *that* make it the case that – the coin having just landed heads – she decides to steal the car freely? It would seem not – at least if we hang on to the idea that acting freely underpins moral responsibility. For while Carly is now not *determined* to steal your car – after all, the coin *might* have landed tails – she doesn't seem to have any *control* over whether or not she steals it either: it just seems to be a matter of luck. So, she still doesn't seem to be morally responsible for stealing it.

The rest of this book is devoted to trying to figure out how to answer these questions – not an easy task, as we'll see, and that's one reason why the debate about free will continues to rage. The rest of this chapter is devoted to some necessary scene-setting: getting clear on some basics, and fleshing out the arguments for incompatibilism briefly described above in some more detail.

A note on 'freedom of the will'

The problems that are the topic of this book tend to be advertised as problems concerning 'freedom of the will'. But this is a somewhat arcane expression, and it's worth spending a moment explaining it. From the outset, it was an assumption in modern philosophy that the mind is composed of several 'faculties', which were typically thought to include the faculty of reason, the imagination, the faculty of perception, and the will. ('Modern' in the context of 'modern philosophy' doesn't mean 'recent': the 'modern' period started in the sixteenth and seventeenth centuries with philosophers such as Francis Bacon (1561–1626) and René Descartes (1596–1650).) Each of these faculties has its own distinctive role to play in our mental lives: the job of reason is to acquire knowledge, for example, and the role of perception is to acquire information about our surroundings. So, the different faculties correspond to different kinds of mental activity. In the case of the will, the relevant mental activity is mental *action*; as Descartes puts it in the fourth of his *Meditations on First Philosophy*, 'the will...consists simply in the fact that when something is put forward for our consideration by the intellect, we are moved to affirm or deny it, or pursue or avoid it' (1641, 101–2).

In ordinary usage, 'the will' has come to be more narrowly associated with desires. Thus, someone's will, in the legal sense of 'last will and testament', is an expression of what they *want* to happen to their possessions after they die; or someone might be described as 'strong-willed' (stubborn or unlikely to change their mind about what they want) or 'weak-willed' (acting contrary to their judgement about what is the best thing to do, and so unable to align what they *want* to do with their judgement about what they *ought* to do).

In philosophy, talk of 'the will' has mostly disappeared; if you read contemporary philosophical texts that claim to be about free will, you will typically find little if any reference to 'the will' or 'willing' (though as we'll see in §2.5, Harry Frankfurt is one exception to this rule). By and large, philosophers these days talk exclusively about freedom of *action*, where action includes both overt, bodily actions, such as switching on a light or picking up a wallet or declining an invitation (a bodily action in that it involves speaking or writing or emailing), and – especially – mental actions such as *deciding* or (perhaps equivalently) *forming an intention* to do something.

1.2   Determinism v. indeterminism

Given the centrality of the question whether *determinism* is compatible with acting freely, we need to get clear on what the thesis of determinism – and its denial, indeterminism – amounts to. So, what *is* determinism? Well, imagine watching a game of snooker on television. If the players are good, you'll often be able accurately to predict what's going to happen when they take the shot: you can tell by the way the player is lining up the shot that he intends to get the black in the corner pocket and have the cue ball bounce back off the cushion and come to rest aligned with a particular red ball for the next shot, or whatever, and – if he's a good player and it's an easy shot – you can therefore predict that that's exactly what will happen. Of course, our predictions aren't always right – snooker would be a *really* boring game if they were. But when we get them wrong, it's reasonable to suppose that that's because there's some further fact about the situation that we didn't know about when we made our prediction. For example, if you make the prediction just after the player hit the cue ball, maybe you didn't know that he hadn't put quite enough power into the shot to do what he wanted to do, or that he hit it at slightly the wrong angle. If we knew those things (which one can't always discern from watching on TV), then – maybe – we'd be able to predict with total accuracy and certainty what the final position on the table will be when all the balls have come to a standstill.

Imagine that *in principle* we can predict the outcome of the snooker shot with total accuracy and certainty. What is it that we would need to know in order to be able to do this? First of all, we would need to know all the relevant facts about the situation we're looking at: where all the balls are on the table, exactly how hard, and at what angle, the player hits the cue ball, and also a lot of things that we normally simply take for granted – e.g. that the playing surface is felt and not satin and that the balls are regular snooker balls and not made of cheese. But, of course, knowing all that isn't enough; we also need to know *how* things – primarily, snooker balls – behave. We need to know that *if* the player hits the ball with such-and-such force at such-and-such an angle, then the ball will move in such-and-such a direction at such-and-such a speed; that if a ball hits a cushion at a certain speed and angle, it will bounce off at a particular angle with a particular speed. In other words, we need to know some of the *laws of nature* – namely, those laws that are relevant to snooker.

Now, to say that the relevant laws of nature are *deterministic* is to say that for any given starting position or 'initial conditions' – the player hitting the ball with such-and-such force at such-and-such an angle, together with all the other facts about the positions of the balls, what they're made of, and other details – those laws will specify a unique outcome: given a particular starting position, given the laws of nature only one thing *can* happen. For example, the laws will not (again, given a particular starting position) leave it open whether the white ends up aligned with a red or whether it overshoots. By contrast, if the relevant laws are indeterministic, they will *not* specify a unique outcome for a given set of initial conditions. So, in order to be able to predict the outcome of the shot with total accuracy and certainty – never to get it wrong (which of course in practice is pretty much impossible because we are never able to know *everything* about the starting point) – the laws of nature that are relevant to our game of snooker must be deterministic. Or, to put it another way, they must leave nothing to chance. For if the laws were to leave more than one final outcome open, we would have no way of knowing – short of getting in a time machine, zipping a few seconds into the future and taking a look – *which* outcome would result, even if we knew everything there was to know about the initial conditions.

Determinism is the thesis that (i) *all* the laws of nature have this feature – they always specify a unique outcome for a given set of initial conditions – and (ii) everything that happens in the Universe falls under some law of nature or other. In other words, the entire Universe is just like our imagined snooker table: for any given total state of the Universe, the laws of nature specify exactly what the total state of the Universe will be in, say, five seconds' time. For example, if determinism is true, then, if you knew *all* the relevant facts about the wasp that is currently cruising around my study, and you knew all the relevant laws of nature, you'd be able to figure out exactly where the wasp will be in five seconds' time. Of course, wasps are *much* more complicated than snooker balls, and it's a much more difficult – not to mention dangerous – matter trying to find out what state they're in at any given time, and so in practice we're much worse at predicting their movements. But that's just a practical difficulty: if determinism is true, the laws governing the behaviour of the wasp, together with the current state of the wasp and its surroundings, specify a unique outcome. Given the laws, together with current facts about the wasp and its environment, there's only one place the wasp *can* be in five seconds' time.

We, in turn, are much more complicated than wasps; and, in particular, we have a rich inner mental life that wasps lack. In particular, we, unlike wasps, often deliberate about what to do and form intentions as a result of that deliberation. Nonetheless, again, if determinism is true, this merely a practical difficulty when it comes to predicting human behaviour. It's still true that the laws plus all the relevant current facts about me, right now, entail some fact (I don't know what it is) about exactly what I'll be doing, thinking and feeling in five seconds' time.

Indeed, the laws plus current facts specify exactly what the total state of the Universe will be in an hour's time, and a month's time, and in ten billion years' time – including all the facts there will be at that time about me, including facts about what I'll be doing, thinking and feeling. (Well, it's pretty easy to predict that I won't be doing *anything* in ten billion years' time; we can safely assume that the laws plus current facts *don't* leave open the possibility that I'll still exist then.) So, while it's obviously *practically* impossible to predict exactly what I'll be doing in exactly one month's time, again – just as with the wasp – that's only because we lack relevant knowledge.

If determinism is true, then, given the precise state of your brain (or perhaps the precise state of your mind, if you want to resist identifying your state of mind with a particular state of your brain) at this moment, together with the total state of your environment, the laws of nature uniquely determine what will happen next – and not just what will happen next (e.g. whether you'll decide on a sandwich or some soup for lunch), but what you'll be doing at noon a week on Thursday, the exact moment of your death, whether you will have any grandchildren and whether those grandchildren will ever steal any cars. (It's not hard to see why this might make you worry about freedom of the will, but let's ignore that for now.)

To put it a bit more formally, suppose proposition P_0 is a proposition that specifies the entire state of the Universe at time t_0 (now, say), and suppose L is a proposition that states all the laws of nature. Determinism is the thesis that there is some proposition, P_1, which specifies the entire state of the Universe at some later time, t_1 (noon a week on Thursday, say), such that the conjunction of P_0 and L *entails* P_1. (So if you *knew* P_0 and you knew L – which of course nobody does, and perhaps nobody could do, even in principle – you would be able to *derive* P_1, and you would therefore know exactly what you, and everybody else on the planet, will be doing at noon a week on Thursday.)

So much for determinism. *Indeterminism* is simply the denial of determinism: if indeterminism is true, then it is *not* the case that the precise state of the entire Universe at a given time, together with the laws of nature, specifies a unique outcome for the entire unfolding of the rest of the life of the Universe. How might this work? Well, without getting too far into the deeply puzzling realms of quantum physics, let's consider the concept of radioactive decay. Radioactive atoms, such as strontium-90, have a 'half-life': the period of time such that there is a 50 per cent probability that the atom will decay during that period. (High doses of radiation – that is, a lot of radioactive atoms decaying – are very bad indeed for humans: they cause radiation sickness and longer-term health problems such as leukaemia. And some radioactive atoms have a very long half-life: in the case of strontium-90, it's 28 years. That's the reason why nuclear waste has to be stored safely over a very long period of time, but not indefinitely: after enough time has passed, it's overwhelmingly likely that almost all of the radioactive particles will have decayed. It's also part of the reason why nuclear accidents are to be avoided.)

Now, what does it mean to say that there's a 50 per cent probability of a strontium-90 atom decaying within 28 years? Often, when we ascribe probabilities (or 'likelihoods' or 'chances') to events, our doing so merely reflects our ignorance of further facts. For example, if you have just shuffled a deck of cards, tell me you're going to deal me the top card, and ask me the probability that it's an ace, my answer is 1/13: I know there are 52 cards and four of them are aces. If you had already dealt out the first 20 cards and there were no aces amongst them, my answer would be

4/32 (that is, 1/8). But, of course, in each case, my answer only reflects my *ignorance* of what the top card is. There is a fact of the matter about whether it's an ace; it's just that I have no way of knowing what that fact of the matter is. So, there is also a perfectly good sense in which the probability of the top card being an ace is either 1 (it's an ace) or 0 (it isn't) – I just don't know which. While this is a perfectly good sense of probability, however, you're unlikely to win at cards if you don't adopt the former, ignorance-based, not-1-or-0 probabilities as a basis for your play!

So, is the case of strontium-90 like the case of being dealt an ace? That is, is there some further fact of the matter that determines the precise time at which a given strontium-90 atom will decay? Are seemingly-identical strontium-90 atoms actually different to one another in some way that explains why some decay after 47 days and some after 12,689 days? The safest answer is to say: We don't know. If there *is* some further fact of the matter, physicists certainly haven't yet figured out what it is. Perhaps there is some further fact of the matter (as Einstein, who famously said that 'God does not play dice', believed) – in which case, the laws of nature governing radioactive decay are deterministic, it's just that we don't (yet) know what they are. If there is *no* further fact of the matter, then the laws governing radioactive decay are indeterministic, and so – given that indeterminism is simply the denial that everything is governed by deterministic laws – indeterminism is true, and determinism is false. (Actually, some philosophers – myself included – think that we shouldn't really hold that the laws *govern* what happens at all; see §3.5. But let's ignore that for now.)

There are two really important points to grasp when it comes to thinking about the connection between indeterminism and freedom of the will. The first is that *we don't know* whether or not determinism is true. Perhaps one day the sciences will answer that question, but as things currently stand, we're a long way from knowing. (See Balaguer 2010, Chapter 4 for a good survey.) So – in particular – simply assuming that determinism is true, or indeed that indeterminism is true, is not a good thing to do! However plausible determinism (or indeterminism) might seem to you, whether or not it is true is not, in fact, something you can discern just by considering how plausible it seems to you. Quite a lot of the time in philosophy, we adopt or reject theories on the basis of how plausible they are: by the extent to which they accord with our 'intuitions' or pre-theoretic judgements. I'll come back to the issue of the status of intuitions in philosophical methodology in §7.4, but that issue isn't really relevant here, because determinism is not a *philosophical* thesis at all – it's an empirical thesis. So, the question of whether or not it is true is a question for scientific investigation, not philosophical reflection.

Second, if you think that free will is incompatible with determinism, then the mere fact (if it is a fact) that indeterminism is true does not, just by itself, secure freedom of the will. Grant that, say, radioactive decay is – and perhaps the laws of quantum mechanics more generally are – genuinely indeterministic. That, just by itself, has no implications for whether or not anybody ever acts freely; all it does (if incompatibilism is true) is remove one possible obstacle. But obstacles remain. We'll come back to this point in Chapter 5.

1.3   Determinism, indeterminism and causation

To avoid confusion later on, it's very important to note that determinism is *not* equivalent to the thesis that every event has a cause. Prior to around the middle of the twentieth century, most philosophers – including philosophers writing about free will – *did* take determinism to be the thesis that every event has a cause, presumably because they simply assumed that all causation must be *deterministic* causation. Thus, for example, G.E. Moore says: 'if everything is caused, it must be true, in *some* sense, that we *never could* have done, what we did not do' (1912, 110).

One possible explanation of this conflation is that indeterminism only really started to be taken seriously by scientists in the early twentieth century, when quantum physics began to be developed. It was only at that point that the question of whether events that are not fully determined by the laws of nature plus facts about the past may yet have causes began to be addressed; and these days, most philosophers would agree that undetermined events *can* have causes.

Take our example of radioactive decay. It is surely obviously true that the nuclear accident at Chernobyl in 1986 *caused* people to suffer (and indeed die) from acute radiation sickness in the same year: the accident caused a vast quantity of radioactive material to be released, and that in turn – via radioactive decay – caused acute radiation sickness. But, as we've seen, radioactive decay is (so far as we know) indeterministic. So, the release of the radioactive material did not *determine* that anyone would get sick during 1986, since it's entirely consistent with the laws of physics – though admittedly extremely unlikely – that *none*, or very few, of the radioactive particles decayed that year; and if none or very few had decayed, there would have been no radiation sickness.

To take a more humdrum example, suppose that coin-flipping is indeterministic, so that whether the coin lands heads or tails isn't determined by the starting position (e.g. how you flip the coin) plus the laws. If I bet you £10 that the coin will land heads, you accept the bet, the coin is flipped, and it lands tails, you're £10 better off. Surely your new-found wealth has causes, including my offering you the bet and the flipping of the coin: if I hadn't offered you the bet, or no coin had been flipped, you wouldn't have got the money. So, again, it looks like we can have *indeterministic* causation: you can *cause* something to happen without *determining* it to happen.

As I said, it's important to be aware that much of the older (by which I mean before about 1970) literature on free will assumes the contrary – that all causation is deterministic causation. Here, for example, is an argument of Carl Ginet's (1962) for the incompatibility of free will and determinism. (a) If our decisions were caused, it would be possible in principle to know in advance what one were going to decide, before one decided it. But (b) it is impossible to decide to do something if you already know what it is you're going to decide. (After all, how can you deliberate about whether to go to the shops or stay in and watch TV if you already somehow *know* you're going to decide to go to the shops? What exactly would you be deliberating about?) Conclusion: Decisions cannot be caused. (Thus, Ginet is sometimes described as defending a 'contra-causal' account of free will.)

We can see that premise (a) above presupposes that all causation must be deterministic causation: it is only if our decisions are *determin-istically* caused, or, equivalently, *causally determinined*, that we could in principle – by knowing the laws and all the relevant facts about the past – know what we're going to decide. For if our decisions were *inde-terministically* caused – say your deliberation still left it open whether you would decide on going to the shops or staying in – then you could *not* in principle know what you were going to decide, even if you knew the laws and all the relevant facts about the past. So, in fact, assuming Ginet is right about premise (b), his argument only really shows that our decisions cannot be *deterministically* caused – which does not, of course, entail that they cannot be caused *at all*. (We'll briefly come back to the question of the relationship between free will and foreknowledge in §7.2.)

1.4 The Consequence Argument

Now that we've got clear on what the thesis of determinism is, we're in a position to be able to get to grips with perhaps the most famous argu-ment for incompatibilism, which I briefly introduced in §1.1. This argu-ment has been around for a very long time in various different forms, but its best-known formulation is that of Peter van Inwagen (1975). Van

Inwagen's formulation is quite technical. We'll get back to the technicalities in §3.1, but for now we'll just stick to the basic idea, which goes
something like this:

First of all – and, as we'll see, this is a crucial premise – van Inwagen
assumes that doing something freely requires that I *could* have acted
differently. So, for example, in order to freely make a cup of tea, it must
be the case that, at some time prior to my actually making the tea, I
could have refrained from making it.

Now, as we've seen, if determinism is true, then a proposition stating
all the laws of nature (call this proposition L), together with a proposition that describes the precise state of the Universe at a given time t_0 –
say, 1 p.m. on 2 January 2004 (call this proposition P_0) – jointly entail a
proposition that describes the precise state of the Universe at some later
time t – 6 p.m. on 26 March 2012, say. Now, as a matter of fact, one thing
that happened at t is that I made a cup of tea. Let P be the proposition
that I made a cup of tea at t. So – assuming determinism – P is entailed
by (L & P_0). Now, *could* I have refrained from making the tea then, even
though in fact I did not refrain and did, in fact, make the tea?

Well, P is entailed by – that is, P is a *consequence of* – L & P_0. So, if I
could have refrained from making the tea – in van Inwagen's terms, if
I could have 'rendered P false' – then it must be the case that I could
also have rendered L & P_0 false. Why? Because if you can render some
proposition R false, and R is entailed by Q, then you can also render
Q false. For example, suppose there are nine people in the room (Q).
That entails that there are fewer than ten people in the room (R), so
Q entails R. Suppose I can render R false, for example, by entering the
room, thereby increasing the number of people in it to ten. Then clearly
I can also render Q false – I can also render it false that there are nine
people in the room. Of course, this is just *one* case where some proposition Q entails another, R, and where it's true that if I can render R false,
I can also render Q false. Van Inwagen is claiming that this is true of
all propositions Q and R, where Q entails R. The fact that one instance
of this general claim is true does not, of course, demonstrate that the
general claim is true. If you doubt that the general claim is true, you
need to find a case where (i) Q entails R, and (ii) someone can render R
false, but they cannot render Q false. Go ahead and try!

So, if we want to know whether I could have rendered P false, we need
to know whether I could have rendered L & P_0 false. Given the above
principle, and given that L & P_0 entails P, if I could *not* have rendered
L & P_0 false, then it must be the case that I could not have rendered P
false – otherwise we'd be contradicting the principle we've just assumed

to be true. So, the question is: *Could* I have rendered L & P_0 false? Well, clearly I could not, at any stage later than t_0 (1 p.m. on 2 January 2004), have rendered P_0 false: what's past is past, and you can't do anything about that. I can't now render false the fact that I had toast for breakfast this morning, or the fact that I just typed the word 'breakfast'; I can delete the word, but I can't make it the case that I never typed it in the first place.

It follows that I could *only* have rendered L & P_0 false if I could have rendered L false. But nobody can render the laws of nature false: if proposition is a law of nature (e.g. if it's a law of nature that nothing travels faster than the speed of light), then nothing we do can possibly render that proposition false. To put it more simply, we cannot break the laws of nature. So, in fact, I could not have rendered L false. And, as we saw above, I could not render P_0 false either. So, clearly I could not have rendered their conjunction – L & P_0 – false. But in that case, I could not have rendered P false either. (Remember: If I could have rendered P false, then I could have rendered L & P_0 false. But since I could not have done the latter, I could not have done the former either.) Hence, if determinism is true, I could not have refrained from making a cup of tea at t. And, since being such that I could have done otherwise than make a cup of tea at t is a requirement on my making it freely, it follows that if determinism is true, I did not make the cup of tea freely.

To put things much more straightforwardly, though rather less rigorously: the laws of nature and facts about the past aren't up to me. So, the consequences of the laws of nature and facts about the past can't be up to me either. So, if (as determinism entails) everything I do is a consequence of the laws of nature and facts about the past, nothing I do is really up to me. Hence, acting freely is incompatible with determinism.

Recall that compatibilists think that acting freely and responsibly is compatible with determinism, and incompatibilists don't. Many – but not all – incompatibilists reject the claim that acting freely and responsibly is compatible with determinism because they are convinced by the Consequence Argument. We'll come back to the highly contentious question of whether or not the Consequence Argument really works in Chapter 3; below, however, I turn to a different kind of argument for incompatibilism.

1.5 Sourcehood and manipulation arguments

Whether we're compatibilists or incompatibilists, it's plausible to think that at least *some* kinds of manipulation restrict our freedom. In the film *The Truman Show*, Truman Burbank thinks he's an ordinary guy in an ordinary town with an ordinary job. What he doesn't know is that he's spent his whole life living on a giant soap opera set, and all of his supposed friends and family and colleagues are actors. Truman is deliberately placed by the director and scriptwriters in situations that will make for good TV. Truman is clearly the victim of a kind of constant manipulation. While his behaviour in any given situation is not generally any more predictable than yours or mine (by people who know us very well), his circumstances are frequently engineered in such a way as to make it likely that he'll behave in the way that the director wants him to behave. In particular, Truman unfortunately develops the desire to get outside the cosy but restricting (literally restricting, in fact, but Truman doesn't know this) town of Seahaven. The director manipulates Truman in two ways: by thwarting his desires (e.g. cancelling flights, making the bus break down) and by affecting his desires themselves through external circumstances (e.g. putting news reports on TV about the dangers of travelling and killing off Truman's 'father').

What should we say about Truman's predicament? Clearly, in one sense his freedom has been restricted. In particular, he is not free to leave the set: this is something he cannot do (although he does – spoiler alert! – eventually manage to escape). But we might still say, at least up to the point where the director has to start (apparently) cancelling flights and so on, that he freely remains – even though his *desire* to remain has itself been manipulated by circumstances. After all, our desires are manipulated by circumstances all the time – it happens every time we watch an advert or walk around the supermarket. But we still want to say that we freely buy the things we buy, and are morally responsible for those purchases.

But what about more extreme cases of manipulation? Remember Joe the laptop thief from §1.1, whose brain has been interfered with by evil alien neurosurgeons so that Joe's previous good and law-abiding nature has been replaced with a concern only for his own short-term material gain in such a way that he is now determined to steal the laptop. Does Joe freely do so? A simple 'manipulation argument' against compatibilism runs like this. Clearly Joe does *not* freely steal the laptop, and is therefore not blameworthy for doing so. But in that case, the compatibilist needs to explain what exactly the difference is between Joe's case and that of a normal deterministic agent. After all, there are plenty of people who are just like post-manipulation Joe but who have not been the victims of alien intervention, and *they*, according to the compatibilist, are blameworthy for what they do.

Here's a different manipulation-style argument: the 'zygote argument'. Imagine that Ernie lives in a fully deterministic universe. Diana, a goddess with extraordinary powers (and foresight), creates a zygote in Mary – which grows up to be Ernie – in just such a way that Ernie is guaranteed, given the facts at the time plus the laws, to steal his friend's laptop in thirty years' time; and Diana knows this. Indeed, she *intends* for Ernie to steal the laptop, and she knows that by creating the zygote in just the right way she can ensure that this happens, so that's what she does. Ernie grows up in the normal way: he is not subject to brainwashing or alien intervention (aside from the creation of his zygote), Diana does not create the zygote in such a way that Ernie comes to have irresistible impulses or kleptomania, and so on. In other words, creation aside, Ernie is exactly like any normal adult human being (albeit not a very nice one), and hence would seem to satisfy whatever conditions on acting freely that compatibilists might care to name (see Chapter 2).

As with Joe, we're supposed to find it intuitively compelling that Ernie does *not* act freely and responsibly in stealing the laptop. And yet, he would appear to be a normal, fully functioning deterministic adult, and so the compatibilist would apparently have no grounds for *denying* that Ernie acts freely. Hence, since Ernie does not act freely, neither does any other normal, fully functioning deterministic adult. Hence compatibilism must be false. Note that while Diana does not directly intervene in Ernie's life (post-conception) in any way, there still a sense in which Ernie is the victim of manipulation. After all, Diana brought him into existence *intending* that he would steal his friend's laptop, and – given determinism – there was nothing, at any stage, that Ernie could do to stop this happening.

It's clear that the compatibilist faces a difficult choice here: accept that Joe and Ernie are morally responsible for what they do, which is (allegedly) implausible, or else try to find some way of distinguishing between Joe's and Ernie's predicaments on the one hand and, on the other, the situation that normal deterministic agents are in, so that Joe and Ernie get off the hook, but the rest of us (or at least most of us, most of the time) do not. There are various moves the compatibilist might try and make at this point. For example, in Joe's case we might try to claim that there is something about the sudden and wholesale alien intervention that is (obviously) completely unlike what happens to normal deterministic agents, and so we just need to add some kind of historical condition – perhaps a condition that specifies that one's psychology develop in the 'normal' way – in order to deal with Joe's case. Unfortunately, even if we manage to come up with such a condition to deal with Joe's case, we're not going to be able to apply it to Ernie's case. After all, Ernie's psychology *does* develop in the 'normal' way. Ernie's *zygote* certainly didn't come into existence in the normal way, but it's unclear why facts about *that* aspect of Ernie's history should be thought to render him unfree.

We'll consider manipulation arguments in more detail in Chapter 4. For now, it's worth noting that incompatibilists generally take manipulation arguments, such as those described above, to connect with the issue of *sourcehood* raised in §1.1. Remember Wally, who is determined by his good character to hand the wallet in to the police station so that he cannot, now, do otherwise than hand in the wallet. And recall the worry that if determinism is true, his character in turn was determined to be the way it is by factors that were ultimately outside Wally's control. There is no point at which the buck stops with Wally; the buck passes right through Wally and right out the other side. Manipulation arguments describe cases, such as Joe's and Ernie's, where, again, it seems that the buck doesn't stop with the agent. (Perhaps in Joe's case the buck stops with the evil alien neuroscientists, and in Ernie's case it stops with Diana: these are the people who are *ultimately* responsible for Joe and Ernie behaving as they do.) The force of manipulation arguments lies in the thought that, if determinism is true, there isn't *really* any relevant difference between Joe and Ernie on the one hand, and the rest of us on the other. After all, they are (or perhaps just Ernie is) just like us in all *relevant* respects. So, if the buck passes right through Ernie and out the other side, then the same is true of us, since there is nothing in *us* to stop the buck that is not present in Ernie. If there were, then Ernie would not be the normally-functioning deterministic agent that he is stipulated to be.

1.6   Conclusion

This main point of this chapter has been to introduce you to some of the broad questions and themes that will get discussed in a lot more detail later on. In particular, the various ways in which the compatibilist might respond to the Consequence Argument are discussed in Chapter 3, and compatibilist reactions to 'sourcehood' arguments, such as the kinds of manipulation argument just described, are considered in Chapter 4. But these arguments only address the very general question of whether there are good reasons for thinking that acting freely is incompatible with determinism.

The more significant question, I think, is whether we have any good reasons to think that *we* act freely – we real, flesh-and-blood agents – as we go about our daily lives. This is a really important question. After all, if we never (or hardly ever) act freely, then we are never (or hardly ever) entitled to hold people responsible for what they do: nobody is ever praiseworthy or blameworthy, so nobody is ever *deserving* of praise or blame or – for example – gratitude or forgiveness. That might (conceivably) not make much of a *practical* difference to our lives; perhaps, even in the absence of moral responsibility, we would still have good grounds for rewarding people who treat us well and incarcerating criminals. But it would, or so I think, make a significant *moral* difference to our lives. If there is no such thing as moral responsibility, then there would appear to be no *moral* difference between the friend who misses your wedding because she has a pathological fear of flying and just can't make herself get on the plane despite really not wanting to let you down, and the friend who misses it because, well, she knew it was important to you, but she just couldn't be bothered to make the effort.

So, *is* there a moral difference between the cases? To answer that question, we need to have settled a lot more than just the question whether acting freely is compatible with determinism – we need a *theory* of what acting freely consists in. That will be our concern in Chapter 2, where I consider compatibilist theories, and Chapter 5, where I consider incompatibilist theories.

Chapter 6 returns to the question of whether acting freely requires the *ability to do otherwise*, in the sense of my doing otherwise being an alternative possibility that is left open by the past plus the laws. The claim that acting freely *does* require this ability is, as we've seen, a central premise in the Consequence Argument for incompatibilism, but it is thrown into serious doubt by a famous argument of Harry Frankfurt's, and we'll see how incompatibilists have responded to that argument. Finally, in Chapter 7, I briefly consider some additional issues and draw attention to some loose ends.

2
What Does Acting Freely Require? Some Compatibilist Views

2.1 Introduction

By and large, as we've already seen, philosophers fall into two opposing camps when it comes to free will: compatibilism and incompatibilism. But note that these two theses are merely claims about whether or not free will is *compatible* with determinism, and that's not the same as having a theory about what acting freely *consists in*.

One way to think of this is in terms of *necessary and sufficient conditions*. Let's switch examples to make it easier, and consider something more humdrum than free will: chairs. A *necessary* condition for something's being a chair is a condition that it *has* to satisfy in order to be a chair: anything that doesn't satisfy the condition just isn't a chair. So, for example, we might think that *being such that people can sit on it* is a necessary condition for being a chair: if you can't sit on something, it definitely isn't a chair. (You can probably think of counter-examples to this claim, but let's ignore the complications!) However, *being such that people can sit on it* certainly isn't a *sufficient* condition for being a chair; that is to say, satisfying that necessary condition on being a chair doesn't *guarantee* that something is a chair. People can sit on all kinds of things that aren't chairs: you can perfectly well sit on a tree stump, or a table, or a stool, or a wall, or…. If we wanted a list of conditions that are collectively or jointly *sufficient* for being a chair, we'd have to think of a list of conditions such that tree stumps, stools, and various other items fail to satisfy at least one of those conditions. So, for example, we might try adding the condition that the thing in question is an artefact – something that someone has made. That would rule out tree stumps but not walls. We could add, further, that it must be an item of furniture. That would rule out walls but not tables. We could add the further condition that it must have been designed to be sat on, ruling out tables but not stools. Finally, we could add the condition that it has a back: *that* would rule out stools. Job done! (Or let's assume so, anyway.)

So, what we've got now is a list of conditions, each of which is, individually, *necessary* for something's being a chair (being an item of furniture is a necessary condition, for example, because if you're not an item of furniture, you can't be a chair). Moreover, our conditions are collectively *sufficient* for being a chair: anything that meets *all* the conditions on the list is guaranteed to be a chair. (I'll have a little more to say about necessary and sufficient conditions in §5.2.) Philosophers sometimes call such a list of individually necessary and jointly sufficient conditions a *conceptual analysis*. In this case, I've proposed an *analysis* of the concept *chair*: I've proposed a list of conditions such that, if you can figure out whether or not a given object satisfies all the conditions in the list, you can figure out whether or not it satisfies the concept *chair* – or, to put it more simply, you can figure out whether or not it is a chair. (Of course, you might be able to think of objections to my proposed conceptual analysis. Maybe you can think of something that satisfies all the conditions in the list but still isn't a chair, or maybe you can think of something that *is* a chair but doesn't satisfy all of the conditions. Given how hard it is to come up with necessary and sufficient conditions for being a chair, it's hardly surprising that philosophers have found doing the same thing for free will to be somewhat challenging!)

So, let's get back to free will. In effect, the dispute between compatibilists and incompatibilists is a dispute about whether indeterminism is a *necessary* condition of acting freely: incompatibilists think it is, and compatibilists think it isn't. But, whoever is right, we're still a long way from providing *sufficient* conditions for an act's being free, since, so far, we have, at most, one necessary condition – and not even that, if the compatibilists are right.

Since the focus of this chapter is compatibilism, let's forget about indeterminism for now. As we just saw, compatibilism just by itself – the view that determinism is no bar to acting freely – imposes no necessary conditions whatsoever on acting freely. It's a *claim* about free will, but it's certainly not a *theory* of free will: a *theory* of free will must tell us what the individually necessary and jointly sufficient conditions are for acting freely. In fact, most compatibilists think that ordinary adult human beings act freely most of the time and hence are mostly morally responsible for what they do, whereas only people who are subject to pathological aversions or certain kinds of psychiatric disorders, or are in prison, or perhaps are victims of coercion, *don't* act freely. But what we need is a theory of free will that explains what the difference is between the two kinds of case. What exactly is it that free will requires? For example, what is the necessary condition for acting freely that someone subject to a pathological aversion fails to satisfy, but which ordinary people, most of the time, *do* satisfy? This chapter surveys some compatibilist answers.

2.2   Compatibilist control and reasons-responsiveness

Compatibilists and incompatibilists generally agree that *being in control* of one's action is a necessary condition of that action's being performed freely. As we saw in Chapter 1, it is easy to see that determinism raises a *prima facie* worry about control. How can Carly or Wally be in control of their respective actions, if they are fully determined to behave as they do by their genetic makeup, their upbringing, their environment and other factors – things over which they manifestly don't have any control? The compatibilist's response to this worry is to argue that if we pay attention to what it *means* to say that someone is in control of their actions, having such control turns out to be fully compatible with determinism.

What the compatibilist needs, then, is an account of what it is to be in control of one's actions. David Hume famously said: 'By liberty ... we can only mean *a power of acting or not acting, according to the determinations of the will*; that is, if we choose to remain at rest, we may; if we choose to move, we also may'; and he goes on to note that 'this hypothetical liberty is universally allowed to belong to every one who is not a prisoner and in chains. Here, then, is no subject of dispute' (1748, §8). In effect, then, for Hume, freedom of action amounts merely to being able to do what one chooses to do. Or, to put it in terms of control, freedom is constituted by the fact that we are *in control of* our actions, in the sense that what we do is sensitive or responsive to our choices, intentions and decisions.

Despite Hume's optimism, however, philosophers have found a great deal to dispute here. In particular, his definition of liberty would seem to be far too relaxed, for surely we need to be in control of our *choices* as well in order truly to act freely. The kleptomaniac or the heroin addict most likely steals or injects in accordance with her choices – it's not as though the addict chooses not to inject and then finds her body acting against her will while she helplessly looks on. Nonetheless, we would want to say that the kleptomaniac and the addict are not acting freely, or, at any rate, that their freedom is compromised in some way.

More sophisticated compatibilist accounts of the nature of the control required for acting freely are provided by, for example, Dennett (1984) and John Martin Fischer and Mark Ravizza (Fischer 1994; Fischer and Ravizza 1998). Let's start with Dennett, who notes that the ordinary notion of control is (to put it rather loosely) one according to which the extent to which an agent or other entity *A* controls some agent or entity *B* (where *A* and *B* can be the *same* entity, as when I control my own behaviour) is a matter of the extent to which *A* can get *B* to conform to what *A* wants or is designed to achieve, across a range of different circumstances (1984, Chapter 3).

Take a thermostat. It's true, of course, that thermostats control the temperature; but they aren't really very *good* at it. A thermostat is sensitive to precisely one kind of environmental input – the temperature – and can respond to that input in just two ways: it can turn the heating on (if the temperature gets too low) or off (if it gets high enough). That's it. And this lack of sensitivity and range of responses makes it pretty easy for the thermostat to fail in what it's 'trying' to do. The thermostat in my house is supposed to keep the temperature of the whole house at a steady twenty degrees, let's say. But the thermostat is located in the hallway, so if I leave the front door open for a while, the thermostat will turn the heating on, thereby making the rest of the house too warm. A better temperature-controller would be able to shut the front door, or turn just the heater in the upstairs bedroom off, or whatever. Thermostats just aren't that good at controlling the temperature – better than nothing, but still not that good.

To get a better handle on what being more or less in control amounts to on Dennett's view, compare a robot dog with a real dog. Imagine I throw a stick to my robot dog, and it manages to fetch the stick by running exactly twenty paces in a north-easterly direction, to just the place where the stick is, biting the stick, and returning to where it started. Good robot dog! This might lead me to think that the robot dog has a high level of control over the location of the stick. But on further investigation, this turns out not to be so. When I throw the stick different distances or in a different direction, the robot dog runs exactly twenty paces in a north-easterly direction, bites and returns to where it started – with no stick. It turns out that the robot dog was programmed to respond to stick-throwing in exactly one way: it is insensitive to the distance and direction of the throw. I conclude that the robot dog just got lucky with that first throw; it is, in fact, pretty useless at controlling the location of the stick. A real dog, needless to say, is *much* better in this regard. It *is* sensitive to the direction and distance of the throw; it can successfully negotiate obstacles in its way; and, by and large, it doesn't come back until it's actually picked up the stick.

Of course, dogs aren't perfect stick-fetchers – they're not *that* bright. Normal adult human beings, by contrast, are generally much better than dogs at controlling the locations of thrown sticks. You can't fool *me* with a dummy throw; nor am I apt to mistake an algae-covered pond for a nice patch of grass and run straight into it. And I am generally much better at retrieving lost sticks from bushes than the average dog is.

Similarly, adult human beings are generally much better than dogs – and some dogs are better than others – at controlling *themselves*. Some dogs will obediently follow the command to sit, even if you've just thrown a juicy bone that they really, really want down to the bottom of the garden; others just won't be able to help themselves and will run off to fetch the bone. Sean finds the offer of a chocolate irresistible even though he's on a diet – he just can't help himself – whereas Sinead, who has just as strong a desire for the chocolate as Sean does, is able to resist. Sinead thus exhibits self-control, while Sean does not.

As with Hume, Dennett's central thought is that the truth of determinism doesn't pose any threat to the idea that we are in control of what we do, given the notion of control in play. As Robert Nozick notes, 'No one has ever announced that, because determinism is true, thermostats do not control temperature' (1981, 315). Similarly, we can distinguish between Sean's and Sinead's respective levels of self-control when it comes to chocolate, without even considering whether either of both of them are determined to act as they do by the past plus the laws. If you were to claim that if Sean and Sinead are both determined to behave as they do by the past plus the laws, then Sinead exhibits no more self-control than Sean does, Dennett's response would doubtless be that you appear to have misunderstood what 'self-control' actually *means*.

Nonetheless, we might legitimately ask for a bit more information about *exactly* what kind of control – and how much of it – is required in order to act freely. This question becomes especially pertinent when we consider not merely our overt physical behaviour (fetching the stick that the dog failed to retrieve, say) but mental actions: deciding and forming intentions, for example. The control we need to be able to exert over our *mental* lives is not so much a matter of responding appropriately to *environmental* inputs, such as one's owner throwing a stick; it is, rather, a matter of responding appropriately to our own mental goings-on. To use Fischer's term, we should think of the kind of control that's needed in terms of being *reasons-responsive*.

The idea of reasons-responsiveness seems, at least at first sight, to exclude from acting freely just the kinds of cases we want to exclude. Consider Kevin the kleptomaniac, for example. Here's Kevin, stealing a bag of peanuts from the corner shop. Kevin really has no reason at all to steal the peanuts: he's allergic to peanuts, so he's not going to get any benefit from stealing them; nor does he expect to get any pleasure out of the act of stealing itself. And, of course, he runs the risk of being arrested for theft. His behaviour is clearly not responsive to reasons, since all the reasons he has are reasons *not* to steal the peanuts. Hence, Kevin lacks the kind of control over his action that would render that action free.

Sometimes, however, it's not clear from someone's *actual* behaviour whether or not they are being reasons-responsive. For example, suppose that Kira decides to put the kettle on as a result of a very strong desire for a cup of tea. That sounds like a sensible decision in the circumstances. But what if, in fact, Kira *would* have made exactly the same decision if she'd instead wanted a drink of cold water, *and* if she'd believed that the kettle is extremely dangerous, *and* if she'd just been threatened in some way ('I'm warning you: If you put that kettle on, the kitty gets it!')? In that case, we would probably want to say that there is something very badly wrong with Kira – and in particular that she was not, in fact, in control of her decision at all, for she would have made exactly the same decision whatever her reasons, or lack of reasons, may have been for making it. In other words, Kira, like Kevin, fails to be reasons-responsive. In fact, she wants a cup of tea, and so it *seems* as though she's putting on the kettle in response to that reason. But in fact, she isn't: no matter what her reasons had been, she would have done the same thing.

Here's an analogy to help make it clearer why we need to think about 'counterfactual' scenarios – what *would* have happened in different circumstances. (For more on counterfactual scenarios, see §3.4.) The thermostat is set to turn the heating on when the temperature drops below 20 degrees. It's now 21 degrees, and the thermostat hasn't turned the heating on. That's just the way you'd expect a working thermostat to behave – but is it *really* controlling the temperature? That depends on what it *would* do if the temperature were to drop below 20 degrees. If it *still* wouldn't turn the heating on in that situation, then in fact the thermostat isn'tcontrolling the temperature at all, since it lacks the capacity to *respond* appropriately to the temperature.

Accounts of 'reasons-responsiveness' are developed by Fischer and Ravizza (Fischer 1994; Fischer and Ravizza 1998). The basic idea is to consider whether or to what extent the agent's decision is sensitive to the reasons she has for making that decision. Kira, as we've just seen, is not being very reasons-responsive at all. Maybe, for all I've said, there are *some* possible reasons that she might be responsive to. Perhaps if someone had put a gun to her head and threatened to kill her if she put the kettle on, she would have desisted. So, she might be a *little bit* reasons-responsive – but not very. Most of us, most of the time, are a lot more reasons-responsive than that. When *I* decided to put the kettle on just now, I really did it *because* I wanted a cup of tea; if I'd wanted cold water or I'd thought I was in danger of electrocution, I certainly would not have made that decision.

The tricky part is explaining just *how* reasons-responsive an agent's decision has to be in order for it to count as one that they freely made and for which they are morally responsible. Set the bar too high, and there is the danger that any decision that is not fully rational will fail to count as freely made – but surely we can at least sometimes be morally responsible for our decisions even when they are irrational. For example, imagine that Matthew promises to meet his friend Jane at the cinema at 8 p.m. He knows that it's really important to Jane that he isn't late – she loves all the trailers and doesn't want to miss any of them – and he sincerely doesn't want to annoy her. Unfortunately, however, he spends too long replying to some non-urgent emails and arrives late. Jane is not pleased with him. Matthew's behaviour was not fully reasons-responsive – he really did want to arrive on time, and he knew that sending those emails right away just wasn't important, but he failed to respond appropriately to those reasons. But Jane would rightly judge it to be an exceptionally lame excuse, were Matthew to try to argue that his lack of full reasons-responsiveness rendered him blameless for Jane missing the trailers.

On the other hand, if we set the bar for reasons-responsiveness too low, we'll count as morally responsible decisions that we shouldn't. For example, in the case where the *only* reason Kira would respond to – the only thing that would stop her putting the kettle on – would be a direct threat to her life, it seems a mistake to claim that she acts freely and responsibly.

One additional issue here is what counts as a 'reason'. If we go fully 'internalist' about reasons, so that a reason for action is just any relevant belief or desire the agent happens to have, then, again, we might be setting the bar too low. If I think that the little green men are coming to get me, and I consequently spend the day hiding under the bed, my doing so might well be fully responsive to *my* reasons. After all, I certainly wouldn't be hiding under the bed if I *didn't* think the little green men were coming to get me – that would be crazy! On the other hand, my reason itself – my belief about the little green men – itself fails to be appropriately responsive to my environment: there really is (we may suppose) no evidence whatsoever that there are any little green men intent on abducting me. So, in a different, 'externalist' sense of 'reason', in hiding under the bed, I am *not* being responsive to reasons. From the point of view of the way the world is, I have every reason to do the things I was supposed to be doing today, and no reason at all to hide under the bed instead. But if we deploy this externalist sense of 'reason' in defining reasons-responsiveness, we may well be setting the bar too high. Plenty of us sometimes act on the basis of beliefs for which we don't really have any good evidence, after all. Last night, for example, I unthinkingly walked to the supermarket to buy some milk, even though – as I realised when I got there to find it shut – I had no reason at all to suppose that it would be open. So, my decision to walk to the supermarket failed to be reasons-responsive in this externalist sense. Nonetheless, it would be very odd to say on that basis that I failed to make that decision freely. More generally, we might reasonably assume that in this externalist sense of 'reason', there is *always* a good reason not to perform an action that is morally wrong – *viz*, the very fact that it is morally wrong. So, it looks as though if we characterise reasons-responsiveness in an externalist way, nobody who does the wrong thing is ever reasons-responsive – or at least, they cannot be *fully* reasons-responsive. (For a brief discussion of a closely related issue, see §3.3.)

Just to make things more complicated, here's a minor wrinkle: Fischer's official view is actually what he calls 'semi-compatibilism'. Fischer distinguishes between two kinds of control that one might have over one's actions: *regulative control* and *guidance control*. Regulative control is control of *whether or not* one performs the action in question, and thus requires that the agent could have done otherwise. Fischer (2006b, 8) thinks that the Consequence Argument shows regulative control to be incompatible with determinism (though see Chapter 3 for ways in which compatibilists have tried to get the ability to do otherwise to turn out to be compatible with determinism). On the other hand, he thinks that *moral responsibility* requires only a weaker kind of control, namely guidance control.

We might think of Fischer's distinction between regulative and guidance control as disambiguating two distinct meanings of 'free', so that (if Fischer is right about regulative control being incompatible with determinism) there is *a* sense of 'free' (a sense that requires regulative control) according to which acting freely is incompatible with determinism, but there is a different, weaker sense of 'free' (a sense that requires only guidance control) that captures what is required for moral responsibility, according to which acting freely is *compatible* with determinism. (Note, however, that Fischer himself doesn't do this; he reserves 'free' for cases of guidance control.) Putting this distinction together with the idea that reasons-responsiveness is what is required for moral responsibility, we might conclude that reasons-responsiveness just *is* the kind of guidance control that is required for acting freely, in the sense of 'free' that underpins moral responsibility.

2.3   Dennett's 'personal stance'

As we've already seen, Dennett claims that acting freely is (at least in part) a matter of having control over our actions, where the kind of control at issue is not one that is threatened by determinism. However, Dennett (1973) also has a more sophisticated positive account of what acting freely consists in. This account connects with a much larger view about the nature of the mind, of which we only have the space for a very short summary.

At the heart of Dennett's account is the notion of a 'stance'. The basic idea is roughly this: Suppose we want to explain some bit of behaviour (not necessarily human behaviour – it might be the behaviour of a thermostat or a chess program or a robot or a dog). What would be the most appropriate 'stance' to adopt when giving such an explanation – in other words, in what kinds of terms would the best explanation of the behaviour be couched?

Consider desires, for example. When you get the dog lead out, and your pet dog starts wagging its tail and getting very excited, you'd naturally explain that behaviour by saying that the dog *wants* to go for a walk. Now, dogs are just biological, and indeed physical, entities; and so in principle, alternative explanations of your dog's behaviour are available. For example, if you knew a whole bunch of facts about the way the dog's visual system and brain worked, and you were tracking its visual input and neurological states, you might be able to explain its behaviour by saying, 'Well, it had visual input X, and this triggered neurological processes Y and Z, and this caused signals to be sent to various muscles, hence the wagging and barking'.

Now, suppose that this broadly physical explanation were available to you. Would it be a *better* explanation of why the dog started barking and wagging its tail than the explanation in terms of the dog's *wanting to go for a walk* – an explanation that deploys distinctively mental vocabulary? Dennett's thought is: No, it wouldn't. The explanation in terms of what the dog *wants* is a better explanation. In other words, we should explain the dog's behaviour from the perspective of the 'intentional stance' – a stance that attributes to the dog 'intentional' states such as intentions and desires. ('Intentional' states are, broadly speaking, psychological states that are *about* something, such as the world (so, the belief that it's raining is an intentional state) or oneself. So, for example, the desire to go for a walk is a desire *about* oneself – it is a desire *that* one go for a walk. Similarly for the intention to make some tea, or the decision to water the garden.)

Now here's the crucial move: The fact that ascribing an intentional state to the dog (it *wants* to go for a walk) is a better explanation than the rival, neurophysiological explanation is what *makes it true* that the dog *has* such an intentional state. There is no more to the dog's *having* desires than the fact that our best explanations of its behaviour are ones that *attribute* desires to the dog.

Other 'stances' that feature in Dennett's system are the 'physical stance' (which is the stance we adopt when we explain the dog's behaviour in neurophysiological terms), the 'design stance' and – crucially in the present context – the 'personal stance'. So, for example, if you want to explain why a fairly basic chess computer just moved the king one place to the left, you might in principle adopt either the 'physical stance', which would give you an explanation in terms of the mechanism – the electrical circuitry, for example – that caused the move, or the 'design stance', which would give you an explanation in terms of what the *point* of the move was ('It moved the king like that in order to keep it out of the danger posed by the other player's bishop', say). Note that this is not an *intentional* explanation; it doesn't appeal to the chess computer *wanting* to get the king out of danger. Most likely, the design stance would be more appropriate in this case. (Why wouldn't the intentional stance be better? Presumably because attributing a desire to the computer is no more explanatorily helpful than ascribing a purpose to its move. Note that, for Dennett, the reason would *not* be a philosophical thesis to the effect that computers can't have desires.) Similarly, when explaining why cats have whiskers, say, the design stance might well be the most appropriate: that would involve giving an explanation in terms of what the whiskers are *for*.

The important point here, again, is that the appropriateness of the design stance – as applied to chess computers, say, or cats' whiskers – is not determined by there being a further fact of the matter about whether the computer or the whiskers were 'really' designed to perform the relevant function. Chess computers do, in fact, have designers – whoever built the software built it *in order* to make the computer good at chess. Cats, on the other hand, do not have designers. But this does not make the design stance inappropriate for explaining why they have whiskers. It's simply a fact about biological organisms in general that it's often appropriate to adopt the design stance when explaining their behaviour.

When it comes to moral responsibility and hence freedom of the will, it's the *personal* stance that is important. To give an explanation of behaviour from the personal stance is to give an explanation in terms of features that we take to be constitutive of personhood. These might include, for example, appealing to 'reactive attitudes' (for more on these, see the next section) – 'She gave you the flowers because she was really *grateful*', or 'He did it out of *spite*' – or rationality ('She decided it was the *best thing to do* in the circumstances'). And if you put that together with the very widely held idea that personhood is itself a requirement of moral responsibility – only *persons* are capable of being morally responsible for their actions – you get the result that it's appropriate to attribute moral responsibility to someone for their action just when the best explanation of that action is one that invokes the personal stance, as opposed to merely the intentional or design or physical stance.

It looks as though this approach latches on fairly well to our ordinary attitudes to moral responsibility. For example, a baby might cry because it wants attention (intentional stance), but it wouldn't be appropriate to say that it's crying because it wants to annoy you (personal stance); hence, it's inappropriate to attribute moral responsibility to the baby. Or imagine that someone is so scared of flying that they refuse to board the plane. The best explanation of their behaviour is simply that the person is terrified – an explanation that doesn't involve the personal stance. (Dogs can be terrified, too). This isn't to say that the person who can't get on the plane isn't really a person; just that in this situation, our regarding them as not responsible for their actions and so unfree is due to the fact that we are not regarding them as persons when it comes to understanding this particular bit of behaviour.

The fear of flying case highlights an important aspect of Dennett's view, which is the idea that one retreats to a different, lower-level stance (taking the physical stance as the lowest level, and the personal stance as the highest) when things have gone *wrong* in some way. For example, most of the time, if you want to explain why your computer does the things it does, the design stance is the most appropriate. But when it goes wrong – say, the 'k' key stops working – the design stance is no longer appropriate. If we want to explain why nothing happens when you press the 'k' key, we'll need to adopt the physical stance: The best explanation will be the fact that a wire has come loose, say. The same point applies to human beings and their behaviour: We retreat from the personal stance just when someone's behaviour becomes *more* intelligible by adopting some other stance, and this will generally be when something, somewhere has gone awry. For example, we *might* take the view that the behaviour of Joe, our laptop thief from §1.5 whom the evil alien neuroscientists have rewired in such a way that he ends up stealing your laptop, is best understood not by adopting the personal stance, but instead by regarding him as the unwitting puppet of the evil aliens, so that the design stance is more appropriate. (Joe has, in effect, been wired up by the evil aliens *in order* to behave badly.) Or, of course, we might not. Dennett, I presume, would not. Nor do I, for that matter.

Dennett's view is often regarded as a 'pragmatist' view because it locates the having of certain features (e.g. having mental states such as intentions, or having free will) in the appropriateness of certain kinds of *explanation* of behaviour. You might think the appropriateness of attributing desires to a dog, say, depends upon an independent, objective fact of the matter, namely whether or not dogs really do have desires. But Dennett thinks the order of dependence runs in the other direction: It's true that the dog has desires just *because* attributing desires to it is the most appropriate way of explaining its behaviour. Similarly, whether or not someone acts freely is not some independently establishable metaphysical fact about them; instead, it's a matter of whether our best explanation of why they behaved as they did requires the adoption of the personal stance.

2.4   Reactive attitudes

Dennett's account bears some affinity with the compatibilist account of moral responsibility offered by P.F. Strawson (1962). Strawson begins by reminding us how very central what he calls the 'reactive attitudes' are to our understanding of ourselves and others. As the name suggests, the reactive attitudes are the kinds of attitudes we take to other people in response to their behaviour: gratitude and resentment, for example. And he notes that such attitudes aren't just a matter of how we *feel*; they are also *manifested* in a good deal of our behaviour. Thus, when we act with good manners or kindness or studied indifference or deliberate rudeness, we are manifesting a certain kind of reactive attitude to the object of our behaviour. (Thus, for example, if you are deliberately rude to me, you are manifesting an attitude of contempt towards me.) Such attitudes permeate our relationships with other people, whether they are the people we care most about or complete strangers whose toes we accidentally tread on. They are, as Strawson puts it, 'participant attitudes': attitudes that are required in order for us to engage in normal interpersonal relationships.

Now, Strawson notes that in certain special cases, we can and do legitimately set aside the participant attitude towards a particular person. This might happen because of the particular circumstances the person happens to be in. For example, I might resent you for missing our appointment, but on discovering that I had forgotten to send the email confirming the time, I withdraw my resentment: I regard that particular reactive attitude as inappropriate on this particular occasion. Or we might regard the participant attitude as largely or wholly inappropriate when it comes to a particular individual: someone might be so psychologically damaged, for example, that it would be inappropriate to regard them as an object of gratitude or resentment. Instead, it is appropriate in such cases to adopt the 'objective' attitude: to regard the person in question as (as Strawson puts it) 'an object of social policy; as a subject for what, in a wide range of sense, might be called treatment; as something certainly taken account, perhaps precautionary account, of; to be managed or handled or cured or trained; perhaps simply to be avoided' (1962, 66).

Now, to get back to free will, the question Strawson is interested in is: If determinism were true – as it may well be for all we know – would, could or should that lead to the total repudiation of participant reactive attitudes? It seems that the incompatibilist must say 'Yes' – at least to the 'should' part. Reactive attitudes are distinctively *moral* attitudes, and such attitudes will be entirely inappropriate if a necessary condition for moral responsibility, namely indeterminism, is not satisfied. Strawson takes this recommendation to be simply incredible. First of all, repudiating the participant attitude wholesale is something that is 'practically inconceivable' (1962, 68): a 'sustained objectivity of inter-personal attitude, and the human isolation which that would entail, does not seem to be something of which human beings would be capable, even if some general truth were a theoretical ground for it' (1962, 68). So, even if we had rational grounds for abandoning the participant attitude – say, through a combination of the Consequence Argument and evidence for the truth of determinism – we could not, as a matter of psychological fact, actually go ahead and abandon it. After all, try to imagine what it would be like. There would be no interpersonal relationships of any but the crudest kind – perhaps the kind enjoyed by other higher primates that live in social and family groups, such as chimps and gorillas. We might enjoy some people's company more than others', be afraid of some people and not others or develop a system of rules and punishment to encourage people not to go about killing and stealing. But we would not be able to treat people with respect (or disrespect), or make a moral distinction between people who hurt us on purpose and those who do it by accident, or form genuine friendships; we might be happy that someone has helped us, but we would not feel gratitude; we might feel regret for something we have done (if, for example, we think the injured party might retaliate) but not remorse. It's a pretty bleak prospect. But Strawson's point is not merely that it would be bleak, but that we cannot really seriously entertain it as something that we *could* do.

Second, and perhaps more importantly, Strawson asks whether giving up on the participant attitude could be rationally justified (as opposed to being psychologically possible). His answer is No: 'if we could imagine what we cannot have, *viz*, a choice in this matter [about whether or not to abandon the participant attitude], then we could choose rationally only in the light of an assessment of the gains and losses to human life, its enrichment or impoverishment; and the truth or falsity of a general thesis of determinism would not bear on the rationality of this choice' (1962, 70). The implication here is that the loss to human life involved in abandoning the participant attitude would be so enormous that it could not *possibly* be rational to choose to do so. (The claim that the absence of moral responsibility would be catastrophic is disputed by Derk Pereboom, however; see §5.8. I'll also raise a worry for Strawson's view in §3.6, in the context of the Consequence Argument.)

Dennett and Strawson thus both take the view that whether or not someone acts freely and morally responsibly is not a matter of how things 'ultimately' or 'objectively' *are* – and in particular it is not a matter of whether or not their action is deterministically caused. Instead, it is a matter of how well their action coheres with certain ways of thinking about or conceptualising their behaviour. For Dennett, the focus is on *explanation*: when someone behaves in a certain way, what is the best 'stance' to adopt with respect to that behaviour, where our aim in adopting a stance is to explain the behaviour? For Strawson, by contrast, the focus is on whether someone's behaviour is such that it would be appropriate for us to regard them as, as it were, a participant in our moral community – as someone towards whom it would be appropriate to adopt the reactive attitudes, and hence as someone with whom it would be appropriate to enter into the normal interpersonal relationships that depend upon those attitudes.

Dennett and Strawson share the idea that we should retreat from the relevant stance or attitude only when things go *wrong* in some way: when we cannot make sense of someone's behaviour from the perspective of the personal stance and hence have to retreat to a 'lower' stance (Dennett), or when it is appropriate to regard someone as an 'object of social policy' or a 'subject for treatment' (Strawson). And they also share the idea that such a retreat is something that should only be done in exceptional circumstances: *no* argument for incompatibilism could possibly establish that the personal stance or the participant attitude is *never* appropriate. And, since the appropriateness of that stance or attitude is what acting freely and responsibly *consists* in, no argument for incompatibilism can succeed.

2.5   Frankfurt's hierarchical model

Harry Frankfurt's (1971) account is sometimes called 'hierarchical compatibilism'. Frankfurt, unlike most authors in the free will literature, draws a distinction between freedom of *action* and freedom of the *will*. His is a compatibilist account because it entails that neither freedom of action nor freedom of the will depends upon the falsity of determinism: one does not need the ability to do otherwise in order to enjoy either freedom of action or freedom of the will. (Actually, things are a little more complicated than that – we'll see why presently.) And it's a 'hierarchical' account because Frankfurt thinks that enjoying freedom of the will requires that one's 'will' have a certain hierarchical structure. The account isn't entirely straightforward, but here's a brief summary of its main elements.

First, we need to distinguish between 'first-order' and 'second-order' desires. A first-order desire is just a common-or-garden desire – the desire for beer, or the desire to go to the cinema, or whatever. A second-order desire is a desire *to have a certain first-order desire*. A lot of the time, we don't bother reflecting on our second-order desires, so it might not be immediately obvious that we really have them. For example, if I want a cup of tea, it might seem odd to ask whether I also *want* to want a cup of tea. But when we reflect on cases where our first-order and second-order desires conflict, it's easy to see that we *do* generally have second-order desires. For example, you might *want* to want to quit smoking, or want to want to go to the gym twice a week, or want to want not to leave writing your essays until the last minute; these are all second-order desires. But it doesn't follow that you actually want to quit smoking or to go to the gym twice a week or to start writing your essays earlier; these are all first-order desires. For example, I *do*, in fact, want to want to go to the gym twice a week – that's a first-order desire I'd like to have. But I just don't have it, unfortunately.

The important point here is that our first-order desires might or might not line up with our second-order desires. In the gym case above, they don't. In other cases, they do match up: I want to buy my friend a nice birthday present, and that is a desire that I *do* want to have. Or I might be just neutral about a particular first-order desire: I currently want a cup of tea, for example, and I don't really care one way or the other whether I have that desire (though it's a desire I might not want to have if, say, my train were due to depart, and the queue at the station café were very long).

Second, we need to distinguish between someone's first-order desires and their *will*. Acting in accordance with your will is a matter of the relevant first-order desire's being 'effective'. Plenty of our desires aren't effective. One reason for this is that we often have *conflicting* desires, and, when we deliberate about what to do, often we are attempting to figure out which of those conflicting desires should motivate us to act. For example, I currently want to finish this chapter, but I also want to watch my favourite TV programme. When I resolve to finish the chapter rather than turning on the TV, and hence do exactly that, the former desire is effective, and the latter is not. So, the former desire, and not the latter, is my will.

Finally, we need to distinguish between a second-order desire and a second-order *volition*. As we've seen, a second-order desire is just a desire to want something (i.e. to have a first-order desire). A second-order volition is a desire *to have a certain will* – that is to say, it is a desire for a certain first-order desire to be *effective*. Plausibly, most of our second-order desires are really second-order volitions. Consider the gym case again: I really do want to have the first-order desire to go to the gym twice a week, but the *reason* I want to have this desire is that if I had it, then I probably would, in fact, go to the gym twice a week – something I think would be good for me. In other words, I don't just want the first-order desire for its own sake. Rather, I want that desire to be *effective*: I want it to motivate me to action. Wanting to *have* a certain first-order desire is much less demanding than wanting that desire to be your will. Consider the gym case again. Suppose that my second-order desire to want to go to the gym is effective, in that I do, indeed, manage to get myself to want to go to the gym. That first-order desire may yet itself fail to be effective; for example, suppose that I also have the desire to stay at home and watch TV, and that it's *that* first-order desire that's effective. So, my second-order *desire* is satisfied – I do, indeed, have a first-order desire (to go to the gym) that I want to have – but my second-order *volition* – my desire that my desire to go to the gym be my *will* – is not. My inner couch potato triumphs.

So much for the background; let's get back to the issue of freedom. Frankfurt holds that whenever our first-order desires are 'effective' – I want to do something and I then do it *because* I want to do it – we *act freely*. (This is more or less Hume's view of freedom: 'If I choose to remain at rest, I may'. See §2.2 above.) However, Frankfurt thinks this isn't the whole story. What Frankfurt calls 'enjoying freedom of the will' is altogether different: it is a matter of your *will* (those first-order desires that motivate you to act) conforming to your *second-order volitions*. (Note: Frankfurt means 'enjoying' here in the sense of 'having for one's use or benefit', and not in the sense of 'taking pleasure in'.) To put it simply, *acting* freely is a matter of doing what you want to do; enjoying freedom of the will is a matter of having the will you want to have. So, for example, in the gym case, I fail to enjoy freedom of the will. The will I want to have is to go to the gym: that's the desire that I want to be effective. Unfortunately, it's not: I do have that desire, but the desire to stay home and watch TV is the one that, in the end, motivates me to act.

More generally, part of Frankfurt's thought is that things like psychological compulsions need not undermine freedom of *action*, but they *do* undermine one's enjoyment of freedom of the will. The person who's unwillingly afraid of flying does what she wants – *viz*, she doesn't get on the plane. So, not getting on the plane is her will. (Though she may have conflicting first-order desires: she may also want to get on the plane. She bought a ticket, after all, which would be an odd thing for someone who has *no* desire to get on the plane to do.) But she does not *want* the desire not to get on the plane to be her will; she wants her will to be that she *does* get on the plane. And she is unable to get her will to conform to this second-order volition. Hence, she doesn't enjoy freedom of the will with respect to flying.

Note that this is a *compatibilist* position because nothing in the story requires determinism to be false. Fully deterministic agents are, in principle, perfectly capable of conforming their will to their second-order volitions, i.e. not only doing what they want to do, but having the will they want to have. Of course, not all deterministic agents succeed in doing this, but when one fails, the reason one fails has nothing to do with the fact that one's will is determined to be what it is by the past plus the laws. It is *what* determines one's will to be what it is that's important: whether one's will is what it is because of one's second-order volition, or whether it is determined by something else (addiction, say, or a psychological compulsion – or, in the gym case, deep-seated laziness).

It should be stressed that the above account is something of a rational reconstruction of Frankfurt's 1971 position because his terminology is somewhat confusing. In particular, he *does*, in fact, suggest that determinism may prevent one's will from being free: 'A person's will is free only if...with regard to any of his first-order desires, he is free either to make that desire his will or to make some other desire his will instead. Whatever his will, then, the will of a person whose will is free could have been otherwise: he could have done otherwise than to constitute his will as he did' (1971, 18–19). But he immediately goes on to say both that 'although this question is important to a theory of freedom, it has no bearing on the theory of moral responsibility', and that being morally responsible entails that 'the person did what they did freely, or that he did it of his own free will' (1971, 19).

This position looks dangerously close to being self-contradictory. How can it be that someone does something 'of his own free will' (which, according to Frankfurt, is required for moral responsibility) and yet their will is not free (which is *not* required)? Frankfurt later describes the 'distinction between a person who acts of his own free will and a person whose will is free' as 'clumsy' (1999, 369). That's a fair assessment in my view. Nonetheless, he clearly thinks that there *is* a distinction to be made here, and I suggest that we interpret Frankfurt's position as follows. There is *a* sense in which determinism may preclude freedom of the will, *viz*, if someone's will could not have been otherwise, then their will is not free. (Whether or not determinism does preclude this depends, of course, on whether one thinks that the ability to do otherwise in the sense relevant to freedom is incompatible with determinism; see Chapter 3.) Roughly, someone's will is free only if they are able to take *any* of their current first-order desires and make that desire be their will – that is, the desire that motivates them to action.

For example, suppose that Jane, perusing the lunch menu, currently *both* desires the lamb (yum!) *and* desires the vegetarian lasagne (she's a vegetarian). For her will to be free, in the sense that may be incompatible with determinism, it must be the case that she *could* make *either* of these desires her will. In fact, Jane has the second-order volition that her desire for the lasagne be her will. She's a vegetarian after all, and so – let's suppose – whenever she is faced with the opportunity to eat meat, she wants the desire to take the vegetarian option to be her will. However, she *could* instead form the second-order desire volition that her desire for the lamb be her will.

For Jane's will to be free in this way is not, however, a requirement on moral responsibility; nor, correspondingly (if confusingly), is it a requirement on Jane's choosing the lasagne 'of her own free will', or her 'enjoying freedom of the will' in choosing the lasagne. In order for *that* requirement to be satisfied, Jane merely needs to be such that her *actual* second-order volition – that her desire for the lasagne be her will – is effective. There need be no *other* second-order volition that Jane is, in the circumstances, able to acquire. Abstracting away from the details, we might think of the distinction between 'having a will that is free' on the one hand and 'enjoying freedom of the will' (or 'acting of one's own free will') as roughly analogous to Fischer's distinction, described briefly at the end of §2.2, between regulative and guidance control: the former is a *kind* of freedom, but not the kind of freedom that is required for moral responsibility. (In the rest of this section, when I say 'freedom of the will', I'm talking about the kind of freedom of the will that Frankfurt takes to be compatible with determinism.)

Does Frankfurt's account succeed? Here are two potential problems. One problem arises when we consider moral responsibility. Should we hold that moral responsibility goes along with *acting* freely, or with enjoying freedom of the *will*? The former is clearly not demanding enough, while the latter seems rather *too* demanding.

That acting freely is not sufficient for moral responsibility is clear from the fact that even non-human animals can act freely, in the sense of being able to do what they want to do ('an animal may be free to run in whatever direction is wants', for example (Frankfurt 1971, 14)). Frankfurt himself takes moral responsibility to require not only freedom of *action* but, in addition, freedom of the will. Note that the former is a separate and additional requirement to the latter. Suppose I hear a cry for help outside my office. I want to go and help, I want this desire to be my will, and it is: my desire to go and help motivates me to act. So, I enjoy freedom of the will here. Unfortunately, the door is locked, and I cannot get out. I am not morally responsible for failing to help because my *action* – remaining in my office – is itself not free. (To put this in Frankfurtian terms, we might say that while I am enjoying freedom of the will, I am not *acting* of my own free will: acting of one's own free will requires *both* acting freely *and* enjoying freedom of the will.) But requiring freedom of the will, in Frankfurt's sense, in addition to freedom of action may be too demanding. I consistently fail to enjoy freedom of the will with respect to going to the gym, for example; but it seems slightly odd to maintain that I am not morally responsible for my repeated failure to go.

Of course, it may seem a little strange to ask whether I'm morally responsible for failing to go to the gym, since I'm harming nobody but myself by sitting in front of the TV instead. So, let's change the example. Imagine your friend is arriving at your house at 4 p.m., and you want to be home in time for her, or she'll have to wait outside in the rain. However, you also want to stop at the shop on the way home from work and buy yourself a nice cake. You really want the first desire to be effective, but it isn't: your desire for the cake is what motivates you to act, you stop at the shop, and your friend gets wet. She's not happy at all. Does the fact that you didn't get your will to conform to your second-order volition really get you off the hook?

Here's a second potential problem. Imagine that an evil alien neuroscientist has managed to implant in your friend Joe – normally a perfectly nice, law-abiding citizen – an irresistible urge to steal your laptop. Is Joe morally responsible for doing so? Intuitively not – and Frankfurt's account gives us the right answer because our alien neuroscientist has left Joe's second-order volitions intact: he doesn't *want* the desire to steal your laptop to be effective, but he just *can't help* acting on it. Thus on Frankfurt's account, Joe is not acting of his own free will. So far, so good. But what if the alien neuroscientist engages in some more drastic manipulation, so that they affect Joe's second-order desires as well, and as a result he becomes someone who *wants* to be motivated by entirely selfish desires? (In fact, this was implicit in the way I set up this case in §1.1 above.) In that case, it seems that Frankfurt's account makes Joe morally responsible for stealing the laptop, since Joe has the will he wants to have. And that might seem rather unfair on Joe. Of course, we could try holding that Joe's second-order volitions must conform to his *third*-order volitions in order to be morally responsible, so while he has the will he wants to have, perhaps he fails to have the will he wants to *want* to have. But then we can just change the example so that the alien neuroscientist affects his third-order volitions as well.

In other words, Frankfurt doesn't appear to have a good response to 'manipulation arguments' (see §1.5) – although, as we'll see in Chapter 4, his response in effect is simply to deny that Joe lacks responsibility for stealing the laptop – and I'm inclined to agree with Frankfurt here. But setting aside manipulation arguments for now, we can raise a related worry without invoking evil alien neuroscientists: Why should it be that, on Frankfurt's hierarchical model of the structure of our desires, the buck should stop at level two? What's so special about our *second*-order desires, as opposed to our third- or fourth-order desires? Frankfurt anticipates this question, saying:

> When a person identifies himself *decisively* with one of his first-order desires, this commitment 'resounds' throughout the potentially endless array of higher orders... The decisiveness of the commitment

he has made means that he has decided that no further questions about his second-order volition, at any higher order, remain to be asked. (1971, 16)

What on earth does this mean? Well, Frankfurt later (1988) gives us an analogy. Imagine doing a maths calculation – say, just adding up a long list of numbers. You get to the end, but you're not sure you haven't made a mistake, so you check it by doing it again. If you get different answers, obviously you'll have to check again. Or maybe you get the same answer the second time around, but you're still not totally convinced. ('Did I really remember to carry the 2? I'd better check again.') Of course, no matter how many times you do the sum, it's not *guaranteed* that you haven't made a mistake – you could just be making the same mistake every time and not noticing. There isn't some magic number such that if you check *that* number of times you can be sure you've got it right: there's no principle that says that if you check it *five* times, say, then you'll be justified in stopping and accepting your answer, but if you only check it four times you won't. But you have to stop somewhere. Does that mean that wherever you stop – at the second check, say – you are stopping at an *arbitrary* point, and so stopping there isn't really justified? (See Watson 1975, §3.)

Frankfurt says no. At some point (unless you've simply run out of time, or got bored and just decide to stop because you've got more important things to do), you'll become confident that you now *know* what the answer is. You have *committed* yourself, as it were, to that answer (though, of course, you may yet be wrong; nobody's infallible). The fact that you're now confident that the answer is right means that you can now happily *predict* that, if you were to carry out the calculation again (at any rate if you were to do it without making a mistake), you'd get the same, right answer – whether you did it once more, or ten more times, or whatever. At this point, you have made a 'decisive commitment', and this commitment 'resounds endlessly' in the sense that you're convinced that any further enquiry would be pointless because it wouldn't make you change your mind.

So – to return from the analogy to the case we're interested in – the idea is just this. 'Identifying myself decisively' with one of my first-order desires is just like deciding to stop checking my maths – not because I've run out of time, but (in the maths case) because I've got things *right*. For example, I want the desire to go to the gym to be my will: the desire to go to the gym is the desire that I want to be effective. So, I have a second-order volition: a desire that a certain desire (going to the gym) be my will. Now, I *might* proceed to have reservations about this. By hypothesis, I definitely want the desire to go to the gym to be my will. But is this second-order desire *itself* a desire I really want to be effective? This is a third-order question, and the answer to that question might, in principle, turn out, on reflection, to be 'No'. Maybe the kind of person who religiously trots off to the gym three times a week (as people who consistently have the relevant second-order volition tend to be) is not the kind of person I really want to be. Maybe I'd get really obsessed about it and start boring my friends with how fast I managed to do 500 metres on the rowing machine yesterday, or start spending so much time in the gym that I'd neglect other things I should be doing. So I might, on reflection, come to have the third-order desire that my second-order volition *not* be effective. And then I might (though this may make my brain explode) start worrying about whether I want that *third*-order desire to be effective.

On the other hand, I might happily stop at the second-order stage rather than ascending any higher up the hierarchy, because I just don't see any reason to think that ascending will make any difference – just as one might stop after the second check of the calculation because one is now confident that one has got the answer right. This is to 'identify decisively' with my desire to go to the gym. Or, if I've gone through the bit of reflection described above, I might instead stop at level three, having fixed on the desire that my second-order volition *not* be effective. In that case, I will – if all is well with my psychology – revise my second-order desires so that they don't conflict with that third-order desire, and come to desire instead that my first-order desire *not* to go to the gym be my will. And so I will 'identify decisively' with *that* desire and wholeheartedly embrace my inner couch potato.

Frankfurt's overall claim, then, is that we do not have to choose between an infinite regress and an arbitrary stopping-point in the case of the will, any more than we do in the case of checking our arithmetic – though whether that claim is defensible is, of course, a matter for dispute (see Fischer 2012).

2.6 Conclusion

In this chapter, we've seen some attempts by compatibilists to explain what it is that acting freely requires. You may have noticed that they fall into two broad categories. On the one hand, we have the kind of account – described in §§2.2 and 2.5 – that focuses, either explicitly or implicitly, on the kind of *control* that is required for acting freely.

Thus, Fischer holds that the kind of control required for acting freely (in the sense of 'free' required for moral responsibility) is a matter of being responsive to reasons. (Well, that's my way of putting it. Fischer himself thinks that guidance control doesn't get us *free* action but does get us morally responsible action. But perhaps we can think of this as a mere terminological difference.) Frankfurt, in effect, takes the kind of control that is required to be a matter of getting one's hierarchy of desires to cohere in the right kind of way – though he is interested in freedom of the *will* rather than in *acting* freely. *Acting* freely is something dogs can do, on Frankfurt's view.

On the other hand, we have accounts – represented by Dennett's and Strawson's views discussed in §§2.3 and 2.4 – that deal directly with moral responsibility and, in effect, infer facts about freedom. One way to think about such accounts is as follows. Grant that acting freely is required for moral responsibility. Then we can figure out what the requirements are on acting freely by considering the requirements on being morally responsible. Thus, for example, on Strawson's account, the fact that the possibility that we are *never* morally responsible for our actions (and hence that our reactive attitudes are always and everywhere inappropriate) is not to be countenanced implies that we *must*, ordinarily at least, be acting freely, since if we were not acting freely, those reactive attitudes *would* be inappropriate.

It remains to be seen, however, whether any compatibilist account of free will can overcome the obstacles put in their way by the various arguments for incompatibilism. These are the topics of the next two chapters.

3
Compatibilism and the Consequence Argument

3.1 Introduction

In §1.4, I introduced The Consequence Argument, so-called because it trades on the fact that if determinism is true, our acts are *consequences* of the laws of nature plus facts about the past – that is, the laws plus the past *entail* that we perform them. As I said in §1.4, a very rough summary of the argument goes like this: The laws of nature and facts about the past aren't up to me. So, the consequences of the laws of nature and facts about the past can't be up to me either. So, if (as determinism entails) everything I do is a consequence of the laws of nature and facts about the past, nothing I do is really up to me. Hence, acting freely is incompatible with determinism.

Van Inwagen's rather more rigorous rendition of the argument (1975) runs as follows. Suppose that J is a judge who, were he to raise his hand at time T, would thereby grant clemency to a criminal. J, in fact, decides (after careful deliberation, and without any of the standard impediments to acting freely in place, e.g. he was not coerced or acting under hypnosis) not to raise his hand, thus sentencing the criminal to death. L is a proposition stating all the laws of nature, P_0 is a proposition stating all the facts that obtained at some arbitrary time prior to J's birth, and P is a proposition stating all the facts that obtain at T. Now, here's the argument, with a very brief explanation of each premise inserted in square brackets:

(1) If determinism is true, then the conjunction of P_0 and L entails P.

[This just follows from the definition of determinism; see §1.2.]

(2) If J had raised his hand at T, then P would be false.

[Since P states all the facts that obtain at T, the fact that J does not raise his hand at T is included in P. So, 'J raised his hand at T' is inconsistent with P. Hence, if the former proposition were true, the latter would be false.]

(3) If (2) is true, then if J could have raised his hand at T, J could have rendered P false.

[Another example: suppose Q is the true proposition that I ate no biscuits yesterday. So, if I had eaten a biscuit yesterday (which you know I didn't, because I just told you that Q is true), Q would have been false. So, if I *could* have had a biscuit yesterday, I *could* have rendered it false that I ate no biscuits yesterday – since if I could have had a biscuit yesterday, I could have rendered 'Helen ate a biscuit yesterday' true, and hence rendered 'Helen ate *no* biscuits yesterday' false.]

(4) If J could have rendered P false, and if the conjunction of P_0 and L entails P, then J could have rendered the conjunction of P_0 and L false.

[This is an instance of a general principle discussed in §1.4.]

(5) If J could have rendered the conjunction of P_0 and L false, then J could have rendered L false.

[Clearly J could not have rendered false any true propositions about the state of the world before he was born; e.g. I cannot now, and could never have, rendered it false that the Battle of Hastings took place in 1066. Likewise, J could not have rendered P_0 false. Hence if J *could* have rendered the conjunction of P_0 and L false, it must be that he could have rendered L false.]

(6) J could not have rendered L false.

[Nobody can render any law of nature false!]

Therefore,

(7) If determinism is true, J could not have raised his hand at T. (Van Inwagen 1975, 191)

Add to this the premise that J desists from raising his hand freely *only* if he could have done otherwise than desist – that is, only if he could have raised his hand at T – and you get:

(8) If determinism is true, J did not (in desisting from raising his hand) act freely.

(In fact, the essence of the above argument was already presented in §1.4, so if you're not following it, you might want to go back to §1.4 at this point for a refresher.)

Note that, while the argument concerns a specific agent, J, and a specific action, nothing specific to J's situation is appealed to in the argument. So, the argument *generalises*: it applies to any agent, any action and any time whatsoever. And of course, the generalised version of the conclusion, (8), is that if determinism is true, nobody ever acts freely – which is the thesis of *incompatibilism*.

The Consequence Argument might look as though it sounds the death-knell for compatibilism, the view that acting freely *is* compatible with determinism. After all, the argument would appear to be valid, and its premises would appear to be very plausible. In fact, however, compatibilists have been pretty resourceful in looking for ways to criticise it. In this chapter, I'll survey some of those criticisms.

3.2   What does 'could have done otherwise' mean?

The Consequence Argument (henceforth 'CA' for short) aims to show that if determinism is true, no agents could ever have done otherwise than what they actually do – and hence, assuming that the ability to do otherwise is required for acting freely, no agent ever acts freely. But notice that CA presupposes that 'could have done otherwise' means something very specific: in effect, in order to be such that they could have done otherwise – or, as it is sometimes put, in order for them to be *able* to do otherwise – the agent's act must *not* be a consequence of the laws of nature plus a fact about the entire state of the Universe at some past time. (I'll shorten this to 'the laws plus the past' from now on.) One line of compatibilist response to CA has been to offer an alternative definition of 'could have done otherwise' (or 'is able to do otherwise') – one that *is* compatible with determinism. The thought here is that while, doubtless, the sense of 'could have done otherwise' at work in CA is *a* legitimate sense of the expression – and indeed one that cannot be satisfied, ever, if determinism is true – that is *not* the sense of 'could have done otherwise' that is relevant to whether or not we are capable of acting freely and morally responsibly.

The 'conditional' account

Some compatibilists, taking their lead from Hume's claim that liberty merely requires that 'if we choose to remain at rest, we may; if we choose to move, we also may' (see §2.2 above), and also from G.E. Moore, define 'could have done otherwise' in terms of a 'counterfactual conditional'. A counterfactual conditional (or 'counterfactual' for short) takes the form 'if *X had been* the case, then *Y would have been* the case' – or, alternatively, 'if *X were* the case, then *Y would be* the case'. Counterfactuals are so-called because the antecedent (the proposition between the 'if' and the 'then') is *contrary to fact*: when I say, 'If Aguero hadn't scored a goal in stoppage time, United would have won the League', I'm saying something about what would have been the case if some fact or facts (here, the fact that Aguero scored a goal in stoppage time) had not obtained, and some other fact or facts obtained instead.

According to Moore (1912, Chapter 6), we often make what would appear to be perfectly sensible distinctions between what we can and cannot do – distinctions that we would want to preserve even if it turns out that determinism is true. For example, I might perfectly reasonably say that, while I could have gone for a long walk this morning and been home in time for lunch, I couldn't have walked all the way to Leicester and back and been home in time for lunch. Moore concludes that there are 'good reasons for thinking that we *very often* mean by "could" merely "would, *if* so and so had chosen"'. So. when I say that I *could* have gone for a long walk this morning and been home in time for lunch, I am saying something true, because if I had chosen to go for a long walk and be back in time for lunch, that's what I would have done. By contrast, when I say that I could *not* have walked to Leicester this morning and been back in time for lunch, I am also saying something true, because I mean that even if I had (rather rashly) chosen to walk to Leicester this morning and be back in time for lunch, I would not have succeeded in doing what I had chosen to do.

This sense of 'could have done otherwise' is certainly consistent with determinism: even if my choosing to stay at home instead of going for a walk was itself determined by the past plus the laws, that doesn't undermine the fact that if I *had* (contrary to what the laws plus the past entail) chosen to go for a walk and be back in time for lunch, that's what I would have done. So, Moore's account of 'could have done otherwise' – unlike the account presupposed by CA – is compatible with determinism; and, Moore argues, it is his sense of 'could have done otherwise' that is relevant to attributions of moral responsibility.

Taking their cue from Moore, some philosophers (e.g. Aune 1967) have defended the view that '*S* could have done *A*' means '*S* would have done *A*, had *S* chosen to do *A*'. (It's not clear that this is exactly Moore's view, since Moore only says that the two only 'very often' mean the same thing, not that they *always* do.) This account is sometimes known as the 'conditional account' because the proposed analysis defines 'could have done otherwise' in terms of a *conditional*: '*if S* had chosen to *A*, she *would have* done *A*'.

Unfortunately, however, this claim appears to be subject to an obvious objection (see Lehrer 1968). Imagine that I have a pathological aversion to spiders: I find them terrifying and repulsive, and I just can't go near them. When confronted with a particularly big, hairy, mean-looking spider, can I pick it up? Absolutely not! But if I *chose* to pick it up, would I do so? Arguably, yes I would: if I could somehow get myself into a psychological state where I managed to decide to pick the spider up, arguably I would already have conquered my aversion in making that decision, and so would then succeed in picking it up. It's not that *if* I chose to pick it up I would then find myself unable to follow through, as would be the case if I were to choose to walk to Leicester and be home in time for lunch; rather, it is the choice itself that I am unable to make. (Are you *kidding*? Look at the size of it! There's no *way* I'm going anywhere near it!) So, this looks like a clear case where I could *not* have done something (pick the spider up), but where I *would* have done it if I had chosen to – contrary to the claim that 'I could have done *A*' just *means* 'I would have done *A*, had I chosen to'.

What would the compatibilist need to do in order to get around this objection? Well, it looks like they'd have to revise the analysis, so that '*S* could have done *A*' means '*S* would have done *A* had they chosen to, *and S* could have chosen to *A*'. Since the spider case fails to satisfy the second half of that requirement ('*S* could have chosen to *A*'), it wouldn't count as a counter-example to the revised analysis, which is the result the compatibilist needs. But now the compatibilist is threatened with a vicious regress, because the proposed analysis of '*S* could have done *A*' itself includes the very expression – 'could have...' – that they were trying to analyse! To see this, let's call *S*'s *choosing* to do *A* – a mental action – '*C*'. So '*S* could have done *A*' now means '*S* would have done *A* had they done *C*, *and S* could have done *C*'. But now '*S* could have done *C*' – given the proposed analysis – must itself mean '*S* would have done *C* had they done *X*, *and S* could have done *X*', where *X* is some *other* mental action (choosing to choose to *A*, perhaps). And we can't stop there, because we now have to reapply the analysis to '*S* could have done *X*', and so on, *ad infinitum*. (But see §6.1 for John Locke's attempt to circumvent this vicious regress.)

Compatibilist abilities

A related compatibilist proposal, still in the spirit of Moore but differing in the detail, is that we think about the ability to do otherwise in the context of analysing the notion of an 'ability' more generally. For example, consider whether I, right now, have the ability to play the violin. There is certainly *a* perfectly good sense in which I am able: I was able to play the violin last time I tried, and I have not lost any of the relevant mental or physical capacities since then. On the other hand, you might think that there is also a sense in which I am *not*, right now, able to play the violin, since no violin is to hand. In effect, this is the incompatibilist sense of 'able to do otherwise': the laws plus facts about my current environment rule out the possibility of my now playing the violin.

There is another way to go, however: we can grant that I just *am* able, right now, to play the violin. The problem with my current circum-stances is not that they render me *unable*, right now, to play the violin; rather, they make it the case that my ability to play the violin is an ability that I am not, currently, able to *exercise*, thanks to the fact that there is no violin to hand. The basic compatibilist thought here, then, is that one can have an ability even if circumstances are such that one is unable to exercise it. And, since the fact that I currently have the ability to play the violin in no way requires the falsity of determinism, determinism is not incompatible with the ability to do otherwise (in this case, my ability to play the violin).

More specifically, Michael Fara (2008) argues for a 'dispositional' account of abilities and claims that such an account allows compatibil-ists to hold that determinism is no bar to possessing the ability to do otherwise. Dispositions certainly look to be pretty compatibilist-friendly. Consider the fragility of a wine glass. A wine glass uncontroversially retains its fragility – that is, the disposition to break when dropped – even when it is safely stored in the cupboard. It doesn't suddenly *acquire* that disposition when it's dropped; it had it all the time – it's just that the disposition is not *manifested* when it's in the cupboard. (So, the glass's disposition to break when dropped is not the disposition to break – a disposition it only has when it's dropped; rather, it's the disposition to break-when-dropped – a disposition it has all the time. If I were to point to a glass in the cupboard and ask you whether it was fragile, you'd say 'Yes'; you wouldn't say 'Oh, not at the moment – but if I were to drop it, *then* it would be fragile'.) If my ability to, say, make a cup of tea is akin to the glass's disposition to break-when-dropped, then it looks as though this might be an ability I can retain even when

I'm not in a position to make the tea, just as the glass retains its fragility when stored in the cupboard.

Fara's proposal (2008, 849) is roughly this: I am *able* to do *A* if and only if I am *disposed* to do *A* when I try. (As with the fragile glass, we need to read 'disposed to do *A* when I try' as a disposition that I have all the time – the disposition to do-*A*-when-I-try – and not as a disposition (the disposition to do *A*) that I have *only* when I try.)

Does Fara's dispositional account get around the objections raised against the conditional analysis? Well, the spider problem can be recast as follows. I am (let's agree) unable to pick up the spider, and yet I seem to satisfy Fara's definition of 'ability': I *am* disposed to pick-up-the-spider-if-I-try; it's just that I can't *try* to pick it up any more than I can *choose* to pick it up. So far, so bad. But Fara argues that we have independent reasons to deny that something has a disposition to do-*A*-in-circumstances-*C* if circumstances *C* are themselves impossible (2008, 851–2). For example, a rubber ball is not disposed to bounce when dropped if, in fact, it is nailed to the wall and so *cannot* be dropped. So, since I can't *try* to pick the spider up, I am not, in fact, disposed to pick-up-the-spider-if-I-try – which is the right result.

Of course, one might worry that, given determinism, the relevant circumstances – namely, my *trying* to do something I, in fact, don't do – are *always* going to be impossible, since my failing to try (if that's how things *actually* are) is determined by the laws plus the past. If the laws plus the past determine that, say, I do not try in five minutes' time to make the tea, then surely my trying to make the tea then is impossible. In that case, the ability to do otherwise, understood in Fara's sense, is going to turn out to be incompatible with determinism after all. Fara's dispositional account fares better here than a Moore-style conditional analysis, however, because it would be very implausible to insist that *in general* circumstances that are incompatible with the laws plus the past count as 'impossible' in a sense of 'impossible' that makes sense of the existence of unmanifested dispositions in general. If we adopt this sense of 'impossible', it turns out that determinism is incompatible not just with the ability of agents to do otherwise but also with the existence of *any* unmanifested dispositions whatsoever. For example, the fragile glass is just as determined to be sitting in the cupboard right now as I am determined not to try to make the tea. So, if we count circumstances that are incompatible with the laws plus the past as 'impossible' circumstances in the relevant sense, then the glass lacks the disposition to break when dropped, just as rubber ball that's nailed to the wall lacks the disposition to bounce when dropped. And that surely isn't right: it would be bizarre to claim that if determinism is true, none of the glasses in my cupboard are really fragile!

So, if – as seems eminently plausible – the existence of unmanifested dispositions quite generally (e.g. the fragility of the undropped glass) is compatible with determinism, the incompatibilist cannot insist that it is 'impossible' in the relevant sense for me to try to make the tea on the grounds that my trying is incompatible with the laws plus the past. Of course, this still leaves undone the task of explaining what the relevant sense of 'impossible' *is* – that is, one that counts as impossible my trying to pick up the spider if I have an aversion to spiders, or the ball's being dropped if it is nailed to the wall, but does *not* count as impossible the glass's being dropped or my trying to make the tea – and this may not be easy. But the point is that this is an issue to be resolved by thinking about dispositions generally, and – since incompatibilists will presumably concede that determinism is compatible with undropped glasses being fragile – the burden of providing such an account does not fall on the compatibilist specifically.

It's not entirely clear that the dispositional analysis is entirely off the hook, however. This is because the analysis implicitly focuses on overt actions, such as picking up spiders and making the tea. But what about mental actions, and in particular, what about *trying* itself? Fara's account (implicitly) seeks to sideline the issue about the possibility or impossibility of trying into the question just discussed, concerning whether or in what sense the relevant 'circumstances' are 'possible'. But trying is itself, arguably, a kind of action, and so it would seem to be an entirely legitimate question whether, assuming that determinism is true and I don't try to make the tea, I am *able* to try to make the tea. It looks as though on Fara's account, the answer to this question will be that I am able to try to make the tea if and only if I am disposed to try to make the tea *if I try to try* to make the tea. And now the worry is that we get into a vicious regress similar to (though not quite the same as) that faced by the Moore-style conditional analysis: if my ability to try to make the tea depends on my being disposed to try to make the tea if I try (to try to make the tea), then we have to postulate a further mental action – that of trying to try to make the tea. But then we can ask of *that* mental action whether I am able to perform *it*, and to answer that question we will have to postulate the further mental action of trying-to-try-to-try to make the tea, and so on. But, of course, there simply are not, and cannot be, infinitely many tryings that we perform when we go about our mundane tea-making activities.

3.3   Dennett on the Principle of Alternate Possibilities

Dennett (1984, Chapter 6) takes a much more straightforward approach to CA than those discussed above. Rather than try to interpret 'could have done otherwise' so that deterministic agents *can* do otherwise than they actually do (though he does this as well – see his 1984, 139–44), he simply denies that the ability to do otherwise, in the sense at work in CA, is required for acting freely and morally responsibly.

Dennett gives us a simple example: that of Martin Luther, a sixteenth-century theologian who challenged the authority of the Pope. When pressed to recant, Luther is reputed to have said, 'Here I stand. I can do no other'. Luther took himself to be *unable* to recant: his conscience made it impossible for him to deny, in public, things that he really believed and that he took to be extremely important truths. According to Dennett, Luther's 'declaration is testimony to the fact that we simply do not exempt someone from blame or praise because we think he could do no other. Whatever Luther was doing, he was not trying to duck responsibility' (1984, 133). In other words, Luther's subtext was not, 'Hey, don't blame *me*! I just don't have a choice here – I am at the mercy of my conscience!'. Rather, it was more like, 'I wholeheartedly stand by what I have said. I cannot recant because doing so would be wrong. But go ahead and blame me if you really think I *should* be recanting'. Moreover, understanding Luther's assertion in this way simply doesn't incline *us* to think that if he is right that he can do no other, then he gets to be exempted from responsibility. (Of course, he may be wrong; maybe he *can* recant. But that isn't the point. *He* doesn't think that the ability to recant is necessary for moral responsibility; if he did, then he *would* be trying to duck responsibility by saying that he can't recant. And – Dennett thinks – we don't think that either.)

In fact, the Luther case is simply a more vivid, and perhaps therefore more compelling, version of the case of Wally from Chapter 1. Wally, remember, finds a wallet that someone has dropped and unhesitatingly hands it in to the police station. Wally, we may suppose, doesn't feel *compelled* by his conscience to hand in the wallet; he just goes ahead and does it without really thinking about it. Luther, on the other hand, *does* feel compelled. Even so, Dennett thinks, our intuitive reaction is to hold him responsible for his behaviour. And, of course, Dennett thinks that that reaction is entirely appropriate. Hence, the central premise of CA, that acting freely requires the ability to do otherwise, is false.

It may be significant that both the Wally and Luther cases focus on potentially *praiseworthy* actions, while examples that incompatibilists tend to focus on when defending the claim that alternative possibilities *are* required for moral responsibility tend to focus on *blameworthy* actions. Susan Wolf (1980) has argued that the 'alternative possibilities' requirement does not, in fact, apply to freedom – and hence to moral responsibility – *simpliciter*; instead, it is a requirement only on blameworthy, but not praiseworthy, free actions. Wolf holds that when someone says, 'she couldn't hurt a fly!' or 'I just couldn't resist buying you that present – I knew how much you'd like it!', we don't think that undermines their praiseworthiness. But when people can't help doing *bad* things, we *do* think it undermines their *blame*worthiness.

How might we cash out the notion of acting freely in a way that makes sense of these (allegedly) asymmetrical intuitions? Wolf, who calls her position the 'Reason View', thinks it's because moral responsibility requires 'only the ability to do the right thing for the right reasons' (1990, 81). So someone who *does* do the right thing for the right reasons is *a fortiori* morally responsible (and hence praiseworthy), while someone who does the *wrong* thing must – in order to satisfy the above requirement – be *able* to do the right thing for the right reasons. Hence, blameworthiness, but not praiseworthiness, requires the ability to otherwise.

More precisely, Wolf claims that an agent is morally responsible only if she 'could have done otherwise if there had been a good and sufficient reason' (1980, 159). How does this work, and why does it deliver the required asymmetry? Well, let's start with praiseworthy actions. Suppose I couldn't resist buying you the present – even though it was expensive, and it was pretty inconvenient to carry it around with me for the rest of the day – because I knew how much you'd like it. Nonetheless, probably I *could* have resisted buying it (indeed I *would* have resisted) if I'd thought that you'd hate it – that is, if I'd had a 'good and sufficient reason' not to buy it. Hence I satisfy Wolf's requirement that I 'could have done otherwise if there had been a good and sufficient reason', and am therefore morally responsible (and hence praiseworthy) for buying you the present.

By contrast, when someone does something bad, there is *in fact* a 'good and sufficient reason' for them to desist, namely the fact that it's a bad thing to do. So, when someone does something bad, the only way to satisfy the requirement that one could have done otherwise *if there had been a good and sufficient reason to do so* is to *actually* be such that one could have done otherwise. For example, suppose Colin accidentally spills Jim's drink, and Jim thumps Colin as a result. There was a good and sufficient reason for Jim *not* to thump Colin: accidentally spilling someone's drink just doesn't merit being thumped. Does Jim satisfy Wolf's requirement? That requirement says that he's morally responsible only if he could have refrained from thumping Colin if there had been a good and sufficient reason to do so. But there *was* such a reason for him to refrain. Hence, he's morally responsible only if he could have refrained – only, that is, if he could have done otherwise.

So, Wolf's requirement – the idea that moral responsibility requires the 'ability to do the right thing for the right reasons' – implies that acting freely (in the sense of 'free' required for moral responsibility) requires alternative possibilities when one does the wrong thing, but it doesn't when one does the right thing. Her account connects with the idea that acting freely requires 'reasons-responsiveness', in the sense described in §2.2, in interesting ways that I won't explore here; but note that Wolf's is a more demanding account, in that reasons-responsiveness does *not* require the ability to do otherwise, while on Wolf's account only praise-worthiness lacks that requirement.

Wolf's view has come in for criticism (see, for example, Mele 1995, 162–4), but let's get back to my basic point in mentioning it in the first place. Dennett, remember, thinks that the ability to do otherwise just isn't a requirement on moral responsibility *at all*, independently of whether the act in question is praiseworthy or blameworthy. (After all, Dennett is a compatibilist – and not just a compatibilist about praise-worthy actions.) But, as I said, the case that Dennett uses to get us to agree with him – the case of Martin Luther – is one of praiseworthi-ness. My point in mentioning Wolf's asymmetry thesis is really that, if she is right about our *intuitive* reactions to cases of putative praisewor-thiness and blameworthiness (*viz*, we tend to count not being able to do otherwise as undermining the latter but not the former), then we need to be rather careful to avoid being overly impressed by carefully-chosen examples. For it Wolf is right about our ordinary intuitions, then we are liable to find ourselves inclined to agree with incompatibilists when they provide cases designed to show that an agent who could not have done otherwise isn't really blameworthy for doing something bad (where this is supposed to be evidence that they didn't act freely), but also to agree with compatibilists when *they* provide cases designed to show that an agent who could not have done otherwise is praiseworthy for doing something good (where this is supposed to show that they *do* act freely). In other words, our intuitive reactions to cases of putative praiseworthiness and blameworthiness may not all point us in the same direction – so we need to be careful not to over-generalise from our intuitive reaction to a single case.

Be that as it may, I myself am inclined to side with Dennett when it comes to the ability to do otherwise: Luther and Wally are both praiseworthy for their actions despite lacking the ability to do otherwise. Equally, people who do bad things are often blameworthy even if they, too, lack the ability to do otherwise. Someone who is suitably responsive to reasons and who nonetheless does something wrong (of course, we need an account of reasons-responsiveness that can make sense of this, and this isn't terribly straightforward – see §2.2 above) is blameworthy even if there was nothing else they could have done in the circumstances.

3.4   Local miracle compatibilism

One premise of CA, remember, is that nobody can render false the laws of nature. Hence, if some proposition P is a consequence of the laws of nature plus a complete description of all the facts at some particular past time, then nobody can (after that time) render P false, since they cannot render false facts about the past, and nor can they render false the laws. So, in particular, if the laws plus facts about what happened a hundred years previously entail that Sue will make a cup of tea at 10 a.m., then Sue cannot, at any time (she's less than a hundred years old), render it false that she does exactly that at 10 a.m.

David Lewis (1981) argues roughly as follows. While it's true that there is *a* sense in which we cannot render the laws of nature false, it simply doesn't follow that we cannot do things such that, were we to do them, a law of nature would be false. So, if Sue's making a cup of tea, say, is entailed by the laws plus the past, it doesn't follow that Sue could not do otherwise than make the tea, in a perfectly good sense of 'could have done otherwise'. The key idea is that the premise that nobody (Judge J, for example) can render false the laws of nature – premise (6), 'J cannot render L false', in van Inwagen's argument (see §3.1) – is ambiguous. It could mean either:

(6a) J cannot do or cause anything that would itself constitute a law-breaking event,

or it could mean:

(6b) J cannot do anything such that, were he to do it, some actual law L would be false.

In other words, there are two kinds of law-breaking ability that one might, in principle, have: one might have the ability to do or cause something that would be a law-breaking event (call this kind of ability A1), or one might have the ability to do something such were one to do it, some law *L* would be false. (Call this kind of ability A2.)

Lewis's basic claim is that, while nobody has the A1 kind of ability – for example, nobody can run faster than the speed of light, or levitate, or make a table move just by willing it and without exerting any kind of force on it – it doesn't follow that nobody has the A2 kind of ability. Indeed, we routinely *do* have the A2 kind of ability, even if determinism is true. Just now, I could have made a cup of tea, or turned on the TV, or had another biscuit, even though I didn't, in fact, do any of those things. If I *had* done any of those things, then, assuming determinism, an actual law of nature would have been false. But that in no way compromises the fact that I was *able* to do those things.

Putting this in a way that connects directly with CA, if we disambiguate premise (6), we'll see that, while (6a) is true, it does not entail (6b) – but it's (6b) that CA needs in order to be a sound argument. So if we plug (6a) into CA, we'll get an argument with true premises, but it won't be valid, since the fact that *J* cannot do or cause a law-breaking event does not (together with the other premises) entail that *J* cannot raise his hand. But if we plug (6b) into CA, the argument will be valid, but it will have a false premise, since it is simply false that *J* cannot do something (*viz*, raise his hand) such that, were he to do it, *L* would be false. Either way, then, CA fails.

The reasoning here is a little tricky, and we're going to have to cover a fair bit of background theory in order to be able to make sense of it, so let's take a detour into Lewis territory. As we saw in §2.2, we routinely make *counterfactual* claims: claims about what *would* have happened, had things been different. For example, I might say: 'I'm glad I made it on time; *if* I'd missed the bus, I *would have* been late'. And we take it for granted that such claims are sometimes true and sometimes false; indeed, we often feel pretty confident in being able to sort the true ones from the false ones. For example, in the situation where *in fact* the next bus didn't arrive for another hour, the counterfactual is clearly true: If I'd missed the bus, I would have had to wait a full hour for the next one, and (since I only arrived five minutes early as it was) I would certainly have been late. On the other hand, in the situation where *in fact* there was another bus five minutes behind the one I caught, the counterfactual is false (at least, it is if we assume that I in fact missed the bus by less than five minutes): If I'd missed the bus I *actually* caught, I would caught the next one, and I would still have arrived on time (just).

On Lewis's account of counterfactuals (1973, 1979), the *truth conditions* for counterfactuals – what makes them true – are as follows. Suppose we have the counterfactual, 'if *A* had been the case, *B* would have been the case' (so if *A* is 'I miss the bus' and *B* is 'I'm late', this counterfactual just says, 'if I'd missed the bus, I would have been late'). This counterfactual will be true if and only if, *at the closest possible world to the actual world* at which *A* is true, *B* is also true. So, our sample counterfactual, 'If I'd missed the bus, I would have been late', is true if and only if: *at the closest possible world to the actual world* at which I miss the bus, I'm late.

What on earth is a 'possible world', and what makes one closer than another to the actual world? Well, to cut a very long story short, we can think of possible worlds as *ways the world might have been*. As with counterfactuals, we routinely say that things *could* or *might* have been different: 'The extinction of the Tasmanian Tiger could have been prevented', 'I could have been a contender', 'You could have made the effort to show up on time', or whatever. In Lewis's terms, such claims amount to saying that *there is* a possible world in which the Tasmanian tiger is not extinct in 2013, or in which I am a contender, or in which you made the effort to show up on time.

(That doesn't answer the question of what a possible world *is*. Lewis himself thinks that they are real, concrete entities, just like the actual world, so that a possible world in which Tasmanian tigers aren't extinct really does exist, and the Tasmanian tigers that inhabit it are real, flesh-and-blood animals (Lewis 1986c). Other philosophers think this is crazy, and give alternative accounts. Some hold, for example, that a possible world is really just a kind of *story*. I could easily write an internally consistent story according to which the extinction of the Tasmanian tiger was prevented; hence, there's a possible world in which Tasmanian tigers exist in 2013. But we'll leave this thorny issue aside.)

The *actual* world, unsurprisingly, is the world we *in fact* inhabit – the one in which Tasmanian tigers *are* extinct, and (we're supposing) you didn't make the effort to arrive on time. So the actual world, according to Lewis, is just one among very many *possible* worlds. (If we think of a possible world as a way the world might have been, then clearly the actual world is a possible world, since things obviously *might* have been the way they in fact *are*.) And the *closeness* of one possible world to another goes by how *similar* the two possible worlds are to one another. Thus, for example, a possible world where the Tasmanian tiger isn't extinct in 2013 is a lot closer to the actual world than is a possible world where *The Hobbit* is an accurate historical account of the adventures of Bilbo Baggins. It's not much of a departure from reality to imagine a concerted effort in Tasmania in the early twentieth century to save the Tasmanian tiger; it's quite a big departure from reality to imagine hobbits and trolls and wizard existing, the casting of spells being effective, etc.

So, let's get back to our sample counterfactual: 'If I'd missed the bus, I would have been late'. In order to see whether this is true, we have to see whether or not, at the *closest* possible world where I miss the bus, I arrive late. If I do arrive late at that possible world, then the counterfactual is true, and if I don't, it isn't. So, *is* it true that I'm late at the closest possible world where I miss the bus? In order to answer that question, we have to consider what the closest possible world where I miss the bus is like.

Let's set aside the question about closeness of possible worlds for a moment, and think about how we *actually*, implicitly, imagine things to be different when we go around making counterfactual claims such as 'If I'd missed the bus, I would have been late'. In effect what we do, it seems, is imagine a situation that's quite a lot like the *actual* situation, but where things are a *little* bit different: just different enough so that I miss the bus. So, for example, I might imagine the bus having arrived a bit earlier (and hence having already departed by the time I got to the bus stop) by not getting caught at the traffic lights just down the road. Or I might imagine my having left the house a little later because I couldn't find my keys. In effect, what we imagine is the past up until very recently being just the same as it *actually* was, but *something* at some recent point in time going a little bit differently to what actually happened; and then we consider whether or not, in our imagined scenario, I arrive on time.

Lewis's claim about the truth conditions of counterfactuals works in just the same way. The closest possible world where I miss the bus – the possible world where I miss the bus that is the most *similar* to the actual world – is one at which the past up until very recently is the same as it actually was, but then something goes a little bit differently so that I end up missing the bus. So, our counterfactual, 'If I'd missed the bus, I would have been late', is true just if, in that closest possible world, I also arrive late. Which possible world is closer: the one in which the bus doesn't get caught at the lights, or the one in which it takes me a couple of minutes to locate my keys? It's not clear what the answer to that question is, but, luckily, it probably doesn't matter. Let's assume that the next bus didn't, in fact, arrive for another hour. Then – since closeness requires as much similarity to the *actual* world as possible – the closest possible world where the bus doesn't get caught at the lights *and* the closest world where I don't find my keys right away are *both* possible worlds where the next bus doesn't arrive for an hour, and so they're both possible worlds at which I arrive late. For the sake of simplicity, however, let's just assume from now on that the closest possible world where I miss the bus is the (closest) possible world at which the bus doesn't get caught at the lights. Call this world *w*.

Now – to bring us slightly closer to the point of all this – note that if determinism is true, then *w* is a possible world in which some (unspecified) *actual* law of nature is *false*. After all, facts about the distant past plus the actual laws entail that the bus *did* get stuck at the lights. So, somewhere in the counterfactual scenario we're imagining – somewhere in the recent history of world *w* – the actual laws must have been broken.

In Lewis's terms, *w* involves a 'local miracle', which is why his view is often referred to as 'local miracle compatibilism'. Note, however, that the 'miracle' in question isn't quite as miraculous as it sounds. We might define a 'miracle' in the usual sense of the word as follows: event *M* is a miracle if and only if *M* occurs *at possible world W*, and *M* is contrary to some law (or combination of laws) of nature *L that obtain at W*. (Whether a miracle in this sense is even a conceptual possibility is a good question, but not one we'll dwell on here.) This is not what *Lewis* means by a 'miracle'. If determinism is true, then – given facts about the distant past – the bus managing to get through the traffic lights (call this *m*) *at w* is contrary to some *actual* law of nature *L*. This is what Lewis means by a 'miracle': event *M* is a miracle if and only if *M* occurs *at possible world W*, and *M* is contrary to some *actual* law (or combination of laws) *L*. The point here is that while *m* is a miracle in Lewis's sense, it is *not* contrary to any *of w's* law of nature. At *w*, *L* simply isn't a law in the first place. So, as things *actually* happened – in the *actual* world – *L* is a law, and *m* does not occur, so there is no miracle in the usual sense of 'miracle'. In *w*, *m* does occur but *L* is not a law, so, again, there is no miracle in the usual sense of 'miracle'. *m* is only a 'miracle' in Lewis's special sense of 'miracle': something (*m*) happens in *w* that is contrary to the laws of nature of the *actual* world.

That's the rather lengthy excursion into the background theory over with; let's get back, finally, to the ability to do otherwise. Recall the distinction between what I'm calling 'A1' abilities and 'A2' abilities: the distinction between the ability (A1) to *do or cause* a law-breaking event and the ability (A2) to do something such that, *were you to do it*, a law would have been false. Now, a 'law-breaking event' is just a *miracle*, in Lewis's sense: an event (at some possible world *w*) that is, in the circumstances, incompatible with the *actual* laws. So, another way to draw the distinction between A1- and A2-abilities would be to distinguish between the ability (A1) to *perform* or *cause to happen* a miracle (in Lewis's sense of 'miracle', obviously) and the ability (A2) to do something such that, were you to do it, a miracle *would have occurred*.

Now, on Lewis's view, miracles (in his sense) *can happen*; indeed, assuming determinism, they routinely happen at close possible worlds. For example at *w*, where the bus doesn't get caught at the lights, there really is a miracle – something that is incompatible with the actual laws – hidden somewhere in the scenario. If there were no such event, then (assuming determinism), *w* would pan out exactly like the actual world, where the bus *does* get caught at the lights. Crucially, however – in our bus case and indeed in general – when we evaluate the counter-factual 'If event *a* had happened, then event *b* would have happened' by considering whether *b* happens at the closest world where *a* happens, we *don't* have to assume that *a itself* is the miracle. In the bus case, my missing the bus *itself* (if we can stretch the ordinary notion of 'event' and think of this as an event, which occurred, let's say, at the moment when I reached the bus stop) was no miracle; I just showed up at the bus stop, entirely non-miraculously, and the bus had already left. The miracle occurred *earlier*, at some point just before the bus got to the traffic lights.

This being so, consider the ability (A2) to do something such that, were you to do it, a miracle *would have occurred*. Lewis thinks we routinely have *this* kind of ability. Let's consider Sue's ability to make a cup of tea at 10 a.m. (something she doesn't, in fact, do). Of course, given that Sue doesn't, in fact, make a cup of tea at 10 a.m., the closest possible world in which she *does* make a cup of tea is one that involves some actual law of nature being false: it's a possible world in which a miracle occurs *somewhere* along the line. But we do not need to suppose that the miracle is *Sue's making a cup of tea* itself. We can (allegedly) reasonably assume that the miracle occurs *before* Sue makes the tea, just as, in the bus case, the miracle occurs before I get to the bus stop. So, Lewis thinks, Sue is able to do something, namely make the tea, such that, *were she to do it* (that is, make the tea), a law of nature would have been broken: a miracle would have occurred. (Let's assume that, say, in the closest possible world where Sue makes the tea, some neurons fire in her brain in a way that's contrary to the actual laws, and their firing leads her to think that a cup of tea would be nice.) But that does *not* imply that she has the ability (A1) to *perform* or *cause to happen* a miracle. The firing of those neurons (in that possible world) is not something that Sue *does* or that she *brings about*. (Remember the bus case: *Had I missed the bus*, a law would have been broken. It doesn't follow that *my missing the bus* would *itself* have been a miracle.)

To put it the other way around, Lewis thinks we lack A1-abilities: nobody is able to run faster than light or to stop a speeding bullet with the power of their mind. We don't, unfortunately, have magical powers. But, given what we've just seen, it does not follow from this that we lack A2-abilities. For, as we've just seen, Sue's inability to *perform* (or cause) a miracle (in Lewis's sense) is entirely consistent with her ability to make the tea.

The upshot of all this, according to Lewis, is that while there is a *sense* in which van Inwagen is right to say that we cannot break the laws of nature – *viz*, we have no A1-abilities – it would be a mistake to conclude that we cannot do things that are *consequences* of the laws of nature (plus facts about the distant past). We *can* do such things, that is, we have lots of A2-abilities. We can do things – for example, Sue can make a cup of tea – such that, were we to do them, a law of nature would be broken.

Of course, it's a matter for debate whether Lewis's defence of compatibilism really works (see e.g. Fischer 1994, Chapter 4; Beebee 2003; Oakley 2006; Graham 2008). And even if it does work in principle, notice that he hasn't provided an account of the circumstances in which we do and don't have A2-abilities. For example, we can't simply stipulate that someone has the ability to do X just if there is some possible world in which they X, for it would follow from this definition that we all have the ability to run really fast or sing the Russian national anthem or walk a tightrope. It is surely true that there are possible worlds in which I can do these things; at any rate, I can certainly coherently imagine having learned the Russian national anthem or, at a push, how to walk a tightrope. But, of course, only some people actually have these abilities – and unfortunately I am not one of them. Similarly, our arachnophobe (let's assume) is *unable* to pick up the big, hairy spider. Nonetheless, there are possible worlds where she *does* pick up the spider – for example, one in which she has just been hypnotised and temporarily lost her fear of spiders. So, it looks like some constraints on what it is to have an ability are needed. (See Smith 1997 for an attempt to cash out some plausible conditions on possessing a Lewisian A2-ability.)

3.5 Humean compatibilism

As we've seen, Lewis takes issue with van Inwagen's claim that we cannot render the laws of nature false. Lewis thinks that while there is a sense in which this claim is true (we do indeed have no A1-abilities), there is also a sense in which it is simply false (we have at least some A2-abilities), and so the compatibilist can avoid the conclusion of CA.

A more radical proposal than Lewis's, which Alfred Mele and I dub 'Humean compatibilism' (Beebee & Mele 2002; see also Berofsky 1987), denies that we lack even A1-abilities – or, to put it in terms of CA, rejects the premise that nobody can render the laws of nature false, however we disambiguate it. (Remember, Lewis thinks that premise is true if taken to mean that nobody has A1-abilities.) This may sound crazy, but bear with me! The starting point of this proposal is to consider *why* one might think that we cannot render the laws of nature false. Laws of nature – or, more carefully, propositions that *state* laws of nature – would seem to be *universal generalisations* of a special sort. Newton's Second Law of Motion, for example, says that for *every* object, the force acting on it (*f*) is equal to its mass (*m*) × its acceleration (*a*): *f=ma*. (Actually this 'law' is, strictly speaking, false, although it gets things roughly right for things that aren't moving too quickly. Let's ignore this complication and pretend that it really is a law.) Einstein's Special Theory of Relativity entails that *nothing* travels faster than the speed of light, or, in other words, that *everything* travels at the speed of light or slower – a universal generalisation that is as good a candidate as any for being a law.

What marks the laws of nature out from common-or-garden true universal generalisations, such as the fact (let's assume it is a fact) that every human being, past, present and future, dies before the age of 160, or that I never (past, present or future) eat a kumquat? We'll come back to that question presently. For now, though, notice that it's entirely plausible to suppose – or at least it is unless we've already accepted the conclusion of CA – that even if determinism is true, we *can* render plenty of true universal generalisations false. Even if it's true that, in fact, I will never eat a kumquat, this is a fact that I *could* render false by finding a kumquat and eating it. Supposing that the oldest-ever human lives to age 159, it's entirely possible that the fact that all human beings die before they're 160 *could* be rendered false, even though – since we're supposing our universal generalisation to be true – nobody *will* render it false. Perhaps the 159-year-old dies on the day before her 160th birthday because that's when her life-support machine gets turned off. In that case, someone *could* render our universal generalisation false by leaving it switched on for another day.

Aside: Of course, if CA has already persuaded you that if determinism is true then nobody can do anything other than what they actually do, then you will think that nobody *can* render any true common-or-garden universal generalisation false, since doing so would involve doing something, e.g. my eating a kumquat, that is incompatible with the past plus the laws. But in the current context, to claim this would be to beg the question. The position I'm in the middle of trying to explain – Humean compatibilism – rejects a *premise* of CA, namely the claim that we cannot render the laws of nature false. It's a presupposition of Humean compatibilism that we *can* render false common-or-garden universal generalisations. So, you're not entitled to reject Humean compatibilism by using the *conclusion* of CA to argue that we can't, in fact, render false common-or-garden universal generalisations. If you were to do that, you would implicitly be appealing to the very premise of CA – the premise that we cannot render the laws of nature false – that Humean compatibilism rejects. So hold that thought!

Back to the main point. If we can render false universal generalisations such as 'Helen never eats a kumquat', why can we not render false those universal generalisations that are laws of nature? What's so special about the *laws* that makes them unsusceptible to being rendered false? To answer that question, we need to think about what laws of nature are supposed to be. Philosophical views on the matter fall into two broad camps: the 'Humean' camp and the 'anti-Humean' or 'necessitarian' camp. (Actually, things are much more complicated than this, but let's keep things simple.)

According to necessitarians, the laws of nature, unlike other universal generalisations, *govern* what happens in the Universe. Actually, strictly speaking, it isn't right to say here that the laws *are* universal generalisations; generalisations, after all, are just facts *about* the world, and therefore can't possibly govern anything. Rather, the idea is that the laws are features of the world whose existence *entails* the relevant universal generalisations. So, for example, on David Armstrong's view (1983), the laws of nature are relations of necessitation between universals.

What does this mean? Well, universal generalisations (let's suppose) have the form 'all Fs are Gs', where (at least sometimes) 'F' and 'G' refer to *universals*: genuine multiply-located features of reality. So, supposing that *weighing exactly 1kg* is a universal, it is a real element of reality that is wholly located wherever a thing weighing exactly 1 kg is to be found. Not all predicates refer to universals, however. '…is smaller than the average car' doesn't refer to a universal: there is no feature of reality, *being smaller than the average car*, that is to be found in both Reliant Robins and coffee cups. (See Armstrong 1980 for a lot more on universals.)

According to Armstrong, sometimes two universals F and G are related by the higher-order relation of *necessitation*, or N. When this is so, the result is a law of nature. Armstrong writes this '$N(F, G)$', which means: '*F* and *G* are related by *N*', or '*being F* necessitates *being a G*'. And the idea is that if this relation between *F* and *G* obtains, then it's *guaranteed* that all *F*s are *G*s. After all, if being an *F* necessitates being a *G*, then whenever you find something that is an *F*, that thing is surely bound to be a *G*. So if *N(F, G)* obtains – if those universals really do stand in that relation – then that entails the universal generalisation 'all *F*s are *G*s'. By contrast, in the case of common-or-garden universal generalisations, the universals (if any) that they refer to *don't* stand in relation *N* to one another. Even supposing that *being a human being* and *dying before the age of 160* are universals (which they probably aren't – at least, *dying before the age of 160* certainly doesn't look like a plausible candidate for being a universal), those two universals are certainly not related by *N*, or at least, they certainly aren't if the only reason why the generalisation is true is that someone's life-support machine one day gets switched off the day before her 160th birthday. It merely *happens* to be the case that all human beings die before the age of 160; being a human being doesn't *guarantee* that you'll die before you hit 160.

This being so, we have the makings of an explanation for *why* it is that we *can* (intuitively and, again, without having presupposed the conclusion of CA) render false common-or-garden universal generalisations, while we *can't* render false those universal generalisations that state laws. If *N(F, G)* obtains, then you just can't 'pull apart' *F* and *G*: the relationship between these universals is something that is completely outside of your control. You can pull apart two pieces of paper that have been joined with a staple: just pull, or remove the staple. But try (metaphorically, of course) getting your hands on two universals related by *N* and prising them apart. It just can't be done. And that's what you'd have to do in order to render false a universal generalisation that states a law. Another way to put the point is to say that on Armstrong's view, the laws *govern* what goes on in the Universe. (This is disputed; in particular, John Foster (2004) argues that the only way to get the laws to turn out to govern what goes on is to think of them as divine edicts. But let's set that aside.)

This 'governing conception' of laws of nature (see Beebee 2000) is not the only view in town, however; there is also the 'Humean' view of laws. On the Humean view, there just *aren't* any relations of necessitation. (Hence, the name 'Humean', named after Hume, who – arguably – thought that the idea that necessitation is a genuine feature of reality made no sense whatsoever.) On the Humean view, then, reality is constituted by lots and lots of things happening – 'just one damn thing after another', as philosophers sometimes say in an attempt to be vaguely humorous. As it turns out – and luckily for us – things happen, by and large, in nice, regular, predictable ways. True universal generalisations capture what those regularities are: the fact that all *F*s are *G*s captures a regular pattern of goings-on in the world, whether it is the fact that all human beings die before the age of 160, or the fact that *f=ma*, or whatever. The laws of nature are merely a special subset of the true universal generalisations. *Which* special subset? Well, on the 'best system' account of laws (sometimes called the 'Ramsey-Lewis' view, or the 'Mill-Ramsey-Lewis' view (Mill 1875, Bk III, Chapter IV; Ramsey 1978; Lewis 1973, 73–5; Lewis 1986b, Postscript C), the idea goes like this: Imagine that Janice (not a human being, we may suppose; she has much more brain power than us), who happens to be around right at the end of the Universe, just before the point where the whole lot is going to blink out of existence, is having a conversation with God:

Janice: Lord, I would really like to be omniscient. I mean, I would really like to know everything that's ever happened in the Universe. (And everything that *will* happen, but there's not going to be very much to say there, seeing as the End of the Universe is upon us.) *You* know all this stuff; can't you just *tell* me?

God: OK, Janice, since you asked, here's something I made earlier. It's my Big Book of Facts. In it, you'll find a full description of every single thing that's ever happened (and ever will happen – but as you say, not much to tell there). It includes absolutely everything, including this very conversation, what you were doing at 10.30 yesterday morning, what Napoleon had for breakfast every day of his life, the precise location of every ant that ever crawled the Earth at every moment in time, and so on and on. Sorry it's rather long. Can't be helped; a lot's happened.

Janice: Um, well, thanks, God, but look, time's running out, and I'm not nearly as clever as you. I'll never get much past the emergence of life on Earth before the End of the Universe is upon us. Can't you give me something, well, *shorter*?

God: Well, yes, I suppose I could. Here's what I can do. I can just give you Chapter 1 – which, as it happens, tells you everything about everything that happened right at the beginning of the Universe – and then I can replace the rest of the book with a big list of universal generalisations. These are the 'axioms'. As it happens, you can derive all the other facts about what happened and when, just from those two things: Chapter 1 plus the axioms. Of course, you don't have the time to derive *all* the other facts; if you did that, you'd just end up with the Big Book of Facts again, and we'd be back where we started. I'm afraid true omniscience is beyond you. However, what you probably *do* have time for is to answer any particular question you might have. So, if you want to know what happened at midnight on 23 October 1723 at a specific location in Paris, you'll be able to figure it out. (Not by any means a trivial exercise, I know. But you're *very* clever, so I think you'll be able to do it.) I'm afraid that's as good as you're going to get. Here you are then.

Janice: Wow, thanks, God! I'm still a bit worried though. I mean, it's still a *really* long book, because there are absolutely *loads* of axioms listed here. Look, here it says, 'Every human being dies before the age of 160'. But presumably that is entailed by various other axioms together with some relevant facts about the initial state of the Universe, since presumably those are going to entail that Napoleon was born on such-and-such a date and died on such-and-such a date, and similarly for everyone else. So, if I know all that other stuff, I can figure out for myself that every human being dies before the age of 160. And there seem to be *vast* numbers of axioms that are in the same boat. Look, here's one that says that every ant within a one-mile radius of the Houses of Parliament on 1 January 1972 was less than 1 cm long, and one that says that every dinosaur in a very specific area on a certain date was a velociraptor, and so on. I really need a way of sorting the wheat from the chaff here! It's just too much information. Can't you do any better?

God: Oh dear, I really am very busy, you know. But, yes, I can, now you mention it. Here's my final offer. I can see that what you need is a system that maximises both *strength* and *simplicity*. There's a sense in which it's handy to have those axioms you mention in there; after all, once you know that everyone dies before the age of 160, and you know that Napoleon existed, you can infer straight off that Napoleon died before the age of 160. Without that axiom, you're going to have to figure it out from other axioms, together with the facts contained in Chapter 1 – you'll have to figure out when Napoleon was born and when he died, and so how old he was when he died, from other information. On the other hand, as you say, you don't really *need* that axiom; that is, the system will be just as strong without it. (By contrast, if I crossed off *f=ma*, you'd be really scuppered; there are all kinds of facts you then wouldn't be able to infer at all. So, *f=ma* is contributing to the system's *strength*.) Moreover, as you say, it is rather a long list. Cutting out a lot of the more boring axioms, such as the ones you mention, will make the system much *simpler*. So, look, here's my new, even shorter version. Happy now?

Janice: Well, I guess so. I mean, I suppose it's not your fault that I don't have a big enough brain to just absorb all of the facts in the original book (actually, it *is* your fault, now I think about it, but I'll let that pass), so, given that we need to do the axiom thing as a short cut, I reckon that what you've given me is as good as it's going to get. Thanks. One last question though: Does this new, shorter list of axioms together with Chapter 1 really entail *absolutely everything*? I mean, don't the axioms leave *any* questions about what's happened or is going to happen unanswered?

God: Oh, no. What you've got there allows you to infer absolutely everything that was in the original book. Which, in fact, is just to say that the Universe is entirely *deterministic*. See, in the shorter version, I crossed out the title 'Axioms' and wrote 'The Laws of Nature'. That's what those humans on Earth used to call them. (Well, that's what they called the generalisations *they* used as axioms; they didn't manage to get them all spot-on.) I kind of like the term, so that's what I've called them, too. (Note, however, that humans also tended to call the *theorems* of the system 'laws' as well – that is, other generalisations that follow just from the axioms. For instance, a generalisation that tells you the acceleration of any body with a specific mass and a specific force acting on it follows from *f=ma*, so that's a theorem and, hence, a law. I haven't listed the theorems, because you can figure them out for yourself. On the other hand, note that the generalisation that all humans die before the age of 160 *isn't* a theorem – you need the facts contained in Chapter 1 together with the axioms to derive *that,* now that I've removed that generalisation from the axiom list. So, it isn't a law.) So, you can infer *all* of the facts about what happened from what you've got in Chapter 1, together with your list of laws. And that's just determinism.

Janice: Wow, that *is* amazing! Did you engineer things so that they'd pan out that way?

God: Good heavens, no, not at all. I just set up the initial conditions – just as I've described in Chapter 1 – and let the Universe get on with it. I didn't tell the Universe what to do; it just went ahead and did what it did. I agree, it *is* pretty amazing that it turned out to be deterministic (except, of course, that I'm omniscient, so I knew it was going to pan out that way, and was therefore not amazed at all). But I had nothing to do with *making* it pan out that way, honest. I guess I *could* have issued a set of decrees – 'Everything with mass, thou shalt obey *f=ma*', and so on – but, well, I didn't.

Let's leave Janice to her calculations. The point here is that the list of axioms that she ends up with, which God has just retitled 'The Laws of Nature', is the best combination of simplicity and strength, in the sense just described. That (together with the theorems that are entailed by the axioms) is exactly what the best system account says the laws are. And, as

God just implied, if the Universe is deterministic, then that best system, together with Chapter 1, a complete list of the facts that obtained right at the beginning (or, indeed, at any other time), will entail all the other facts at all the other times.

With all this in place, let's get back to free will. As we saw earlier, on the necessitarian view of laws, the laws *govern* what happens. And if the laws of nature really do govern what happens, then it seems plausible to suppose that there is no sense in which they are up to us. Similarly, if God had done what he just said he *didn't* do, namely, set the Universe going with a set of decrees about how things had to behave, then it would be plausible to suppose that we would be unable to render those decrees false. In other words, on that kind of view, it seems that the laws place *constraints* on what we can and can't do. Correspondingly, the premise of CA that says that we cannot render the laws false (perhaps disambiguated in the way Lewis proposes, so that the premise only rules out our having A1-abilities), seems to be true.

On the Humean view, by contrast – and on the best system view in particular – the laws *don't* govern what happens. They are just the best way of systematising all the particular facts: all the facts that were listed in God's original gift to Janice, his Big Book of Facts. Nobody and nothing *makes* the facts pan out the way they do; they just *do* pan out that way.

On this kind of view, it's unclear why we should think that the laws place any constraints on what we can and can't do. Consider common-or-garden generalisations again, such as the generalisation that Sam will never eat a kumquat. Let's suppose that that generalisation is true. It follows that Sam will not eat a kumquat at 11 a.m. tomorrow. Now, the compatibilist and the incompatibilist should agree – whatever their view of laws – that the mere fact that a true generalisation entails that Sam doesn't eat a kumquat tomorrow, just by itself, in no way compromises Sam's *ability* to eat a kumquat tomorrow. But now grant that Sam's eating a kumquat tomorrow is incompatible with the laws and the past. According to CA, that *does* compromise Sam's ability to eat a kumquat tomorrow: that is something that he is not able to do, thanks to the fact that, in order to be able to do that, he would have to be able to make it the case that an actual law of nature is false. But on a Humean view of laws, it is unclear why we should think that there is a difference between the two cases. Why should we think some generalisations can be rendered false – e.g. that Sam will never eat a kumquat – but not others, e.g the generalisation in Janice's list of the Laws of Nature that would be false if Sam were to eat a kumquat? After all, the only thing that's special about the generalisations that feature in Janice's list of laws is that they are part of the simplest and strongest system for deriving all the facts there are about what has happened and will happen. On the Humean compatibilist view, there really is no difference between the cases: Sam's ability to eat a kumquat tomorrow is no more compromised by its incompatibility with the laws plus the past than it is by its incompatibility with the true generalisation that Sam never eats a kumquat.

Note that this position is different from Lewis's. Lewis merely *asserts* that we are able to break the laws in the A2 sense – we are able to do things such that, were we to do them, a law would have been broken (or rendered false) – and *denies* that we are able to break them in the A1 sense. (We are unable to do or cause any law-breaking events.) One worry we might have about Lewis's position is that it is unclear what *explanation* there might be for saying that we have one kind of ability but lack the other kind. True, it accords pretty well with our ordinary beliefs (at least before we start worrying about free will, at any rate): We routinely go around attributing A2-abilities to people ('I was worried about you – you could have called!', or 'Why didn't you help when you were perfectly able to?'). But perhaps those beliefs simply aren't justified. In particular, how can I have the ability to do something, the doing of which would *require* a law-breaking event to happen, when I lack the ability to *bring about* any law-breaking event myself? Surely, the incompatibilist may retort, the very fact that I am unable to break the laws in the A1 sense undermines my ability to break them in the A2 sense. In order to address this worry, it looks as though the local miracle compatibilist would have to give a metaphysical story – either about us and our abilities or about the laws – which would explain why our lack of the first kind of ability *doesn't* undermine the second kind of ability. Lewis offers no such explanation. (See Beebee 2003 for more on this line of objection.)

The Humean compatibilist, like my imagined incompatibilist opponent of Lewis, accepts that there is no distinction between the two kinds of ability. However, rather than arguing that since we don't have A1-type abilities, we don't have A2-type abilities either, the Humean compatibilist instead claims that we, in fact, have abilities of *both* kinds. And this claim is motivated by a pretty respectable (which isn't to say universally agreed upon) theory of laws of nature: given their metaphysical nature (or rather, lack of it), *viz*, the fact that laws are *metaphysically* no different from common-or-garden universal generalisations, they no more place constraints on what we are able to do than do common-or-garden generalisations. Hence, the claim, central to CA, that we are unable to render the laws false is itself false. Threat of incompatibilism averted! (Of course, the incompatibilist might retort that if determinism is true, then we are unable to render false even common-or-garden generalisations, since these generalisations are themselves merely consequences of the laws plus the past. But, as we saw earlier, that would beg the question against the Humean compatibilist.)

One major potential problem with Humean compatibilism, however, is that it has the somewhat counter-intuitive consequence that we are able to do exactly the kinds of thing that Lewis thinks we *can't* do. We can clear a tall building with a single bound or run faster than the speed of light. Isn't this *obviously* a mistake? Well, the first thing to note is that there are lots of different meanings of 'ability'; indeed, we've seen a fair few in this chapter. Thus, for example, in one sense I am able to play the violin right now – this is a skill that I have – but in another sense I am not able to do so: there is no violin in my vicinity for me to play. In one sense of 'ability', I am able to go for a long walk, but not as far as Leicester, and be back in time for lunch – whether or not determinism is true. In the incompatibilist sense of 'ability', by contrast, I am not able to go for a walk at all if doing so is incompatible with the past plus the laws.

The Humean compatibilist's response to CA is, in effect, to say that the sense of 'ability' presupposed in that argument – one according to which we are unable to render the laws false – will only seem like a notion of ability that is relevant to our acting *freely* if we buy into a necessitarian or anti-Humean view of laws, according to which the laws *govern* what happens. According to that conception of the laws, the laws are shackles from which we cannot break free: we are *unable*, in an obvious sense of 'unable', to render them false, and this is an impediment to our acting freely. From a Humean perspective, however, while we can grant that there is *a* sense of 'able' according to which we are unable to render the laws false, this sense of 'able' just isn't an important sense when it comes to acting freely. The laws are *not* shackles from which we cannot break free, any more than the generalisation that Sam will never eat a kumquat is a shackle from which *he* can never break free. So, if we want to adopt a sense of 'able' that is relevant to our acting freely, we can happily adopt a sense of 'able' according to which we *can* render the laws false: the laws do not, after all, impede us any more than any more than do common-or-garden generalisations.

On the other hand, as we've seen, there are many different senses of 'able'. In the sense of 'able' according to which (on a Humean view) we are able to break the laws, we are able to jump tall buildings with a single bound. But that is perfectly compatible with there being *other* senses of 'able' according to which we are *unable* to do this. (Remember the violin case. Am I able, right now, to play the violin? Well, yes and no. It depends what you mean, in this context, by 'able'.) Thus, for example, we might define another sense of 'able' – and this harks back to the conditional analysis of 'could have done otherwise' – according to which *S* is able to do *A* just if, were *S* to *try* or *decide* or *choose* to do *A*, then she would succeed. In *this* sense of 'able', I am *not* able to leap a tall building with a single bound, since if I were to try or decide to do it, I would fail.

Why would I fail? Well, remember Lewis's account of counterfactuals from the previous section. Imagine deciding to leap over the Eiffel Tower. What would happen next? You'd fail miserably. That's because when we evaluate the truth of counterfactual claims, such as 'If I decided to leap over the Eiffel Tower, I'd succeed', we hold fixed the laws as far as possible. Assuming determinism, the closest possible world in which I decide to leap over the Eiffel Tower (call it *w*) must contain a 'miracle', since the *actual* laws plus the past determine that I won't make that decision. But thereafter, we reinstate the laws (the laws that *actually* obtain) – that is, the law that is broken in *w* in order to get me to make the decision to leap over the Eiffel Tower only gets broken the once. Thereafter, everything in *w* proceeds in accordance with the actual laws. And those laws most certainly entail that I will fail. Why do we reinstate the laws? Well, the short answer is that, other things being equal, the more miracles there are in a given possible world, relative to the actual world's laws, the less similar it is to the actual world. A possible world in which I decide to leap over the Eiffel Tower and succeed clearly contains more than one miracle, so it is further away from the actual world than is *w*. (Intuitively this sounds right, I hope: it's a much bigger departure from reality to imagine me deciding to leap over the Eiffel Tower and then actually pulling it off than it is to imagine me (bizarrely, admittedly) deciding to do it and then failing pathetically.)

Well, this defence of the claim that we are able to break the laws might not sound too convincing. At a minimum, however, both Humean compatibilism and Lewis's local miracle compatibilism raise the possibility that there is an interesting connection between questions about free will and questions about the nature of laws. And there certainly seems to be *something* right about the thought that the threat allegedly posed by determinism depends upon the idea that the laws of nature *constrain* what we can and can't do. To the extent that that is so, our thinking about free will, in turn, needs to be constrained by what kind of theory of laws of nature we ought to adopt. And that, of course, is another matter for dispute.

3.6   Conclusion

In this chapter, we've seen a variety of ways in which compatibilists have tried to wriggle out of the Consequence Argument. It's worth reflecting on what the connection is between the kinds of responses to CA discussed above and the kinds of compatibilist position discussed in Chapter 2. Those positions all have as a consequence that acting freely does *not* require indeterminism; but they largely remain neutral on how, exactly, we should respond to CA, since their focus is on what acting freely *does* require, rather than on explicitly arguing that it does *not* require the ability to do otherwise in the sense ruled out by determinism.

On the other hand, one might reasonably take it that if we have a plausible-sounding compatibilist position on the table, then that in itself casts some doubt on the plausibility of CA, and in particular it casts doubt on the key premise that acting freely requires the ability to do otherwise (in the incompatibilist's sense). For example, one might argue that the reason why that premise seems *prima facie* plausible is that acting freely requires that we have *control* over our actions, and we might, *prima facie*, think that this, in turn, requires the ability to do otherwise. But once we come to see that we can give a plausible account of what it is to have control over one's actions that does *not* require the ability to do otherwise (e.g. in terms of reasons-responsiveness, as described in §2.2), we can happily side with Dennett and maintain that there is simply no need to think that acting freely requires that ability.

On the other hand, you might think that the ability to do otherwise is required not for *control* but rather for a kind of 'up-to-usness'. Of course, you might think, we are normally in control of what we do, even if determinism is true, just as philosophers such as Dennett and Fischer have claimed; but what is additionally required for acting freely is that it is *up to us* what we do, and *that* is incompatible with determinism.

The compatibilist might respond to this claim in a number of ways. One way would be to question whether something's being 'up to me' is really any different from my being in control. When I say, 'It's not up to *me* what you do this weekend; you'll have to make up your *own* mind', perhaps I mean no more than that what you do is not (or should not be) under *my* control but rather *yours*. This kind of response forces the incompatibilist to say more about what they mean by this mysterious notion of 'up-to-usness' – and their answer had better not simply be 'the ability to do otherwise (in the incompatibilist sense)', because the compatibilist can, again, simply deny that this is required for acting freely.

One rather less obviously question-begging response that the incompatibilist might give at this point is that something's being 'up to me' is a matter of my being *ultimately* responsible for it, or of my being the *ultimate source* of my action – and they might argue that the ability to do otherwise at *some* relevant point in my life is required for such ultimate sourcehood. We briefly came across this idea in Chapter 1, and we'll come back to it again in the next chapter, and again in Chapter 5. As we'll see, however, it is open to the compatibilist to deny that ultimate sourcehood is required for acting morally responsibly and hence freely.

Alternatively, the compatibilist might concede that there may be more to 'up-to-usness' than mere control, and that 'up-to-usness' is, indeed, required for acting freely, while denying that determinism is incompatible with up-to-usness. In a sense, this is the line of thought pursued by the Humean compatibilist. The Humean compatibilist can agree with the incompatibilist that if the laws of nature really *did* constrain what we did in any interesting metaphysical sense, then determinism really would rob us of our freedom, because we would be constrained to do only what we do, in fact, do. Fortunately, however, the laws of nature do *not* constrain us in this sense, and hence we have just the kind of 'elbow room' that the incompatibilist says we need; it's just that we don't need indeterminism to be true in order to have it.

Finally, it's worth returning briefly to P.F. Strawson's position – that it could not possibly be rational to deny that, by and large, people act freely and morally responsibly, since denying that would be tantamount to claiming that it could be rational to adopt a form of life that would undermine most of the things we care about – and how could *that* be rational? One might be somewhat suspicious of this line of argument. After all, consider an analogy. Plenty of people have religious beliefs that are an absolutely essential part of their sense of how they should behave and the purpose of their lives, to the extent that to renounce those beliefs would rob their lives of any meaning – it really might, for them, render life not worth living. Now, that might make it true that from a practical point of view they really ought *not* to renounce their religious beliefs: life would go so badly for them that, in *a* sense, it would be reasonable for them to carry on believing in God. But that doesn't make it *rational*, in a theoretical or epistemic sense, for them to believe in God. Suppose there were a cast-iron, unassailable argument to the conclusion that God does not exist. Would such an argument not make their belief in God *irrational*? Surely it would. Similarly, one might claim that Strawson's attempt to turn the fact that our lives would undoubtedly go much worse if we were to renounce free will into a fact about the *rationality* of belief in free will is something of a sleight of hand: surely the existence of an unassailable argument for incompatibilism cannot be dismissed purely on the grounds that it would be very bad news if the conclusion were true!

Conceived as a response to the Consequence Argument, then, one might be suspicious about whether Strawson's account really succeeds. On the other hand, conceived as a kind of deflationary account of what *is* required for moral responsibility – one that locates the source of moral responsibility (and hence freedom) in our reactive attitudes, rather than in features of agents (such as ultimate sourcehood or the ability to do otherwise) that allegedly *ground* those attitudes and are incompatible with determinism, perhaps Strawson's account is more successful. That leaves the account without the resources to mount a direct response to CA; however, since several such responses are, in principle, available – such as any of those canvassed in this chapter – perhaps that isn't such a problem.

4
Compatibilism, Sourcehood, and Manipulation Arguments

4.1 Introduction

As we saw in Chapter 3, the Consequence Argument appeals directly to the claim that acting freely requires the ability to do otherwise. As we saw in §§1.1 and 1.5, a second way of motivating incompatibilism focuses instead on the notion of 'sourcehood' or 'buck-stopping'. The general idea here is that if determinism is true, then the buck can't stop with the agent, because the inexorable chain of deterministic causes and effects passes right through the agent and out the other side, back to a time before they – or indeed their parents or grandparents – were even born. In other words, if agents are determined to act as they do by factors that are, ultimately, outside their control, then they cannot act freely; and, of course, if determinism is true, then agents *are* so determined.

In this chapter, I discuss a selection of arguments for incompatibilism that appeal in one way or another to this central thought. In §4.2, I discuss what I'll call the 'Sourcehood Argument'; in §§4.3 and 4.4, Pereboom's 'four-case argument'; and in §4.5, the 'zygote argument'.

4.2 Sourcehood and manipulation

Here's a formulation of the 'Sourcehood Argument' due to Michael McKenna, which I'll call 'SA' for short:

(1) A person acts of her own free will only if she is its ultimate source.
(2) If determinism is true, no one is the ultimate source of her actions.

Therefore

(3)   If determinism is true, no one acts of her own free will.

(McKenna 2009, §2.2)

To see why the argument might seem compelling, recall that if determinism is true, all of our actions are determined to happen by the laws of nature, together with facts about the distant past. For example, Sue's making a cup of tea at 10 a.m. is determined to happen by the laws plus facts about some past time before Sue was even born. This being so, how could Sue get to be the ultimate *source* of her action? After all, the chain of deterministic causes and effects traces back right through Sue's decision, her deliberation about whether or not to make the tea, her waking up this morning, all the way back through her childhood, her birth and her conception, and out the other side. At no point, it would seem, does the buck stop with Sue: she is merely the conduit through which the inexorable chain of causes and effects plays itself out.

McKenna puts the point, on behalf of the incompatibilist, in terms of the familiar notion of *control*. According to the 'source model' of control, he says, control 'is understood as being the source whence [the agent's] actions emanate...one's actions issue from one's self (in a suitable manner)' (2009, §2.2). The idea here is that we need to distinguish between things that merely *happen* to an agent – her blood circulating, for example – and things that are '*products of one's agency*' (*ibid.*), such as deciding to make a cup of tea. And determinism threatens control (in this sense), because if determinism is true, 'while it might be true that an agent herself provides a source of her action, that source, the one provided by her, itself has a further source that *originates* outside of her. Hence, she, as an agent, is not the *ultimate source* of her actions' (*ibid.*).

One worry about SA is that it is unclear that *any* remotely plausible thesis about the nature of ourselves and the world can genuinely accommodate the idea that we are ever the 'ultimate sources' of our actions. It's one thing to say that ultimate sourcehood is incompatible with determinism; it's quite another to say what ultimate sourcehood *is* compatible with. Indeed, as we'll see in §5.8, Galen Strawson argues that ultimate sourcehood – and hence free will – is *impossible*. Note in particular – and this point is independent of Strawson's argument – that it is unclear why we should think that we *are*, or even *could* be, 'ultimate sources', in the sense SA seems to require, of actions that we are *not* determined by the past plus the laws to perform. My recent decision to make the tea, for example, has amongst its causes the meeting and subsequent marriage of my maternal grandparents. That is so whether or not my recent decision was fully determined to happen by the past plus the laws. (Remember from §1.3: something's being *caused* is different to its being *deterministically* caused.) So, we should already be worrying that the demands placed on free action by SA are unreasonably high, and hence that we should be wary of endorsing premise (1).

I myself think that ultimate sourcehood is, indeed, too demanding a requirement on acting freely, and so am going to ignore SA for now; we'll return to the incompatibilist worry about 'ultimate sourcehood' in §§5.4, 5.8 and 6.7. In the rest of this chapter, I turn my attention to some related arguments of a kind briefly discussed in §1.5: manipulation arguments. As we shall see, these arguments, like SA, are aimed at motivating incompatibilism; and, like SA, they purport to do this by focussing, though in different ways, on the notion of sourcehood.

Remember Joe, the once-upstanding friend from §1.1 (he appears again in §1.5 and 2.5) who is turned overnight into a laptop thief by pesky alien neuroscientists? The problem Joe poses for compatibilists is that, post-ma-nipulation-by-the-aliens, he seems to satisfy (or rather, can be stipulated to satisfy) all the standard compatibilist conditions for acting freely, of the kind canvassed in Chapter 2. We can stipulate, for example, that he is reasons-responsive, and that he satisfies Frankfurt's hierarchical requirements (so that stealing the laptop really is his will). So, it looks as though the compat-ibilist will have to accept that Joe steals your laptop freely and is hence morally responsible for doing so. But surely he *isn't* – surely it would be wrong to hold him responsible for stealing it. At any rate, this is the imme-diate reaction that many people have to this kind of case. Incompatibilists, by contrast, can embrace the consequence that Joe lacks responsibility: by hypothesis, the alien neuroscientists have fixed Joe up so that he is *deter-mined* to steal the laptop. Hence, he is not morally responsible.

One way in which some compatibilists have responded to 'manipula-tion arguments', such as the little argument above (though we'll consider a more complicated manipulation argument in the next section), is to add a *historical* requirement on acting freely. What's wrong with Joe, such compatibilists say, is not that there's something wrong with his psychology *at the time of the theft* that compromises his free will; rather, it's the fact that his psychology got to be that way through a somewhat non-standard route. To put it crudely, he has ended up with a psychology not of his own making, and that is what deprives him of his freedom.

Given SA, however, it's easy to see that this is something of a slippery slope for the compatibilist to get onto, since if determinism is true, then there is at least *a* sense in which *none* of us has a psychology that is of our own making. As we'll see later on, this idea lies behind both source incompatibilism (§5.4) and the arguments for pessimism discussed in §5.8. This worry about adding a historical requirement is pursued by Alfred Mele in his 'zygote argument' (2006, §7.4). Here, we imagine that Ernie is created, at zygote stage, by a goddess, Diana (who has magical powers, obviously, being a goddess) with the explicit intention of getting Ernie to carry out a particular act later in life. Diana is able to figure out exactly how she has to construct Ernie's zygote so that, given the circumstances he will face throughout the early part of his life, he will act in the kinds of ways that will inevitably lead to him carrying out the act in question. So, this scenario presupposes determinism, since without determinism Diana wouldn't be able to predict with certainty what Ernie will end up doing. (Classificatory point: I'm counting the zygote argument as a kind of manipulation argument, since there is arguably *a* sense in which Ernie is 'manipulated', even though the manipulation occurred before he was even born.)

Mele suggests that Ernie isn't morally responsible for the act he performs and which Diana predicted that he would perform. But, aside from the rather curious way in which he was brought into existence, Ernie (we may assume) is a normal human being. So, he not only satisfies the 'at-a-time' requirements on acting freely at the point at which he carries out the act; he *also* satisfies the historical conditions that some compatibilists have suggested as a way of evading manipulation arguments. He is, by compatibilist lights, as fully in control of his own destiny as any of us is. And yet, he does not, allegedly, act freely.

Just like SA, then, manipulation arguments are arguments for incompatibilism that seem to be independent of the Consequence Argument. While (according to these arguments' protagonists) the underlying reason why Joe, Ernie and their ilk fail to act freely is the truth of determinism, the arguments do not get us to incompatibilism simply by presupposing that acting freely requires the ability to do otherwise. Instead, they try to show that whatever conditions compatibilists try to impose on acting freely – conditions which must, of course, be compatible with determinism – it will always be possible to think of a deterministic agent that meets those conditions and yet fails to act freely. In other words, while compatibilists may have succeeded in identifying some *necessary* conditions on acting freely, they have failed to identify *sufficient* conditions (see §2.1). And the natural conclusion to draw is that the missing condition, whatever that might be (e.g. the requirement that the agent be the ultimate source of the action), itself requires the availability, somewhere along the line, of *alternative possibilities* – a condition that is incompatible with determinism.

4.3   Pereboom's four-case argument

Pereboom's 'four-case argument' (let's call it '4CA' for short) consists in a series of four thought experiments involving different stories about how Professor Plum comes to kill Ms White, ranging from a case a little bit like Joe the laptop thief (Case 1) to the ordinary deterministic case (Case 4) (Pereboom 2001, 110–17). In effect, Pereboom is trying to ease us gently into accepting incompatibilism by starting with an easy case, where Plum is clearly not morally responsible for his act, and arguing that there is no *relevant* difference – no difference relevant to moral responsibility – between each case and the next. Hence, since Case 4 is a case of common-or-garden determinism, we should accept that Plum in Case 4 is not morally responsible either; hence, moral responsibility is incompatible with determinism.

Each of the four cases, Pereboom says, 'features different ways in which Professor Plum's murder of Ms White might be causally determined by factors beyond his control' (2001, 112), and in each of them the standard compatibilist conditions for acting freely are (he claims) met. In particular, Plum is not acting because of an irresistible desire; he would have decided differently had he had reasons (by his own lights) to do so; he is reasons-responsive; and he satisfies Frankfurt's hierarchical requirement. Note also that Plum's reasons for killing White are self-interested ones, that is, he reasons in a rationally egoistic way on this occasion. Perhaps Plum is named in Ms White's will as the beneficiary of her substantial fortune, and he has figured a way to kill her without getting caught – or something like that. The other element common to all four cases is that Plum *normally* (but not always) reasons in a rationally egoistic way, so that his reasoning on this occasion is not out of character. Anyway, here are the four cases:

> *Case 1:* 'Professor Plum was created by neuroscientists, who can manipulate him directly through the use of radio-like technology, but he is as much like an ordinary human being as is possible, given this history. Suppose these neuroscientists "locally" manipulate him to undertake the process of reasoning by which his desires are brought about and modified – directly producing his every state from moment to moment' (2001, 112–13). (Note that the neuroscientists have been doing this kind of thing to Plum ever since they created him – they don't *just* intervene in this one particular case.)

Pereboom thinks that Plum-1 (as I'll call him) is clearly not morally responsible for killing White, despite his (allegedly) satisfying the standard compatibilist conditions for acting freely. He suggests that one *might* be tempted to think that it is the 'moment to moment' manipulation that deprives Plum-1 of moral responsibility, so in Case 2 this feature is dropped:

> *Case 2:* Plum was again created by neuroscientists, but this time they cannot control him directly. Instead, they 'programmed him' at the outset 'to weigh reasons for action so that he is often but not exclusively rationally egoistic, with the result that in the circumstances in which he now finds himself, he is causally determined to undertake the moderately reasons-responsive process and to possess the set of first- and second-order desires that results in his killing Ms White' (2001, 113–14).

Pereboom contends that the only difference between these two cases that is even *prima facie* relevant is the length of time that elapses between the programming and Plum's action; but, he claims, the length of time 'seems irrelevant to the question of moral responsibility' (2001, 114). Hence Plum-2 also fails to be morally responsible for killing White. Now we move on to a more homely case:

> *Case 3:* 'Plum is an ordinary human being, except that he was determined by the rigorous training practices of his home and community so that he is often but not exclusively rationally egoistic... His training took place at too early an age for him to have had the ability to prevent or alter the practices that determined his character' (2001, 114). Again, on this occasion he reasons rationally egoistically, and decides to kill White.

The only differences between Case 2 and Case 3 appear to be that Plum-3 was not created by neuroscientists, and that he was determined by 'rigorous training practices' to behave as he did in the particular circumstances in which he found himself rather than being programmed by the neuroscientists. But neither of these differences seems to be *relevant*. After all, what exactly would the relevant difference between having been programmed by neuroscientists and having been subjected to rigorous training practices amount to, given that in both cases these factors causally determine the way that Plum's character develops and the way he turns out, and in very similar kinds of ways? So – if we want to claim that Plum-3 (but not Plum-2) is responsible for killing White – it looks like we can't appeal to this difference. So, we seem to be stuck with the conclusion that Plum-3 isn't morally responsible for killing White either. And so to Case 4:

> *Case 4:* This time, determinism is true and Plum is 'an ordinary human being, generated and raised under normal circumstances, who is often but not exclusively rationally egoistic'. In the particular circumstances Plum now finds himself in, 'the egoistic reasons are very powerful, and together with background circumstances they deterministically result in his act of murder' (2001, 115).

Now, Pereboom notes that one obvious difference between Case 4 and the others is that in Case 4, 'the causal determination of Plum's crime is not, in the last analysis, brought about by other agents' (2001, 115). But he thinks that in the end the reason why Plum-1, Plum-2 and Plum-3 all lack moral responsibility is *not* that the crime *is* 'in the last analysis, brought about by other agents', but rather that Plum's action 'results from a deterministic causal process that traces back to factors beyond his control' (2001, 116). So, for example, if we were to replace the neuroscientists in Cases 1 and 2 with machines that had the same effects but without having themselves been designed by agents (if you can imagine such a thing), Plum-1 and Plum-2 would *still* not be responsible, and this could not be because the murder was 'in the last analysis, brought about by other agents'. Hence, it *must* be because Plum's action 'results from a deterministic causal process that traces back to factors beyond his control'.

  We are therefore left, Pereboom thinks, without a relevant difference between Case 1 and Case 4, and so we must conclude that Plum-4 is no more morally responsible than is Plum-1. Moreover, since Plum-4 is just a normal deterministic agent, the underlying reason *why* he is not morally responsible in Cases 1–3 is the same as it is in Case 4, *viz*, that the deterministic causal process that ultimately leads to the murder of White is one that traces back to factors beyond Plum-4's control. So, while we might have started out assuming that the reason why Plum lacks moral responsibility in the first three cases is that he is *manipulated* in some way, it turns out that his being manipulated is, in fact, *irrelevant* to his lack of responsibility. Ultimately, the reason why *all* the Plums lack responsibility is that they are all causally determined to act as they do.

  One immediate question one might ask is this: In effect, Pereboom's argument is that determinism prevents agents from being the 'ultimate source' of their actions, and hence robs them of the ability to act freely and morally responsibly. But this allegation was already on the table before 4CA came along; as we'll see in §5.4, it's precisely this thought that motivates source incompatibilism. So, what exactly is 4CA adding? Pereboom's answer, in effect (2001, 116–17), is this. We don't presuppose determinism when we ascribe moral responsibility to people – something that we do in real life on a daily basis. Indeed, our inclination to ascribe moral responsibility to normal agents is so deeply entrenched that we fail to notice the undermining effect of adding determinism to the story, as is done in Case 4. So, if we just consider Case 4 on its own, we will be inclined to judge Plum 4 to be morally responsible. 4CA draws us inexorably to the conclusion that determinism *does* undermine responsibility, however, by forcing us to appreciate that the sources of the actions of normal deterministic agents, such as Plum-4, are no more within their control than are those of Plums 1–3.

4.4   Some responses to the four-case argument

4CA has provoked quite a variety of responses, of which I shall survey just a handful in this section. The first response I'll look at focusses on whether *determinism* is really playing the role Pereboom claims it plays in the argument. The second (the 'hard-line' reply) reverse-engineers the argument, so that we start from Case 4 (where it is allegedly intuitively plausible – in the absence of the priming delivered by Cases 1–3 – that Plum *is*, or at least *may* be, morally responsible) and work our way back to Case 1. Trading on Pereboom's own contention that there are no relevant differences among the cases, we can legitimately conclude that Plum-1 is (or at least may be) morally responsible after all. (This is admittedly counter-intuitive. But then it is arguably just as counter-intuitive, at least by compatibilists' lights, that Plum-4 *isn't* morally responsible.) The third (a 'soft-line' reply) argues that we can, *contra* Pereboom, draw a morally relevant distinction between Case 1 and Case 2, so that Plum-1 is not responsible, but Plums 2–4 are. Finally, a different kind of soft-line reply, sometimes going under the heading of *history-sensitive compatibilism*, attempts to articulate an additional compatibilist requirement on acting freely that draws a different kind of morally relevant line between Case 2 and Case 3.

The irrelevance of determinism

Mele (2005) raises a straightforward objection to 4CA. He argues that Pereboom has failed to show that the causal *determination* of Plum's actions in Cases 1–3 is what deprives him of moral responsibility. Mele asks us to consider indeterministic versions of the cases, where the manipulation by the neuroscientists (or machines), or the imposition of 'rigorous training practices' on Plum-3 from an early age, does not *determine* that Plum will decide to kill White. Instead, those manipulative processes leave a tiny chance that Plum will suffer some form of incapacitation rather than deciding to kill White. As it happens, Plum makes the decision to kill; but, in Mele's versions of the cases, that *might* not have happened. And the thought is that this makes no difference to our intuitive reactions to the cases: if we think that Plums 1–3 lack responsibility for killing White in Pereboom's original deterministic cases, we'll think that Plums 1–3 lack responsibility in Mele's indeterministic versions, too. Hence, the causal *determination* of Plum's decision in Cases 1–3 can't be the reason for his lack of responsibility.

Of course, this still leaves Mele with the task of explaining *why* Plums 1–3, or at least some of them, aren't responsible; we'll consider his explanation a little later. But Mele's point is that Pereboom's diagnosis of the lack of moral responsibility in Cases 1–3 is mistaken, and hence cannot be transposed across to Case 4. And that makes it seem very likely that there is some *other* explanation in (some or all of) Cases 1–3 – as yet unspecified – which will not then apply to Case 4, since Plum-4 is just a normal deterministic agent.

One response the incompatibilist might make at this point, however, is to import an incompatibilist claim that we shall come across again in Chapter 6 in the discussion of Frankfurt's 'nefarious neurosurgeon' case. If one holds that alternative possibilities (of the kind ruled out by determinism) are required for moral responsibility, it seems that not just any old alternative possibility will do. In accordance with an argument of Fischer's (§6.6), one might insist that there needs to be a '*robust*' alternative possibility – a possibility whose presence *explains* why the agent is morally responsible (since, according to incompatibilists, if there is no alternative possibility at all, the agent is *not* morally responsible). Or, following David Widerker (§6.8), we might require as a condition on blameworthiness that there be something the agent could have done instead *that it would have been morally reasonable* to have expected them to do.

For example, suppose that Plum is considering whether to kill White, and that determinism is false. Suppose further that the past plus the laws leave precisely two alternatives open – that is, two alternatives such that each of them is compatible with the past plus the laws. One is that Plum decides to kill White; the other is that he is struck by lightning. As it happens, Plum decides to kill White. So, there *is* an alternative possibility here, but it is *not* a 'robust' one: the fact that Plum could have been struck by lightning doesn't seem to explain why we should hold him responsible for his decision to kill White. Similarly, Plum fails to meet Widerker's requirement: there isn't anything else Plum could have *done* instead, since being struck by lightning isn't something you *do*; it's something that *happens* to you.

The alternative possibility that Mele adds to Pereboom's Cases 1–3 – Plum's being 'incapacitated' (being struck by lightning is certainly one way of being incapacitated) – therefore doesn't seem to satisfy either of the requirements on alternative possibilities suggested by Fischer and Widerker. So, the defender of 4CA might concede Mele's point that it isn't the causal *determination* of Plum's action by factors outside his control that deprives him of responsibility; but she can nonetheless retreat to the weaker claim that Plum's lack of *robust* alternatives (or alternative options that it would have been morally reasonable to expect him to take), due to factors outside his control, deprives him of responsibility. And *that* explanation plausibly carries over to Case 4, the normal deterministic case: factors outside Plum-4's control deprive him of *all* alternative possibilities, and *a fortiori* deprive him of *robust* alternative possibilities. (Note for later: Source incompatibilists sometimes claim that robust alternative possibilities aren't required for acting freely, and so would not want to appeal to the response to Mele suggested above. I myself find this claim implausible; see §6.7 for some discussion.)

The hard-line reply

Michael McKenna (2008) draws a useful distinction between what he calls 'hard-line' and 'soft-line' replies to Pereboom's argument, and indeed to manipulation arguments generally. McKenna summarises what we might think of as the standard logical form of manipulation arguments as follows:

(1) If S is manipulated in manner X to A, then S does not A of her own free will and is therefore not morally responsible for A'ing.
(2) An agent manipulated in manner X to A is no different in any relevant respect from any normally functioning agent determined to do A from CAS.

Therefore,

(3) If S is a normally functioning agent determined to A from CAS, she does not A of her own free will and therefore is not morally responsible for A'ing. (2008, 143)

'CAS' here stands for 'Compatibilist-friendly Agential Structure', and we can think of that 'agential structure' as consisting of the kind of compatibilist condition on moral responsibility that we're familiar with from Chapter 2: reasons-responsiveness and satisfaction of Frankfurt's hierarchical conditions, for example. Note that Pereboom's 4CA is, in fact, a kind of iterated version of the above schema: we move first from the claim that if an agent is manipulated in the way described in Case 1, then he is not morally responsible for killing White, via the premise that Plum-1 is not relevantly different to Plum-2, to the conclusion that if an agent is manipulated in the way described in Case 2 then they are not morally responsible; we then run the argument again (if Plum-2 is not morally responsible then, given lack of relevant difference, neither is Plum-3), and then again for Plum-3 and Plum-4, our normally functioning agent who is determined to kill White.

McKenna defines a 'soft-line' reply to a manipulation argument as one that rejects (2): the soft-liner seeks to identify a relevant difference between the manipulated agent and the normal deterministic agent that will explain why the former is not morally responsible even though the latter is. In the case of 4CA, the soft-liner might, in principle, draw the line in between any two of the cases: she might think that Plums 2–4 are responsible and Plum-1 isn't, or that Plums 3 and 4 are responsible but Plums 1 and 2 aren't, or she might even think that only Plum-4 is responsible. A 'hard-line' reply, by contrast, rejects (1): the hard-liner bites the bullet and claims that, contrary to what Pereboom says we ought to think, Plum-1 really is morally responsible for killing White (or, more modestly, that it is *unclear* whether or not Plum-1 is responsible).

McKenna's own reply is a hard-line one, and its main element runs roughly as follows. Pereboom calls the moves through the cases a 'generalisation strategy' (perhaps because the thought is that, since the conditions described in the cases are successively easier to satisfy, more possible agents will satisfy later cases than earlier cases). McKenna deploys a 'reverse generalisation strategy', running the cases backwards from Case 4 to Case 1 and accepting premise (2) – the premise that there is no relevant difference between the cases. (More accurately, what McKenna accepts is the claim that there is no relevant difference between Case 4 and Case 3, or between Case 3 and Case 2, and between Case 2 and Case 1; I'll just stick to saying 'premise (2)' for short.) The crucial question is: What should our initial attitude to Case 4 – which is now our starter case – be? Well, if we start out with the intuition that Plum-4 is not morally responsible, then, of course, we have already placed ourselves firmly in the incompatibilist camp, and we have no need for Pereboom's argument, since that argument is supposed to *persuade* us that Plum-4 lacks responsibility. What if we come into the fray as neutrals, who have not yet made up our minds about Plum-4? Well, in that case, if we run the argument Pereboom's way – from Case 1 to Case 4 – we will end up (granting premise (2)) convinced that Plum-4 is not morally responsible. But if we run it McKenna's way, from Case 4 to Case 1, we'll start out neutral with respect to Case 4 – we'll hold that it's just not *clear* whether Plum-4 is responsible – and we'll end up, via premise (2), holding that it's not clear whether Plum-1 is responsible either. (We might antecedently have suspected that Plum-1 *isn't* morally responsible, but running the argument from Case 4 to Case 1 will have convinced us that, in fact, it just isn't clear one way or the other.) Or, finally, if we start out as committed compatibilists, our initial view will be that Plum-4 *is* responsible. And so, by running backwards from Case 4 to Case 1, we'll end up thinking that Plum-1 is also morally responsible.

McKenna's conclusion is that we are left in a kind of 'dialectical stalemate': run the argument from Case 1 to Case 4, starting with the premise that Plum-1 lacks responsibility, and you end up with the conclusion that Plum-4 likewise lacks responsibility – hence incompatibilism. But if you run the argument from Case 4 to Case 1 – so long as you don't presuppose incompatibilism from the outset, which would beg the question – you end up not with incompatibilism but with the result that Plum-1 is morally responsible (or is not clearly *not* morally responsible, if you started out neutral with respect to Case 4). While this admittedly might strike you as a somewhat counter-intuitive view to take of Plum-1, it is at least a result that is compatible with compatibilism! And, of course, the whole point of the 'generalisation strategy' – whichever direction you run the argument in – is that you end up being forced to agree with something that you might not *initially* have been inclined to accept.

A soft-line reply: drawing the line between Plum-1 and Plum-2

As we've just seen, the hard-line reply does involve a certain amount of bullet-biting. After all, in agreeing with Pereboom that there is no morally relevant difference between Plum-1 and Plum-4, the hard-liner is committed to thinking that Plum-1 is no *less* culpable than Plum-4, and that might strike you as rather too big a bullet to bite. Soft-liners, by contrast, argue that there *are* morally relevant differences between Plum-1 and Plum-4 – although they disagree amongst themselves about where exactly the line should be drawn.

We'll start by considering whether there is, after all, a morally relevant difference between Case 1 and Case 2. One question you might have been asking from the outset is: How *exactly* is it that the neuroscientists in Case 1 are manipulating Plum-1? Now, there has been a lot of discussion of the various ways in which we might flesh this out (see McKenna 2008, §5; Demetriou 2010, §4), and it would seem that how exactly we flesh it out makes a big difference to our judgement about Plum-1's culpability. For example, McKenna considers a way of reading Case 1 according to which 'Team Plum', as McKenna calls the neuroscientists, 'functions like a prosthetic, allowing Plum to deal with his world like any other agent' (2008, 150). This way of fleshing out the case makes it seem rather more plausible that Plum-1 *is* morally responsible, and hence might make you think that the bullet that the hard-liner has to bite isn't such a big one after all.

As Kristin Demetriou (2010) points out, however, fleshing Case 1 out in such a way as to make it seem plausible that Plum-1 *is* morally responsible is rather stacking the deck in the compatibilist's favour, since Pereboom's argument trades on its *not* being plausible that Plum-1 is responsible. So, let's flesh the case out in such a way that it is indeed implausible to suppose that he's responsible. Pereboom says that the 'neuroscientists "locally" manipulate him to undertake the process of reasoning by which his desires are brought about and modified – directly producing his every state from moment to moment'. How, exactly, is this supposed to work? Well, think about the neural processes going on in Plum-1's brain as he deliberates. To simplify, let's suppose there's just one 'process' (the reason for the scare quotes will become apparent in a moment), running from neural state $N1$ through to neural state $N50$, say. Now, we're assuming physicalism here – no immaterial mental phenomena – so (again, simplifying rather a lot) we can think of each of these neural states as 'implementing' or 'realising' a certain mental state, starting with the first moment when it occurs to Plum-1 to murder White (realised by neural state $N1$), through his considering various ways of committing the crime and what his chances of detection would be – culminating in his decision to go ahead with the murder ($N50$). Now, in a *normal* agent, this progression through the successive neural states has a certain *causal structure*. Simplifying yet again, let's just stipulate that in a normal agent going through the same process of deliberation, $N1$ causes $N2$, which in turn causes $N3$, and so on up to $N50$. But, Demetriou argues, if the neuroscientists are 'directly producing his every state from moment to moment', this is *not* the causal structure of Plum-1's mental 'process'. Instead, each of Plum-1's successive neural states is being directly induced by the neuroscientists. There is no *process* running from $N1$ to $N50$. Instead, the neuroscientists directly induce $N1$

(thereby realising Plum-1's initial idea to murder White), and then they directly induce $N2$, and so on, until they finally directly induce $N50$, which realises Plum-1's decision to kill White.

Here's an analogy: Suppose I programme a very basic computer to take the last two numbers that appeared on the screen, add them together, and display their sum, and then to do exactly the same thing again and again, and I kick it off by entering the numbers 1 and 2. Then the computer will generate a long list of numbers that starts 1, 2, 3, 5, 8, 13, 21 and so on. The underlying process, aside from entering the first two numbers, is completely internally generated by the computer: the fact that the first two numbers are 1 and 2 is what *causes* the next number to be 3, which, in turn, causes the next number to be 5, and so on. Now imagine a different case: I am given a long list of numbers and am instructed to type them into the computer so that the numbers display on the screen. That list goes '1, 2, 3, 5, 8, 13, 21, ...'. And so, I dutifully follow my instructions. In this case, there is no internal process in the computer that takes the two most recent numbers as input and the next number – their sum – as output; all the computer is doing is displaying the results of my typing. So, the end result is the same as in the first case, but the mechanism that is producing each number is coming in from the outside – from me typing.

We can see this difference by asking what *would* have happened if I'd accidentally typed a 3 rather than a 2 as the second number. In the first case, where the computer is calculating the sums, the list would have then gone '1, 3, 4, 7, 11, 18, ...', whereas in the second case, it would have gone '1, 3, 3, 5, 8, 13, 21, ...'. So, while the *actual* output (with 1 and 2 as the first numbers) is the same in both cases, the causal *structure* – the mechanism that produces the list – is different. And in particular, in the first case, but not the second, the output at any given stage *causally depends* upon the previous two numbers entered. That's why typing a 3 instead of 2 as the second number would make a difference to subsequent numbers in the first case but not the second.

Demetriou claims, in effect, that the moment-to-moment interference by the neuroscientists makes the causal structure of Plum-1's deliberation just like the second case rather than the first: there is no causal dependence of successive neural states on previous ones in Plum-1's case, just as there is no causal dependence of successive numbers on the previous two in the case where I am just typing in a list of numbers. Moreover, she argues that this means that Plum-1 fails to satisfy the conditions that are required for genuine *agency*. (By analogy, the computer, in the second case, is not *calculating* anything, even though if all you could see was the output – the numbers on the screen – you might mistakenly think that it *was* calculating something.) And she therefore claims that what has gone wrong in Case 1, as far as Plum-1's moral responsibility is concerned, is that Plum-1 is a victim of 'suppressive manipulation'. Plum-1, Pereboom stipulates, is as much like a normal human agent as possible. So, we are not supposed to think of him as a kind of blank slate or a puppet with no ability to act or deliberate on his own without the 'help' of the neuroscientists. So, presumably he *could* have performed his own deliberation had the neuroscientists not intervened. Indeed, we can even suppose that his deliberative process *would* have followed just the same path – *N1* through *N50* – as it in fact did with the neuroscientists' intervention. But, in fact, there *was* no such deliberative process, or at least not conceived as a process *performed by Plum-1*, any more than the computer is performing a calculation in the typing-in-the-list-of-numbers case. It just *looks* that way; and indeed, we may suppose, it even seems that way to Plum-1 himself, who is oblivious to the neuroscientists' intervention.

The point here is that there is, arguably, a relevant difference between, as Demetriou puts it, 'the effects of being causally determined by suppressive manipulation and the effects of being an inhabitant of a causally deterministic world' (2010, 608). Determinism, just by itself, does not suppress our agency – whereas having neuroscientists induce your mental states (by inducing your neural states) from moment to moment clearly *does* suppress agency. Hence, 4CA fails: there is a relevant difference between Case 1 and Case 2.

More soft-line replies: historical conditions on responsibility

Demetriou's soft-line response draws the line between Cases 1 and 2: Plum-1's agency is suppressed, but Plum-2's is not. Other compatibilists have sought to draw the line between Cases 2 and 3 (or, of course, in principle one might try to draw the line between Cases 3 and 4 instead, depending on where in the sequence of cases you think moral responsibility kicks in). Demetriou's response takes issue with the claim that someone who is manipulated 'moment to moment', like Plum-1, can truly be thought of as an *agent*. However, since in Cases 2 and 3 the manipulation is stipulated to have taken place a long time ago, they *don't* look like cases of *suppressive* manipulation; Plums 2 and 3 really do seem to be genuine *agents* with respect to the killing of White. As far as Plum-2's and Plum-3's mental life *around the time of the decision* is concerned, everything seems to be in order: Plum-2 and Plum-3 do, indeed, seem to satisfy the standard compatibilist conditions on acting freely and responsibly. So, if we want to claim that one or both of Plum-2 and Plum-3 lacks moral responsibility for the killing while Plum-4 (and perhaps also Plum-3, depending on where you draw the line) is fully responsible, it looks as though we are going to have to build *historical* conditions into our account of the requirements on acting freely – and, of course, they need to be historical conditions that Plum-2 and/or Plum-3 fails to satisfy, but Plum-4 *does* satisfy. Compatibilist views that do just this are sometimes called 'history-sensitive' compatibilist views or 'historical' views.

Mele (2005), as we've already seen, challenges Pereboom's claim that the reason why Plums 1–3 lack responsibility is that they are causally *determined* to act as they do. But of course that raises the question, what *is* the reason why some or all of Plums 1–3 lack responsibility? Setting aside Plum-1, let's briefly look at Mele's account of the case of Plum-2 – an account that builds historical conditions into the requirements for acting freely.

Mele says that there is a way in which the normal agent's 'deliberative style' undergoes 'evolution' over time, which does not apply to Plum-2 (2005, 78). 'Normal agents', he says, 'learn how to weigh reasons for action. For example, a young agent who weighs reasons very egoistically may suffer as a consequence and learn that things go better for him when he weighs the interests of others more heavily as reasons. His deliberative style might gradually become significantly less egoistic, and, along the way, his less egoistic actions might have reinforcing consequences that help to produce in him increased concern for the welfare of those around him. This increased concern would presumably have an effect on his evolving deliberative habits' (2005, 78). Plum-2, by contrast, is 'programmed' to 'weigh reasons for action so that he is often but not exclusively rationally egoistic'. Hence, since Plum-2's deliberative style has not evolved in the normal way, he lacks moral responsibility for the outcome of his deliberation.

Is this a satisfactory response? Well, it might depend – again – on how we interpret the case. Suppose we think that Plum-2 is programmed to be 'often but not exclusively rationally egoistic' in something like the following way: the neuroscientists have a dial marked *Rational Egoism*, ranging from 0 per cent to 100 per cent, which they set at, say, 80 per cent – thus guaranteeing that, one way or another, Plum-2 will reason in a rationally egoistic way 80 per cent of the time. Then Mele's reply seems appropriate: Plum-2 simply lacks an opportunity that normal deterministic agents have, namely the opportunity to evolve his reasoning style as his character develops: he's stuck on 80 per cent no matter what. Hence

Plum-2 lacks moral responsibility but Plum-3 doesn't, since Plum-3's deliberative habits *have* evolved in the normal way.

On the other hand, we might take Plum-2 to have been programmed in such a way that, *as it happens*, he reasons in a rationally egoistic way about 80 per cent of the time. So, the neuroscientists set Plum-2 up, with no particular intentions regarding the frequency with which he reasons in this way, and let nature take its course – which, in fact, results in him reasoning in this way about 80 per cent of the time. If we interpret the programming like *that*, it's not at all clear that Plum-2 has been denied the opportunity for his style of reasoning to evolve in the way that normal agents' reasoning styles evolve. After all, plenty of normal agents end up reasoning in this way around 80 per cent of the time, we may suppose. So, if we interpret Case 2 in *this* way, it's unclear that there is a relevant difference between Plum-2 and Plum-3, and so it looks as though we can't reasonably claim that Plum-2 lacks responsibility while Plum-3 does not.

Fortunately for the compatibilist, however, if we interpret Case 2 in this latter way, it's unclear that we should think that Plum-2 is not morally responsible in the first place. So – as long as we can think of a morally relevant difference between Plum-1 and Plum-2, perhaps by appealing to Plum-1's lack of agency – 4CA is blocked anyway. (We saw a similar dilemma for Pereboom in the discussion of Case 1 above. If we think of the neuroscientists in Case 1 as agency-suppressors, then Plum-1 isn't morally responsible – but we can provide compatibilist conditions on responsibility that explain *why* he isn't responsible. If, on the other hand, we think of the Case 1 neuroscientists as 'causal prosthetics', then perhaps we should think that Plum-1 *is* morally responsible, and so 4CA cannot get off the ground. Either way, 4CA fails. Or so we might argue.)

Other 'historical' compatibilist conditions on moral responsibility have been developed elsewhere by Mele (1995), Fischer and Ravizza (1998), and others; see Kapitan 2000 for some critical discussion.

Tough it out!

The final kind of response I'll briefly consider is Frankfurt's. Frankfurt is completely unmoved by the thought that we need to introduce historical conditions into a compatibilist account of moral responsibility:

> A manipulator may succeed, through his interventions, in providing a person not merely with particular feelings and thoughts but with a new character. That person is then morally responsible for the choices and the conduct to which having this character leads. We are

inevitably fashioned and sustained, after all, by circumstances over which we have no control. The causes to which we are subject may also change us radically, without thereby bringing it about that we are not morally responsible agents. It is irrelevant whether those causes are operating by virtue of the natural forces that shape our environment or whether they operate through the deliberately manipulative designs of other human agents. We are the sorts of persons we are; and it is what we are, rather than the history of our development, that counts. The fact that someone is a pig warrants treating him like a pig, unless there is reason to believe that in some important way he is a pig against his will and is not acting as he would really prefer to act. (2002, 28)

Frankfurt thus sticks to his guns and insists that manipulation is no bar to moral responsibility – unless, presumably, the manipulation is of a kind that renders the agent unfree according to his own hierarchical account (§2.5). Many philosophers find this response implausible; Mele, for example, says, 'if compatibilists were to have nothing more attractive to offer than Frankfurt's – or any other – ahistorical view of moral responsibility and freedom, compatibilism would be in dire straits' (2008a, 270).

Now, Mele says this in the context of a discussion of a different kind of manipulation case, which we don't have space for here, and perhaps he is right about the implausibility of Frankfurt's defence in the face of *that* kind of case. But let's set that aside and ask whether it is really so implausible in the face of 4CA. Note, first, that there seems to be no bar to Frankfurt's accepting Demetriou's argument that Plum-1 lacks responsibility; any compatibilist (or, indeed, incompatibilist) is entitled to assume that someone whose 'deliberative process' is really a series of individually externally-caused states, and hence not really a deliberative process at all, fails to enjoy freedom of the will. So, the issue is really whether it is so implausible to maintain that Plum-2 *is* morally responsible – something the history-sensitive compatibilist can deny, but which Frankfurt cannot.

A second thing to point out is that, in principle, someone who wanted to bite the bullet, as Frankfurt does, can appeal to McKenna's reverse-generalisation strategy (stopping, if we accept Demetriou's argument, with Case 2 rather than Case 1): if we start out with Case 4 – and, as compatibilists, hold that Plum-4 is morally responsible – then we can agree with Pereboom that there is no relevant difference between Case 4 and Case 2, and conclude that *for that reason* it is entirely appropriate to say that Plum-2 is morally responsible. (Of course, history-sensitive compatibilists will disagree about the lack of a relevant difference between the cases; but in effect I'm trying to argue here that Frankfurt's refusal to embrace historical conditions on responsibility in the face of manipulation arguments is not as implausible as Mele suggests. So, the fact that he disagrees with history-sensitive compatibilists about Plum-2's responsibility is, in itself, no objection to his view.)

Finally, it's worth reflecting on the way that Frankfurt explicitly draws our attention to the fact that we are 'inevitably fashioned and sustained, after all, by circumstances over which we have no control'. 4CA is supposed, according to Pereboom, to draw us to the conclusion that the action of Plum-4, our normal deterministic agent, 'results from a deterministic causal process that traces back to factors beyond his control' (2001, 116), and that Plum-4 is *for this reason* unfree and lacking in moral responsibility. I take it that the point Frankfurt is making in the passage just quoted is that it is just *obvious* that we are fashioned by circumstances beyond our control (and, one might add, this is true whether or not determinism is true), and that there is simply not so much as a *prima facie* reason to think that this undermines our freedom. The history-sensitive compatibilist, who seeks to argue that Plum-2 is not morally responsible, is in a sense conceding something to her incompatibilist opponent: she is conceding that failure to be in control of the formation of one's character does indeed undermine moral responsibility. And, as I said in §4.2, one might worry that this establishes something of a slippery slope, for now we are in the business of distinguishing between being in control of the formation of one's character and *not* being in control of it – a distinction that the compatibilist may find difficult to spell out, given that any compatibilist will have to deny that we are ever (if determinism is true) *ultimate* sources of our actions.

It may be strategically better, therefore, to refuse to get on the slope to start with, as Frankfurt does: to accept that we are – all of us, and not just Plum-2 – products of factors outside our control, and to deny that there is any relevant difference, which would undermine Plum-2's responsibility but not ours, between us (if determinism is true) and Plum-2. (A little more on this is to come in §5.8.)

The point here is that, taking all of the above points into account, Frankfurt's denial that agents whose characters are deterministically formed by manipulative means thereby lack moral responsibility is not obviously implausible. Moreover, as a strategic manoeuvre in the face of incompatibilist arguments such as 4CA, it may well be the wiser course for the compatibilist to take.

4.5   The zygote argument

Mele (2008a) presents a manipulation-style argument that he dubs 'the zygote argument' – and he describes it as 'more promising than any straight manipulation argument I have seen' (2008a, 285) (although he thinks the Humean compatibilist – see §3.5 above – may be able to evade the argument; I'll set that claim aside). Here's the set-up:

> Diana creates a zygote Z in Mary. She combines Z's atoms as she does because she wants a certain event E to occur thirty years later. From her knowledge of the state of the universe just prior to her creating Z and the laws of nature of her deterministic universe, she deduces that a zygote with precisely Z's constitution located in Mary will develop into an ideally self- controlled agent who, in thirty years, will judge, on the basis of rational deliberation, that it is best to A and will A on the basis of that judgement, thereby bringing about E. If this agent, Ernie, has any unsheddable values at the time, they play no role in motivating his A-ing. Thirty years later, Ernie is a mentally healthy, ideally self-controlled person who regularly exercises his powers of self-control and has no relevant compelled or coercively produced attitudes. Furthermore, his beliefs are conducive to informed deliberation about all matters that concern him, and he is a reliable deliberator. (2008a, 279)

Question: is Ernie morally responsible for A-ing? According to Mele, the most plausible answer to this question is 'No'. And so we have a familiar problem for the compatibilist: Ernie satisfies all the standard compatibilist conditions for acting freely and responsibly. But, unlike the conditions assumed by Pereboom to obtain in Plum's case, Ernie also satisfies any *historical* conditions the history-sensitive compatibilist might care to add. Ernie's deliberative style has 'evolved' in the normal way. Other compatibilists propose other historical conditions. But by stipulation, Ernie satisfies all of those, too. Indeed, we can compare Ernie with Bernie, who is *exactly* like Ernie in all respects except that *his* zygote was created in the normal way. Clearly, the compatibilist has to hold that Bernie is morally responsible for A-ing – he is a normal deterministic agent, after all. But there are no compatibilist conditions by virtue of which Bernie is morally responsible and Ernie isn't. Problem.

The zygote argument would seem to be *more* of a problem than 4CA precisely because it's clear that no plausible historical conditions on moral responsibility are going to rule Bernie in and Ernie out. For example, we can't plausibly simply stipulate that only agents who are *created* 'in the normal way' get to be morally responsible; that would be *ad hoc* and in any case would most likely lead to other counter-intuitive results. (What is 'normal' anyway? Do people conceived by IVF count as 'normal'? What about people who have been genetically engineered so that they are blue-eyed or don't suffer from sickle cell anaemia or are clever? These are, of course, not currently possible – unless you count eugenics as a form of genetic engineering – but it's not obvious that they won't become possible at some point, perhaps even in the not-too-distant future.)

Is the zygote argument as compelling as Mele thinks? Certainly, several philosophers have claimed that it is not (see e.g. Kearns 2012). Perhaps the most straightforward compatibilist response comes from Fischer (2011), who simply denies Mele's claim that Ernie lacks moral responsibility for *A*-ing. In effect, Fischer holds that Ernie is not really *manipulated* at all. He asks us to imagine, for example, that rather than Ernie's zygote being implanted in Mary by Diana, it is created in the normal manner by Mary and her partner John, except that they do so in the belief that Ernie will *A* in 30 years' time, and indeed with the intention that he do so. It seems that in *this* case Ernie *is* intuitively morally responsible for *A*-ing. But there is surely no relevant difference between Mele's and Fischer's respective Ernies, since the only difference between them is that Fischer's Ernie is, and Mele's is not, created in the normal way. And, as we just saw, it would be pretty implausible to claim that having been created in the normal way is a requirement on moral responsibility. The zygote argument and its ilk show, Fischer thinks, 'if they show anything, that there is no difference between certain "initial design" scenarios and *ordinary scenarios in which there is no special reason to doubt compatibilism*' (2011, 271).

Of course, you might have compatibilist leanings but find yourself unwilling to bite the bullet and say that Ernie is morally responsible for *A*-ing (though part of Fischer's point is that there really isn't even a bullet to bite here; there is no cost at all associated with taking this view about Ernie). In that case, you have three options. You can embrace your latent incompatibilist leanings, or else try to explain why Ernie's design by Diana constitutes a genuine form of responsibility-undermining manipulation. Or, finally, you can try and find a more nuanced compatibilist response to the zygote argument that involves neither of the above options. (Stephen Kearns, for example, concludes that compatibilists 'need not take a stand on whether programmed agents like Ernie are free or not' (2012, 389).)

4.6 Conclusion

In this chapter, I've surveyed three different but related arguments for incompatibilism, all of which trade, in one way or another, on the idea that if determinism is true, then agents fail to be the sources of their actions, in a sense of 'source' that is allegedly a requirement on acting freely. The Sourcehood Argument makes the argument directly, while the four-case and zygote arguments proceed in a rather more indirect manner, by claiming that there is no relevant difference between a deterministic agent on the one hand and a 'manipulated' or 'programmed' agent on the other. Hence, since manipulated and programmed agents, such as Plum-1 and Ernie, are *not* sources of their actions in a sense of 'source' that is required for acting freely, neither is an ordinary deterministic agent – an agent who, for all we know, may be just like us.

For what it's worth, I'm with Frankfurt on all of the manipulation cases we've considered: If someone is, at the time of their deliberation and decision, a normally-functioning deterministic agent, then they get to be morally responsible for that decision. It might not be their fault that they got to have the character that led them to make that decision, but so what?

I'm not going to argue for that position here, but it is perhaps worth bearing in mind the following thought. Consider again Joe, the friend who is manipulated overnight into becoming someone who cares only about himself and has no qualms about stealing your laptop, which he duly does on Tuesday. Is Joe to blame for the theft? Yes, he is (assuming he meets standard non-historical compatibilist conditions on moral responsibility), and he deserves to be punished accordingly.

But now imagine that, a week after the theft, our evil neuroscientists reconstruct Joe's brain so that he wakes up with his previous good character. (Maybe they excise Joe's memory of his short period of thievery and general nastiness, or maybe they don't – I don't think it matters.) Is Joe *now* blameworthy for stealing the laptop on Tuesday – does he *now* deserve to be punished? You might think that the obvious answer to this question is 'No', and that this shows that I should have answered 'No' to the previous question, which was, in effect, the question of whether Joe *was, at the time he did it*, to blame for the theft. After all, how could he have been blameworthy for the theft at the time, and then suddenly have become not-blameworthy later on? Surely he is either blameworthy or not.

It is not at all clear, however, that we are rationally required to give the same answer to both questions. For example, I think someone – call her Amy – who suffers from total and irreversible amnesia is no longer morally responsible for all the things she did, freely and morally responsibly, prior to the onset of amnesia. (Imagine that Amy freely and responsibly stole a laptop in her pre-amnesia state, for example.) This doesn't involve retrospectively changing my mind about Amy's earlier moral responsibility for the theft of the laptop. She stole it freely and responsibly, but that moral responsibility fails to *transmit* from the earlier time to the later time. Similarly, after the second intervention by the neuro-scientists, Joe is no longer morally responsible for the theft of the laptop, even though he was responsible at the time he stole it. Questions about the *transmission* of moral responsibility over time are different to those about moral responsibility *at the time of action*, and the former questions have nothing to do with freedom of the will. At any rate, that's my excuse for leaving the matter here.

5
What Does Acting Freely Require? Some Incompatibilist Views

5.1 Introduction

In Chapters 3 and 4, we considered some arguments for incompatibilism: the Consequence Argument (CA), the Sourcehood Argument (SA), Pereboom's four-case argument (4CA), and Mele's zygote argument. My own view is that these arguments are by no means conclusive – far from it – but, of course, not everyone agrees with that assessment. And so we come to incompatibilist views of freedom of the will.

Remember that incompatibilism, just by itself, is simply the view that indeterminism is a necessary condition for free action: in a deterministic universe, no agent ever acts freely, and no agent is every morally responsible for what they do. But no incompatibilist should think that indeterminism is a *sufficient* condition for free action. For one thing – as we'll see – the laws and the past need to leave open the *right* alternative possibilities. For another thing, even if we hold that, for example, in order for Carly's decision to steal your car to be free, the laws plus the past must leave it open that she decides *not* to steal your car, that, just by itself, also doesn't seem to secure free action. Suppose that Carly has a miniature coin in her head, such that she decides to steal the car if it lands heads and decides not to if it lands tails. That doesn't seem enough to make Carly morally responsible for stealing your car.

Moreover, incompatibilism just by itself – like compatibilism – makes no claims about whether or not any actual people ever do, in fact, act freely – which you might reasonably think is the million-dollar question, the one that we should really care about most of all. It's an interesting intellectual question whether the various fictional characters we have met in this book – Wally, Carly and Joe from Chapter 1, for example, or Professor Plum or Ernie – are morally responsible for their behaviour. But – having satisfied yourself about what the right answer to that question is – the *really* important question is whether or not *we* are just like Wally, Carly, Joe and their fictional friends in relevant respects, and hence whether or not *we* are morally responsible for our actions as we go about our day-to-day lives. Is it appropriate to resent the friend who just stood you up, or to feel grateful for the thoughtful thing they did for you yesterday, or to blame the person who stole your car? These aren't abstract intellectual questions; they're questions about how we ought to treat our fellow human beings.

In Chapter 2, I considered various compatibilist views about what freedom of the will requires. As to the question whether *we*, as opposed to our fictional friends, are morally responsible for our actions, the answer most compatibilists will give is: 'Normally, yes'. There are, of course, real situations that sometimes deprive people of their freedom – being locked in a room, or held at gunpoint, or suffering from a pathological compulsion, say – but, by and large, most of us act freely and responsibly. (Or, at least, that's the intention of compatibilist theories. As we saw in Chapter 2, actually coming up with a theory that draws the line in just the right place is very far from being a walk in the park.)

In the current chapter, I consider some incompatibilist views about what freedom of the will requires, and whether or to what extent, if those views are correct, it is reasonable to think that we actually do – ever, occasionally, or perhaps routinely – act freely. After some scene-setting below and in §5.2, I'll discuss two basic varieties of incompatibilism, namely leeway (§5.3) and source (§5.4) incompatibilism. In §5.5 I discuss a problem that, at least *prima facie*, applies to both varieties: the problem of luck. I'll then (§5.6) turn to the view that acting freely requires 'agent causation'. In §5.7, I get back to the question just raised about whether, given the incompatibilist views just described, it is plausible to suppose that *we* routinely, or indeed ever, act freely. Incompatibilists who think we do sometimes act freely are known as *libertarians*. Finally, in §5.8, I'll turn to 'pessimism', the aptly-named view that free will is impossible – at least for beings remotely like *us*.

It's worth saying that, in the main (but not universally), incompatibilists tend to be more interested in defending the basic principles of incompatibilism than they are in coming up with a full-blown theory of the necessary and sufficient conditions for acting freely. For some reason this task seems to have fallen squarely on the shoulders of compatibilists. Whatever the reasons for this, one consequence is that you will find no appeal in this chapter to conditions such as reasons-responsiveness. This isn't necessarily because incompatibilists don't think that such conditions are relevant to acting freely, or that they think that the necessary conditions they offer somehow automatically guarantee that, say, the agent is responsive to reasons; it's just that, well, they're happy to leave the hard work to the compatibilists.

Before getting any further, there's an important point to make. You *might* be tempted to think that indeterminism entails that agents generally *could have done otherwise* than what they actually do. This would be a mistake. It is true that indeterminism entails the existence of *alternative possibilities*, where we understand an alternative possibility merely as something that *can* – but doesn't – happen, consistent with the laws and the past being as they actually are. Whenever the laws plus the past fail to determine a unique outcome, there will be an alternative possibility in the offing: something that *could* have happened instead of what actually happened. But the existence of *some* alternative possibilities, somewhere in the history of the Universe, falls a long way short of there being, every time we make a decision, some *other* decision that we could have made.

To illustrate this point, there follow five cases, in all of which indeterminism is true (so there are *some* alternative possibilities in the history of the Universe – and indeed more locally than that), but where the agent fails to be able to do otherwise.

Jemima: Imagine the admittedly far-fetched possibility that the following law *L* obtains: there is a 0.3 per cent chance that, during any half-hour period, any stationary object weighing more than a ton will shift precisely one nanometre in a random direction. All other laws are as close to deterministic as they can be, given the law just stated: for given initial conditions, they specify a unique outcome (except if the specified outcome concerns the location of an object weighing more than a ton, in which case the law will be infected, as it were, by the indeterministic law just stated). This being so, all (or perhaps only *nearly* all) actions that agents perform are determined to happen by the past plus the laws. For example, nothing even slightly relevant to any action of Jemima's in the last ten minutes could have turned out relevantly differently, despite the small dose of indeterminism enshrined in the laws. It was determined, given all the past facts about the Universe ten minutes ago, that Jemima would now decide to make some tea. Given her current location at home, the only thing that could have happened differently is that her house could have shifted a nanometre. But if that had happened, she would *still* have made the same decision. So, there are some alternative possibilities in the vicinity of Jemima's decision – there are various directions in which her house could have shifted – but clearly she could not have done anything different to what she actually did. And, in fact (let's suppose), this generalises: nothing Jemima has ever done is such that she could have done otherwise, despite the falsity of determinism.

Jason: Suppose that the laws plus the past left precisely two possibilities open just now: that Jason decided to eat a banana, or, thanks to some faulty wiring in his brain, he dropped dead. In fact, Jason ate the banana – though, consistent with the past plus the laws, he might *not* have made that decision. Nonetheless, it would wrong to say that he could have *done* otherwise. Were Jason to have dropped dead instead, that would not have been an *act* of his – it would not have been something that he would have *done*. So, Jason is not determined by the past plus the laws to eat the banana; nonetheless, he cannot *do* otherwise.

Wally-2: Wally-2 is just like Wally from Chapter 1, except for the following fact: A some much *earlier* point in his life, he made a significant and character-forming decision to become a better person. Before that moment, he'd been engaged in various acts of petty theft; but he decided that enough was enough and that henceforth he would endeavour always to do the right thing. That decision was not fully determined by the past plus the laws; indeed, he could have done otherwise – he could have decided *not* to become a better person. Since then, however, he has stuck unwaveringly to that commitment, and it is now second nature to him to do the right thing (at least in easy cases). Here is Wally-2, with the wallet he's just found on the pavement. He unthinkingly hands it in to the police station and was determined to do so by his current character (plus the laws). Wally-2 could not, at any time in the *recent* past, have done anything other than hand the wallet in, despite the fact that indeterminism is true (and, indeed, despite the fact that he *earlier* did something than which he *could* have done otherwise).

Jenny: Jenny is thinking about whether to go and watch *Argo* at the cinema this evening. She researches this quite carefully – she doesn't want to waste her time and money – by reading various reviews, trying to remember whether she likes the *Argo* actors in other films. In fact, it is fully determined by the past and the laws that Jenny will decide to go and watch the film. However, it is *not* fully determined how exactly her deliberation will lead to that result. In particular – although this doesn't actually happen – there is a *chance* that, just by luck, it will suddenly pop into her head that she *really* didn't like Ben Affleck in *Pearl Harbor*. The laws plus the past determine that, had that happened, she would *still* have ended up deciding to watch *Argo*; it's just that she'd get there by a different route. (Perhaps, after careful consideration, she'd decide that he wasn't *so* bad in *Pearl Harbor*, and after all, *Argo* did win the Oscar for Best Picture.) So, Jenny is an 'indeterministic agent', in the sense that her process of deliberation is not fully deterministic: there is more than one way it might go, consistent with the laws plus the past. Nonetheless, she cannot *do* otherwise than what she actually does: she cannot decide not to go and see *Argo*.

Jonny: Jonny is also deliberating about whether to go and see *Argo*. Jonny *really* doesn't like Ben Affleck, but he is prone to making daft decisions sometimes, and in this particular case, if left to his own devices, there is indeed some genuinely indeterministic chance that he'll make the daft decision to watch *Argo*. This being so, his fairy godmother is standing by to make sure he doesn't waste his time and money. If she sees that he's about to decide to see the film, she'll wave her wand, which will have the effect of tweaking his neurons in such a way that he makes the sensible decision. In fact, Jonny does the sensible thing all by himself, and his fairy godmother doesn't have to intervene. (This case is a version of Frankfurt's 'nefarious neurosurgeon' case, which is the topic of Chapter 6.) In this case, Jonny, like Jenny, is fully determined by the past plus the laws to make the decision he actually makes. But, again, the deliberative process by which he comes to make that decision, considered by itself, is *not* deterministic: there is a different way it could have gone – namely, the way that would have prompted his fairy godmother to intervene.

The significance of the differences among some of these cases will become clear in due course; in particular, while *some* incompatibilist theories entail that *none* of the characters described above act freely, others hold that one or more of them do, despite lacking, around the time of action, the ability to do otherwise. For now, the take-home message is just this: Indeterminism is a *considerably* weaker thesis than the thesis that agents are always – or even sometimes – able to do otherwise than they actually do (in the sense of 'able to do otherwise' that is incompatible with determinism). There are all kinds of possible situations in which indeterminism is true, and yet agents sometimes, or even always, lack that ability.

5.2 Indeterministic initiators

This section comes with a health warning: it is rather technical. If, as you read on, you find your brain heating up to a dangerous level, don't worry; most of the rest of this chapter will make pretty good sense (I hope) even if you haven't fully absorbed all the technicalities. On the other hand, things are going to get complicated, especially in Chapter 6, and so the technicalities will come in very handy later on. If you find the technical bits of this section difficult, you may find them easier once you've read to the end of Chapter 5.

Now (this bit is *not* technical), we have just seen there is a large gap between the thesis of indeterminism and the thesis that indeterminism is true in just the right kind of way to satisfy incompatibilist demands on acting freely. Remember, my interest in this chapter is in what kinds of condition an incompatibilist might propose as necessary *and sufficient* conditions on acting freely. We know that incompatibilists think that indeterminism is necessary for acting freely, but exactly what are the sufficient conditions? In other words, what is it that agents who act freely have in common, which explains *why* they do? (There may not, in fact, be any such agents, but so long as we think that such agents are *possible*, we ought to be able to articulate what it is that those merely possible agents have in common that explains why *they* act freely.) I hereby stipulate that any incompatibilist *theory* of free will worthy of the name (the name 'theory', that is) must tell us what the necessary *and sufficient* conditions for acting freely are. Anything less than that, and we don't really have a *theory* at all – or, at any rate, we certainly don't have a *complete* theory. So, for example, if the only thesis you subscribe to is the thesis that acting freely requires the ability to do otherwise (in the incompatibilist sense), then you're certainly an incompatibilist, but you don't have a *theory* of free will.

I'm going to propose a 'theory-schema'. Think of it as a kind of template, so that, armed with any given incompatibilist theory of free will, you should (at least if you think hard enough about it, and the alleged theory really is a *theory*, in the sense just stipulated) be able to fill in the details, in such a way as yield necessary *and sufficient* conditions for acting freely, according to that theory. The schema, as you'll find out in a moment, starts: '*S* acts freely *if and only if*...'. A lot of principles that are in play in the free will literature, and we'll see a fair few in Chapter 6, take the form '*S* acts freely *only if*...'. This is all well and good, but to say '*X* only if *Y*' is to state a *necessary* condition (*Y*) on *X*. If we want necessary *and* sufficient conditions – which, if we want a *theory* of free will, we do – we need 'if and only if'.

So, let's get on to the theory-schema, which, as I said, is a kind of template for an incompatibilist theory of free will. Actually, we have a definition-schema, and then a theory-schema that appeals to the definition-schema. So, first, the definition-schema. Call an agent *S* an *indeterministic initiator* of action A – and let's restrict A to a mental action such as *deciding* – just in case some alternative possibility or other arises, somewhere in the process that led to A, that is *relevant* to A. So ('II' for 'indeterministic initiator'):

> (II-Def) S an *indeterministic initiator* of action A if and only if there is some alternative possibility, somewhere in the process that led to A, that is *relevant* to A.

The theory-schema, which appeals to the definition-schema just given, is this:

> (II-Free) S performs act B freely if and only if S is an indeterministic initiator of *some* action A, which stands in the right relation to B (and perhaps, in addition, S satisfies compatibilist conditions on acting freely, such as reasons responsiveness).

Why have I characterised (II-Def) and (II-Free) as a definition-*schema* and a theory-*schema* respectively, rather than just as a definition and a theory? The answer is that both (II-Def) and (II-Free) contain terms that are themselves undefined, and which, in effect, different incompatibilist theories define differently. In particular, there are different views we might take on what counts as a 'relevant' alternative possibility in (II-Def), and different views we might take on what counts as 'the right relation' in (II-Free). (Of course, there are also different views we might take on whether or not S needs in addition to satisfy compatibilist conditions, and, if so, precisely *which* conditions. But I'm just going to ignore this part because it's not going to be directly relevant to any of the discussion of this chapter.)

Slightly more longwindedly, here is what an incompatibilist theory of acting freely needs to do. First, it needs to tell us what counts as a *relevant* alternative possibility. This will tell us what kinds of alternative possibilities need to be in the offing in order for agent S to count as an 'indeterministic initiator' of a given action A, by the lights of that theory, and thus what kinds of agent satisfy (II-Def) – bearing in mind that we're going to go on and appeal to (II-Def), suitably filled in, in our account of what it takes to act freely. So, for example, some incompatibilist theories take Jonny in §5.1 to count as an indeterministic initiator of his decision not to see *Argo*, while some don't – in whatever senses of 'indeterministic initiator' the respective theories are going to plug into (II-Free) to yield an account of free action.

Second, the theory needs to tell us whether, in order to do *B* freely, *S* must be an indeterministic initiator of *B itself* (in which case, the 'right relation' is *identity*), or whether instead it is enough for *S* to be an indeterministic initiator of some *other* (earlier) action that stands in some appropriately-defined *relation* to *B*. So, if, for example, you think that Wally-2 in §5.1 freely hands in the wallet because his handing it in 'traces back' in the right way to his earlier decision to be a better person, you'll think that an agent *S* can freely do *B* (in this case, hand in the wallet) even if they are not an indeterministic initiator of *B* itself – so long as *B* traces back in the right way to some *prior* action of which they *were* an indeterministic initiator.

(Note: I have borrowed the term 'indeterministic initiator' from Mele (2006, 97), but I have deliberately failed to specify precisely what it takes to be one: (II-Def), remember, is a definition-*schema*, and not a definition. Mele's 'indeterministic initiator' *is* precisely specified: it is basically what, in my way of putting things, a 'weak source incompatibilist' defines an indeterministic initiator to be – see §§5.4 and 6.7.)

So much for the theory-schema; let's get back, finally, to discussing some actual philosophical positions. The major (but not the only) axis of disagreement between incompatibilists concerns whether or not, in order to *A* freely, it must be the case that the agent *could have done otherwise than A* (where action *A* is normally considered to be a mental event – normally, a decision). Broadly speaking, incompatibilists fall into two camps: *leeway* incompatibilism and *source* incompatibilism. I'll look at each in turn.

5.3   Leeway incompatibilism

Some incompatibilists – increasingly now referred to as 'leeway incompatibilists' – hold that there must be 'leeway' at (or near) the moment of decision: in order to *A* freely (where *A* is a decision, say, to have lasagne for lunch), the agent must – right before (or near enough) her decision – have been able to do otherwise (choose the fish instead, say). So, if I am to decide freely on what to have for lunch, it must be genuinely undetermined, right up until the decision itself (or near enough), what I'm going to choose. Similarly, in order for Wally to freely (and so morally responsibly) decide to take the lost wallet to the police station, there must have been some moment – somewhere between seeing the wallet and deciding, or forming the intention, to take it to the police station – when he could have done something else (keep it, leave it in the street, or whatever).

We can state leeway incompatibilism by filling in the blanks in our definition-schema (II-Def) and our theory-schema (II-Free) in a nice, straightforward way, as follows:

(II-Def-Leeway) S an *indeterministic initiator* of action A if and only if S could have done otherwise than A.

(II-Free-Leeway) S does A freely if and only if S is an indeterministic initiator of A (and perhaps, in addition, S satisfies compatibilist conditions on acting freely, such as reasons responsiveness).

(Actually, there's an annoying wrinkle: Some leeway incompatibilists actually *don't* actually require that S have the ability to do otherwise than A itself. In particular, recall Jonny from §5.1, who decides not to see *Argo* but whose fairy godmother would have stepped in and *made* him decide not to see it if he had been in danger of deciding to see it. Some leeway incompatibilists think that it is possible for Jonny to freely decide even though he lacks the ability to do otherwise than make that decision. In particular, some think that he will nonetheless decide freely if there is some *other* relevant alternative possibility in the course of his deliberation. Such a leeway incompatibilist will, of course, have to offer a revision to (II-Def-Leeway). But they do still, or so I think, deserve to count as a leeway incompatibilist. We'll get back to this issue in §6.6. If you find what I just said deeply confusing, pretend I never said anything for now; I'm going to ignore it for the purposes of this chapter in any case.)

One way to motivate leeway incompatibilism is to consider how things *seem* to us when we make the decisions or choices, since some philosophers have claimed that how this seems to us – the 'phenomenology' of decision – is the root of our notion of free will. Thus, for example, Timothy O'Connor says that 'it seems ... that I ... could have, in an unconditional sense, decided differently'; this (partly) 'captures the way we experience our own activity' (1995, 196). And John Searle says: 'Reflect very carefully on the character of the experiences you have as you engage in normal, everyday human actions. You will sense the possibility of alternative courses of action built into these experiences ... that we could be doing something else right here and now, that is, *all other conditions remaining the same*. This, I submit, is the source of our own unshakable conviction of our own free will' (1984, 95). (For some other examples of similar claims, see Nahmias et al. 2004, 165–6.) So, the idea here is that our concept of freedom is rooted in the fact that alternative possibilities *seem* to be available to us when we choose or decide; hence the thought that in order to choose or decide freely, things have to be the way they seem: there really must be alternative possibilities open to us.

Doubtless not all leeway incompatibilists would subscribe to this line of argument (to which I return briefly in §5.7). A more direct way to motivate the position would simply be to appeal to the (alleged) intuitive obviousness of the idea that in order to act freely, there must be something else I could have done instead, at or around the time in question. After all, one might try to argue, doesn't the word 'free' imply an absence of constraint, and isn't being determined to do something one way of being constrained to do it? (As we've already seen in Chapter 3, compatibilists argue that being determined by the past plus the laws does *not* constitute the kind of constraint that is incompatible with acting freely. Needless to say, leeway incompatibilists are unmoved by these arguments.) Alternatively, we might focus on the notion of *control*. Recall Fischer's distinction, introduced in §2.2, between 'guidance control' and 'regulative control'. Fischer thinks that moral responsibility only requires guidance control (which, Fischer thinks, should be cashed out in terms of reasons-responsiveness), but that acting *freely* requires regulative control: control over *whether or not* one performs the act in question. Regulative control requires the ability to do otherwise, so we can think of leeway incompatibilism as enshrining the requirement that agents have regulative control over their actions. So far as I can tell, most leeway incompatibilists hold, implicitly at least, that the ability to do otherwise is *all* that is required for regulative control. This is an assumption that I'll cast some doubt on in §5.5, in connection with the 'problem of luck'. Perhaps it would be more charitable to say that leeway incompatibilists typically don't give us a positive story about what *else* might be required for regulative control, aside from the ability to do otherwise – which isn't the same as positively claiming that *nothing* else is required. But if the leeway incompatibilist thinks that something else (nature unspecified) *is* required, then, the way I've set things up, that amounts to failing to provide a *theory* of free will at all, because it amounts to failing to attempt to provide a *sufficient* condition on acting freely.

It's worth connecting the idea that acting freely requires 'leeway' at or near the time of action with the Consequence Argument. While CA assumes that *A*-ing freely requires the ability to do otherwise than *A*, it does not, in fact, assume that in order to *A* freely, *S* must be able *at or near the time of A* to do otherwise than *A*. Since determinism precludes the possibility of there being *any time whatsoever* at which *S* could have done otherwise than *A*, CA can simply remain neutral on *when*, as it were, S could have done otherwise than A. Nonetheless, it's fairly easy to see that CA – *if* it is successful – motivates leeway incompatibilism.

Recall Sue, who is determined by the past plus the laws to make her cup of tea at 10 a.m. But now let's change the example: suppose that, while agents are hardly ever interderministic initiators of their actions (in the sense specified by (II-Def-Leeway)), they *occasionally* are – and so determinism is false. In particular, three weeks ago, Sue was invited to a seminar taking place this morning, and, although she declined the invitation (which she did at time t), she *could have* accepted it. However, since t, *no* feature of Sue's mental life has been undetermined by the past *since t* plus the laws: facts about the state of the world at t plus the laws have fully determined everything Sue has thought and done since then, including her recent decision to make some tea.

Now, if Sue had accepted the invitation at t, she would not have decided to make a cup of tea at 10 a.m. this morning – she would have been in a seminar, after all, with no access to tea-making facilities. So, there is *a* sense in which Sue could have done otherwise than make the tea: prior to t, she could indeed have done something such that, had she done it, come 10 a.m. today she would not have made the tea. But, if you're moved by the thought that acting freely requires the ability to do otherwise, I think it would be very odd for you to claim that Sue's making the tea is free *because* she could have accepted the seminar invitation three weeks ago. After all, we could now run a revised version of CA, which is not obviously any less compelling than CA itself.

Here's the revised version. Recall that in CA, P_0 is a proposition stating all the facts that obtained at some arbitrary time prior to judge J's birth – so that J has been determined by facts prior to his birth, plus the laws, not to raise his arm at time T. But let's change this, so that P_0 is a proposition stating all the facts that obtained at time t, when Sue declined the invitation, so that Sue has been determined *since t* by the facts listed in P_0, plus the laws, to make the tea. It seems to me that, if you are moved by the claim that acting freely requires the ability to do otherwise, you really ought to say that Sue does *not* make the tea freely. Here's Sue, wondering whether to make a cup of tea. Right here and now (I have donned an incompatibilist hat for the purposes of this sentence), there is *nothing she can do* about whether or not she make the tea; she is determined to make it by facts she can now do nothing about. She lacks *regulative control* over that decision. So, *surely* she doesn't make the tea freely.

The point here is that it would, in my view, be very odd to be motivated to adopt incompatibilism by CA, and yet to hold that people can act freely even though *at the time of deliberation* they are completely determined to do what they do and therefore cannot do otherwise. Hence, if you're moved by CA, you should adopt leeway incompatibilism.

Is leeway incompatibilism a well-motivated position? And is it a *viable* position? The motivation question is really, I think, answered by whether there are any good reasons to think that CA is sound. We've already seen some possible reasons to be sceptical about this in Chapter 3; we'll come across another in Chapter 6. As for viability, we'll shortly come to a classic problem for both leeway and source incompatibilism: the problem of luck (§5.5).

5.4   Source incompatibilism

Other incompatibilists – now sometimes called 'source incompatibilists' or 'causal history incompatibilists' – are motivated by the thought that determinism threatens our capacity to be the 'ultimate source' of our actions. We have already seen arguments that are supposed to motivate source incompatibilism in Chapter 4: the Sourcehood Argument (SA), Pereboom's four-case argument, and Mele's zygote argument. Just sticking with SA, remember the basic idea is just this: If determinism is true, then we do not have ultimate control over our actions, since our actions are deterministically caused by factors that were in place long before we were born, and hence over which we have never had any control.

Remember Wally from Chapter 1 (not to be confused with Wally-2), who unhesitatingly hands the dropped wallet in to the police station. Wally, good-natured soul that he is, is determined by his good nature to hand the wallet in. But does he do so freely and morally responsibly? Of course, the *leeway* incompatibilist will say 'No': he could not do otherwise than hand the wallet in. But source incompatibilists don't think the ability to do otherwise is a requirement on acting freely. The *sourcehood* worry about Wally is that if his character was, in turn, shaped by factors that were outside his control – which they were, if determinism is true – then, ultimately, his handing in the wallet is not really under his control either. If determinism is true, then since the beginning of the Universe (or perhaps shortly thereafter), the inexorable flow of causes and effects has been set in stone. It was always determined that Wally would be born and grow up in the way he did to bring him to the dropped wallet and his decision to return it. If we focus hard enough on this, it can start to seem as though we are merely the conduits through which the inexorable flow of causes and effects passes: it seems as though, going backwards in time, the buck passes right through us and out the other side.

What might a positive source incompatibilist account of acting freely consist in? That is, what do we need to add to the mere falsity of determinism in order to get to an account of the necessary and sufficient conditions on acting freely? Well, here things unfortunately start to get extremely murky. To keep things as clean as possible I'm going to invent some more terminology, and distinguish between what I'll call *weak source incompatibilism, strong source incompatibilism,* and *agent-causalism.* Discussion of agent-causalism is deferred until §5.6, but, despite the terminology I'm using, it should still be thought of as a version of source incompatibilism (and, confusingly, it comes in 'weak' and 'strong' varieties, as we'll see). The basic difference between weak and strong source incompatibilist theories is that the latter places a *buck-stopping requirement* on acting freely, whereas the former does not (or so I shall argue). The strong source incompatibilist gives us a story, in effect, about why we should think that the buck fails to stop with Wally if determinism is true, but it *does* stop with Wally if certain conditions – conditions that require indeterminism – are met. For example, you might think that the buck *does* stop with Wally-2, described in §5.1, whose current character was formed by an earlier decision to become a better person. (The same is true of agent-causalism: the agent-causalist also gives us a story about why the buck doesn't stop with Wally if determinism is true, but it does if it's false. But, as I say, I'll come back to agent-causalism later.)

To my mind, anyone who is moved to embrace incompatibilism by the kinds of sourcehood argument discussed in Chapter 4 owes us an account of how someone's being an indeterministic initiator of some specified kind stops the buck from flowing right through them and out the other side. A source incompatibilist account that *doesn't* postulate a buck-stopper – and weak source incompatibilism is just such an account – is *a fortiori* an implausible account of free will, by the source incompatibilist's own lights. If you think Wally isn't morally responsible in the deterministic case *because* the buck doesn't stop with Wally, you'd better come up with an account according to which the buck *does* stop if our agent is an indeterministic initiator of the right kind.

Here's how weak source incompatibilism goes. Look, the *only* problem with determinism is that if determinism is true, then the following principle, (CH) (for 'causal history') is never satisfied:

(CH) An action is free in the sense required for moral responsibility only if it is not produced by a deterministic process that traces back to causal factors beyond the agent's control. (Pereboom 2006, 186)

If determinism is true, agents' actions are *always* 'produced by a deterministic process that traces back to causal factors beyond the agent's control'. If it weren't for that pesky feature of determinism (so says the weak source incompatibilist), compatibilist theories of freedom would be absolutely fine: the only thing wrong with them is that they fail to add (CH) to their list of necessary conditions for acting freely. So, let's just take our favourite compatibilist theory and add (CH) to it. So, any action that satisfies that compatibilist theory (reasons-responsiveness, say) *and* (CH) will act freely (in the sense required for moral responsibility). So, there's our incompatibilist set of necessary and sufficient conditions for acting freely: job done!

To pre-empt an argument that will appear later on (§6.7), it's pretty easy to see, I think, that weak source incompatibilism doesn't postulate a buck-stopper. The weak source incompatibilist thinks that satisfying the *compatibilist* conditions on free will isn't enough to stop the buck; if she did, she wouldn't be a source incompatibilist in the first place. But just adding (CH) to the mix doesn't seem to improve matters. Let's add a dose of indeterminism to Wally's deliberation. (Actually, in the original version of the case he doesn't deliberate at all – he's not in any doubt, even for a second, about what to do. But let's ignore that.) Now he satisfies (CH). Does the buck now stop with Wally? Is he now the 'ultimate source' of his action? Does he now have – when he didn't in the deterministic version of the case – the right kind of control over his action to make him praiseworthy? It's hard to see why we should think that he does.

Of course, you may think that adding a dose of indeterminism *does* make Wally morally responsible, because we've just endowed Wally with the ability to do otherwise. But – first – in that case, it looks as though your motivation for incompatibilism is the Consequence Argument and not the Sourcehood Argument (or some other sourcehood-related argument), so you're really not a source incompatibilist. And, second, I didn't specify that Wally had the *ability to do otherwise* than hand the wallet in. I just specified, in effect, that his process of deliberation wasn't deterministic: that's all that's required by (CH). And that's a *much* weaker requirement – remember Jenny and Jonny from §5.1.

In fact, weak source incompatibilism is something of a straw-man position: generally speaking, incompatibilists who think that (CH) needs to be added to the list of necessary conditions on acting freely *also* think that agent causation needs to be added as well. Nonetheless, I think it's worth carving out the position in logical space, even if it's one that's unoccupied. Having roughly carved it out, however, that's all

I'm going to say about weak source incompatibilism for now. It will get another brief mention in §5.6, but I shall mostly defer discussion of it until Chapter 6, when I consider Frankfurt's 'nefarious neurosurgeon' case (of which the case of Jonny-and-his-fairy-godmother case described in §5.1 is a variant). The basic gist of Frankfurt's argument is that such cases show that acting freely doesn't require the ability to do otherwise. The reason for deferring discussion of weak source incompatibilism until then is that it only becomes clear why one might be tempted to embrace weak rather than strong source incompatibilism once Frankfurt's argument is on the table.

So, let's go back to strong source incompatibilism, which I defined as the kind of source incompatibilism that postulates a buck-stopper. In other words, strong source incompatibilists impose a condition on acting freely that gives Wally his control back: a condition that stops the buck passing right through him and out the other side.

Perhaps the best worked-out version of strong source incompatibilism (bearing mind that I'm treating the agent-causal variety of source incompatibilism separately in §5.6) is due to Robert Kane (1999). Here's the basic motivation for the position. Let's think about Wally again. What kind of thing might count as a buck-stopper for Wally? Well, perhaps we should think as follows. In order for the buck to stop with Wally, there must have been *some* point in his life – perhaps some moment after he'd just done something bad and, after much soul-searching, resolved to be a better person henceforth, or perhaps a moment where he could have given in to temptation but managed to resist, thus strengthening his good nature, or whatever – at which there *was* genuine indeterminacy. That is, there must have been a point, causally relevant to his current decision, where he genuinely could have gone either way (failed to make the resolution, say, or given in to temptation). If there was such a point (as there was in the case of Wally-2 described in §5.1), Wally's current decision is free despite his lacking alternative possibilities, but its freedom *derives* from this previous decision, where there *were* alternative possibilities open to Wally.

According to Kane, what stop the buck passing right through us are what he calls 'self-forming actions' or SFAs – Wally-2's resolution to become a better person, say. These are the ultimate sources to which our actions trace back, and are thus the moments in our lives at which the buck really does stop. But they can only have this status if they themselves are not, in turn, fully determined by what happened earlier on. (Some incompatibilists think that even such undetermined mental acts of self-formation fail to stop the buck, and hence think that we fail to be the ultimate sources of our actions even if such self-forming actions actually exist. We'll get back to the pessimists in §5.8.)

Technical note: Source incompatibilism is sometimes *defined* in such a way as to entail that an agent can act freely even if they are *never* able to do otherwise. (For example, an agent can act freely even if they are only *ever* indeterministic initiators of their actions in the much weaker sense that their processes of deliberation aren't fully deterministic.) This being so, Kane's view is sometimes characterised as being a 'mixed' or 'impure' version of incompatibilism: Kane holds that *many* actions are free despite the agent lacking the ability to do otherwise – namely, those that trace back in the right way to SFAs (that's the source aspect of his view), but that SFAs themselves require the ability to do otherwise (that's the leeway aspect). I myself find this way of carving up the territory deeply confusing, and so I'm not defining source incompatibilism in this way. By my lights, Kane counts as a full-blown source incompatibilist because he thinks that determinism precludes ultimate sourcehood. And his view counts as *strong* source incompatibilism because it clearly postulates buck-stoppers, namely SFAs. (And it isn't an agent-causal view either, because Kane doesn't think we need agent causation to stop the buck.) It's true, of course, that by definition SFAs require the ability to do otherwise or 'leeway'. But they only require leeway *because* leeway is (allegedly) required in order for the demand for ultimate sourcehood to be met.

Kane, in fact, introduces the notion of a self-forming action in order to get around the problem of luck. So, we'll come back to SFAs once I've explained, in the next section, what the problem of luck is. For now, however, let's just accept that Kane requires *more* of an action A, if A is to count as an SFA, than its merely being such that the agent could have done otherwise than A. Without yet specifying what that 'something more' is, we can still roughly characterise Kane-style strong source incompatibilism in terms of (II-Def) and (II-Free), as follows ('SS' for 'strong source'):

(II-Def-SS) S an *indeterministic initiator* of action A if and only if A is a self-forming action.

(II-Free-SS) S performs act B freely if and only if S is an indeterministic initiator of *some* action A, which lies in B's causal history (and perhaps, in addition, S satisfies compatibilist conditions on acting freely, such as reasons responsiveness).

Note that the 'lies in B's causal history' part may, in fact, be a little too weak. For example, let's suppose that, again at an earlier time, Wally-2 resolved to help out around the house much more (*A*), and that that was a genuine SFA – so he was, in the sense that we haven't yet fully defined, an indeterministic initiator of *A*. *A* may well lie in *B*'s causal history, where *B* is Wally-2's forming the intention to hand the wallet in to the police. For example, perhaps, earlier today, Wally-2 decided to do the weekly shop, and he was on his way home from the supermarket when he found the wallet. Then we may suppose that *A* lies in the causal history of *B* because, had Wally-2 not earlier resolve to help out around the house more, he wouldn't have gone to the supermarket and hence would never have found the wallet, and so would never have done *B*. Clearly, however, Wally-2's previously having done *A* in no way underpins his moral responsibility for *B*, even though *A* is an SFA that lies in *B*'s causal history. However, we'll leave it up to the Kane-style strong source incompatibilist to figure out how to formulate a more plausible version of (II-Free-SS).

5.5   The problem of luck

The major problem facing both leeway and source incompatibilism – including agent-causalism, to be discussed in §5.6 – is what has come to be known as the 'problem of luck'. Imagine that Pete is deliberating about whether or not to cheat on a math test. Pete knows it's wrong to cheat and he knows he'll feel bad afterwards if he does it; he also knows he'll get into serious trouble if he's caught. On the plus side, however, he's going to do really badly if he doesn't cheat, and he's pretty sure he can do it in such a way that makes getting caught unlikely. In the end, he decides to cheat. Suppose that, right up until the moment he makes the decision, it's undetermined by the past (including Pete's mental states) plus the laws which decision he'll make – so, the condition for leeway-incompatibilist freedom is met. But in that case, he *might* have gone through exactly the same process of deliberation, considered and weighed up exactly the same options and – consistent with all those facts plus the laws – decided *not* to cheat. But doesn't that make whether or not Pete decides to cheat a mere matter of luck? Isn't the situation essentially the same as there being a tiny coin being flipped inside Pete's head, so that he decides to cheat if it lands heads and not to cheat if it lands tails? And in that case, how can Pete truly be said to have been *in control* of his decision? After all, we're can't control the outcomes of coin tosses; it might be up to us whether we toss the coin, but once it's tossed it's just a matter of luck whether it comes down heads or tails.

To put the problem another way, there seems, *prima facie* at least, to be a tension between demanding *elbow room* in one's decisions – demanding, that is, that we only act freely if we could have done otherwise – and *also* demanding (as any sensible theory of free will surely should) that we have *control* over our decisions. Or, to put it in still other terms, recall Fischer's notion of *regulative control* – control over *whether or not* one performs a given act. Fischer holds, in effect, that *only* indeterministic initiators (of the kind who could have done otherwise) can have regulative control. The problem of luck suggests that not even such indeterministic initiators have regulative control: the fact that there is something else they could have done undermines the claim that they have *control* over the outcome.

Perhaps the best response to the problem of luck comes from Kane (1999). Kane, being a strong source incompatibilist (indeed, he's a source *libertarian*), thinks that only 'self forming actions' or SFAs need be indeterministically caused. SFAs are those decisions that form our character – a character which, having been formed by such SFAs, may well later *determine* us to act in certain ways. Kane thinks that those later determined actions, such as Wally-2's returning the wallet, are freely performed (remember (II-Free-SS) from the previous section), but they are only *derivatively* free: their being free derives from their standing in the appropriate causal relation to earlier SFAs. So Kane himself is only interested in the problem of luck insofar as it pertains to SFAs. In effect, Kane's central claim is that, because of additional constraints on SFAs (additional, that is, to the mere constraint that the agent could have done otherwise), SFAs are *not* subject to the problem of luck, and therefore serve as the kind of buck-stopper that strong source incompatibilism demands.

The first thing we need to note is that there are plenty of cases of indeterminism where we would unhesitatingly say that the agent acted intentionally and voluntarily, and would therefore count them as morally responsible. Imagine that Mila freely decides (whatever that requires) to shoot the Prime Minister. She therefore tries to shoot the PM, and indeed succeeds in doing so. But suppose that there was a *chance* – a genuinely indeterministic chance – that her gun would jam. In a sense, Mila got lucky: as it turned out, the gun didn't jam, and so she was able to carry out her intention to shoot the PM. But the gun might have jammed, and she had no control over whether or not it did. Nonetheless, we do not think that for this reason it was *merely* a matter of luck that she shot the PM, in a sense that deprives her of having done so freely and morally responsibly. On the contrary: Mila is clearly morally responsible for shooting him. (Imagine that Mila tried to argue, on the grounds that it was only a matter of luck that the gun didn't jam, that it wasn't really her fault that she shot the PM. We wouldn't buy the argument. After all, she *tried* to shoot and she succeeded; the fact that she might *not* have succeeded is just irrelevant.)

Now imagine instead that Mila, with her gun at the ready and with the PM in her sights, is having a serious crisis of conscience. She really hates the PM (we might imagine that he is responsible for some policy that indirectly led to the death of a relative, say), she is being paid handsomely for assassinating him, and she is pretty sure she won't get caught. On the other hand, she is very well aware of – and not completely unmoved by – the fact that murder is wrong, and is thinking about the PM's family, who will be left devastated by his murder. Let's assume that it is genuinely undetermined, up until Mila makes her decision, which decision she will make. But she has to settle the matter: shoot or desist? In this kind of situation, Kane claims, there is a perfectly good sense in which Mila is *trying* to make both decisions at once: she is trying to decide to shoot, and also trying to decide not to shoot. But in that case, *whichever* decision she makes, she will have success-fully made a decision she was *trying* to make. So, whatever decision she makes, the case will be similar to the possible-jammed-gun case. In *that* case, remember, we held Mila responsible because she did what she was trying to do, despite the fact that there was some chance she wouldn't, in fact, do it (since there was some chance that the gun would jam). In the crisis-of-conscience case, the same point applies, Kane thinks. If she decides to shoot, then she succeeds in doing what she is trying to do, and therefore does so freely and responsibly despite the fact that there was some chance that she wouldn't do it. And exactly the same applies if she decides *not* to shoot.

Kane holds, then, that in order for an agent S's decision to A to count as a genuine SFA, it must be the case that (a) S could have decided, right up until the moment of deciding to A, *not* to A, and (b) S was, right up until that moment, simultaneously *trying* to decide to A and trying to decide *not* to A. (You can now plug this definition of an SFA back into (II-Def-SS) in the previous section. Note that (II-Def-SS) is a *stronger* requirement on what it takes to be an indeterministic initiator than is (II-Def-Leeway).)

Let's return to the problem of luck. Suppose that Mila's decision (whichever it is) conforms to Kane's requirements on an SFA. Is Kane right to think that it is therefore not a matter of luck that she makes that decision? That's a question that I'm going to leave to you to decide for yourself. That's because I don't think it matters very much what the answer is – and *that's* because I think we have no reason at all to think that any of our *actual* decisions conform to Kane's requirements. So, if we're interested in whether or how often, according to a given theory of freedom – which, primarily, I am – we *actually* act freely and responsibly, the answer to *that* question is 'Probably, never', even if the answer to the first question is 'Yes'. I'll therefore come back to Kane's SFAs in §5.7, when I discuss libertarianism.

5.6   Agent-causalism

Here is a different kind of threat that you might think is posed by determinism. Suppose that the decision I just made to make a cup of tea was fully determined by past facts – let's say, to simplify matters, by facts about my beliefs and desires. I wanted a cup of tea; there wasn't anything incompatible with having a cup of tea that I wanted *more* than I wanted the tea; and I believed that making a cup of tea was something I could easily bring about (there are teabags in the kitchen, there isn't a power cut). Suppose that my possession of these mental states, together with the laws of nature, entailed that I would, in fact, decide to make a cup of tea – that is, they entailed that, shortly afterwards, some mental event would occur, *viz*, my deciding to make a cup of tea.

You might now have the following worry. Doesn't the above story somehow leave *me* out of the picture? If we conceive of my decisions and other actions as merely events that involve my mind or my body, which are in turn deterministically caused by other events (or states) that involve my mind (and perhaps my body and features of my environment), how can it be that *I* am the agent of my own actions? Surely, my actions aren't merely caused by things happening in my mind; rather, they are caused by *me*. It is *I*, and not the mere goings-on inside my head, who ultimately determines whether or not I make a cup of tea.

Someone who is moved by this sort of worry might want to claim that for an agent to truly *act* – or perhaps to act in a way that is distinctive of free and morally responsible beings like ourselves (or so we hope) as opposed to lions and dogs – the *agent herself* must determine what she does, in a way that is not simply a matter of mere happenings in her mind causing it. Two things would seem to be required here. First, facts about the agent's state of mind and external circumstances, together with the laws, must *not* entail that she does what she actually does (decide to make a cup of tea, say) – or, to put it another way, that decision must not be *deterministically caused* by the agent's mental states and external circumstances. After all, if those mental states do deterministically cause her decision, it's hard to see how there can be metaphysical room, as it were, for *her* – as opposed to those mental states – to determine what she does; all the work is being done by her mental states. Second, the agent herself must cause or determine her decision.

Intuitively, the idea here is that the laws plus facts about the agent's mental states (etc.) leave more than one possible decision open to the agent, and it is the agent herself who determines which of these possible decisions she actually makes. Thomas Reid, for example (1788, Essay IV), held that while physical objects and other animals are subject to necessity – that is, they are causally determined to behave as they do by features of themselves and their environments – we human beings are *not* subject to necessity and have 'active powers'. So, while we might *say* that, for example, a rock has the power to break a window, this 'power' really only amounts to the fact that if the rock were to be in the right circumstances – being thrown at a window, for example – then the window would break as a result of the rock's impact. (In terms of dispositions, discussed in §3.2, the rock has the *disposition* to break the window.) But *I* have the power to bring things about in a different sense: I have the power to decide to throw the rock or not, and exercising that power is a matter of *my* directly bringing it about that I make the relevant decision; it is not merely a matter of happening to be in circumstances that determine that I will decide to throw the rock (or, alternatively, in circumstances that determine that I'll decide not to).

Those philosophers who subscribe to the 'agent-causal' view of free will will hold that the two conditions just described are indeed requirements on acting freely. Agent-causalists are therefore incompatibilists, since the first condition is that the action in question not be determined by the past plus the laws. And it is very natural to think of agent-causalism as a variety of source incompatibilism, since being an agent-cause of one's action would seem to be a pretty good buck-stopper. After all, if the *agent* really does cause her action – in a way that is somehow different to her mental states causing it – then it really does seem (at least at first blush) true to say that the buck stops *with the agent*.

The most commonly voiced worry about the agent-causal view is that we really can't make any sense of the idea of an *agent*, as opposed to her mental states, causing anything. Or, more modestly, perhaps we can *only* make sense of that idea if we assume that the agent somehow stands outside the world of physical causes and effects, immune from the dictates of the laws of nature, and yet manages to *intervene* in the world by bringing about her own actions or decisions. But this assumption requires the truth of *Cartesian dualism*, the view that the mind is an immaterial substance (and *hence* not subject to the physical laws), and

Cartesian dualism is itself either incoherent or, at best, highly implausible. Hence, agent-causalism should be rejected.

One way to motivate the former version of the objection, that agent-causalism just doesn't make any sense, is the following thought. We can make sense of causation only as a relation between *events* (or perhaps *states of affairs* or *facts*): things that have spatial and temporal locations. (This is sometimes known as 'event causation' – though we might not want to presuppose that the relata are events specifically, as opposed to, say, facts.) Of course, we often *say* that an *object* caused something: we say that the sun caused my sunburn, that the hailstones caused the damage to the car, or that my neighbour's dog really annoyed me yesterday. But such claims only make sense because what we say is really shorthand for some claim about causal relations between events (or states of affairs or facts). For example, it wasn't really the dog, in and of itself, that annoyed me yesterday; it was something the dog *did*, *viz*, bark incessantly. Strictly speaking it was the *dog's barking* (during a particular period of time) that annoyed me. Similarly, it was the contact of the sun's UV rays with my skin (and not the sun itself) that caused my sunburn, and the impact of the hailstones on the car (and not the hailstones themselves) that caused the damage.

Hence, similarly, while we can, and routinely do, talk about *agents* causing things ('You made me really angry!'), we can only make sense of such claims by taking them to be shorthand for claims about specific features or states or acts of the agent. Thus, when I say, '*I* caused my decision to make a cup of tea', we can really only understand this as an implicit claim about event causation: as the claim that my decision was caused by various beliefs and desires of mine, and/or by my deliberation about what it would be best for me to do. But, of course, this is just to deny that there is really any such thing as 'agent causation', understood as something over and above event causation.

More charitably, we might at least challenge the agent-causalist to explain what exactly agent causation is supposed to be. Dogs don't agent-cause anything, it would seem; so what is it about *us* that makes us capable of standing in this metaphysically distinctive causal relation to our actions? Of course, we have all sorts of mental capacities that dogs lack, and which we might plausibly judge to be relevant to our being bearers of moral responsibility. But the question is, Why should we think that such mental capacities render us capable of bearing a special kind of causal relation to our actions?

This is the point at which it looks like a commitment to dualism might help the agent-causalist out: we, unlike dogs, have *minds*, conceived as distinctively immaterial substances. Once we've made that step, it doesn't seem so implausible to say that our minds stand in different kinds of causal relations to our behaviour to the kinds of causal relations that dogs' 'minds' (which are not really minds at all on a dualist story – just brains) stand in to *their* behaviour. Unfortunately, explaining how immaterial substances (which, for one thing, have no spatial location) can cause anything is a major problem in its own right – indeed, this is one of the standard reasons philosophers give for rejecting dualism. So making this move might make things worse, rather than better, for the agent-causalist.

Finally, one might attempt to undermine the initial motivation for agent-causalism by noting that the question of the difference between *doing* something and something's merely *happening* to one – raising one's arm as opposed to one's arm rising up, say – is one that has been much discussed in the literature on the philosophy of action. One standard way of distinguishing between actions and mere bodily movements is that actions are brought about *intentionally*, whereas mere bodily movements are not. If your arm rises because of a nervous tic, and you thereby spill someone's drink, you might say, 'I'm sorry, I didn't *mean* for my arm to rise just then; it just *happened*'. (See Wilson and Shpall 2012.) But the distinction between *doing* something – intentionally bringing about some bodily movement – and the bodily movement just *happening* doesn't seem to require that the former involve some sort of mysterious causal relation between *you* and the rising of your arm; it just requires that the causal history of your bodily movement involve your psychology in the right kind of way (via forming an intention to move your arm, say – or whatever else acting 'intentionally' might require).

The point here is that the distinction just described *might* serve to scratch the itch that the agent-causalist claims to want to scratch: the thought that we need to account for the fact that my decisions (and other actions) are things that *I* do, rather than things that merely *happen* to me. Indeed, one might think that decisions in particular are para-digmatic intentional actions – they're the kind of thing that *can't* 'just happen' to one. But we can make sense of this by saying that decisions are *always* intentional actions, just as raising one's arm (as opposed to its merely rising) is always an intentional action. Thus, there is no need to postulate any *sui generis* causal relation between the agent and her decision. Agent-causalists, of course, disagree. (See Clarke 1993, 1996 and O'Connor 1995, 1996 for some recent attempts to motivate and flesh out an agent-causal account of free will; O'Connor 2002 provides a good survey. See Steward 2012 for a comprehensive defence of a version of agent-causalism.)

Now for a complication. A question I have glossed over so far in this section is this. We've granted, in effect, that agent causation requires the agent to be *some* kind of indeterministic initiator of her action. But *what* kind, exactly? In particular, recall the distinction made in §5.4 between weak and strong source incompatibilism. The Kane-style strong source incompatibilist requires the agent to be such that she could have done otherwise than decide to *A*, if her deciding to *A* is to count as a self-forming action and hence constitute a buck-stopper for any future actions that might stem from that decision. The weak source incompatibilist, by contrast, requires only that the agent's process of deliberation is not deterministic – a much weaker requirement. We can make a similar distinction when it comes to agent-causal views, which I'll now dub as the distinction between 'strong' and 'weak' agent-causal views. As with the distinction between strong and weak source incompatibilism, this distinction is only going to make some sense once we've got Frankfurt's 'nefarious neurosurgeon' case on the table in Chapter 6, and I'll therefore delay further discussion of the distinction between strong and weak agent-causalism until §6.7.

Before moving on, however, it's worth noting that Ned Markosian (1999) offers a compatibilist account of agent causation. This has not, by any means, become a popular position – virtually all agent-causalists are still incompatibilists. But it's an interesting question – and one that I'll return briefly to in §6.7 – why exactly it is that agent-causalists generally think that agent causation is incompatible with determinism.

5.7 Libertarianism

Libertarianism, as you know by now, is the conjunction of two theses: incompatibilism, and the thesis that at least some actual agents do, at least some of the time, act freely. So, just as there are different varieties of incompatibilism, there are different varieties of libertarianism: leeway, strong and weak source, and agent-causal. As we saw in §5.2, incompatibilists are committed to some version or other of our 'theory-schema' (II-Free), the thesis that in order to act freely, an agent must be an *indeterministic initiator* of at least *some* action or other; and we've seen that different kinds of incompatibilist will flesh out this condition, and the notion of an 'indeterministic initiator', in different ways. Libertarians are therefore committed to holding that at least some actual agents are indeed indeterministic initiators (in some specified sense) of at least some of their actions. That's really all there is to be said about what libertarianism is; we've already done most of the legwork in the preceding sections of this chapter.

Is any version of libertarianism *plausible* – that is, do we have any reason to think that some version or other of libertarianism is actually *true*? Interestingly, this is a question that rarely gets addressed (though Pereboom 2001 and Balaguer 2010 are among the exceptions). In general, incompatibilists seem to be considerably more interested in whether libertarianism is a *coherent* position than they are in whether or not it is *true*. Of course, if libertarianism turned out not to be coherent (say, because there is no *possible* way of getting indeterministically-caused actions to *not* turn out to be a matter of luck), that would entail that libertarianism can't possibly be true – so it's not as though the two questions are completely unrelated. Nonetheless, I think the most interesting questions are these: First, do any of us ever act freely? Second, if we do, is there any way of telling when we do and when we don't? And, third, again if we do, is it something we do routinely or only very occasionally?

So, let's start with the first question: How plausible is it to think that any of us, ever, are indeterministic initiators, in any sense, of our actions? Is it ever *actually* the case that there are relevant alternative possibilities left open by the past plus the laws, at or around the time of any agent's decision? That would appear to be an empirical question, and – I claim – we have no particular reason to think that it's true. For starters, we can't be sure that indeterminism, rather than determinism, is true – and if indeterminism isn't true, then, of course, there is no such thing as an indeterministic initiator, in *any* sense of the term. But even if we think that there is good reason to believe that indeterminism *is* true, because it's what our current best science – at least the quantum physics part of it – seems to indicate, that in itself gives us no reason whatsoever to believe that any of us are ever indeterministic initiators. Suppose, for example, you think that Carly's freely stealing your car depends upon whether, at the time at which she made the decision to do it, she could have done otherwise – that is, it depends upon whether she could have stayed at home, or gone to the cinema, or whatever, instead. Now, quantum phenomena are universal, in that everything – including Carly's brain – is composed of subatomic particles. So, if the laws governing quantum phenomena are indeterministic, then doubtless there are a lot of indeterministic processes – processes governed by indeterministic laws – going on in Carly's head while she's deliberating. But it doesn't follow that the possibilities that those indeterministic laws leave open correspond to the alternatives that Carly is considering. Most likely, the laws don't leave it open that Carly will decide to try and procure a spaceship and fly to the moon, or eat an orange while standing on her head. But why should we assume that they *do* leave it open that she'll, say, decide to go to the cinema? For all we know, they don't leave any possibilities open except the one that actually happens: Carly decides to steal your car.

A related problem – I'm now addressing the second question listed above – is that, even if we grant that *some* decisions are indeterministically caused in just the way that the libertarian requires, we have absolutely no way of telling which ones they are, and so we have no way of telling *which* actions we, or other people, are morally responsible for. Libertarians tend to be rather cagey on the question of *which* of our decisions we make freely and are hence morally responsible for; in principle, they're only committed to the claim that *some* of them are. But from an epistemic point of view, that's not really much help. Is Carly responsible for stealing your car? Is Wally-2 responsible for handing in the wallet? We can't possibly know the answers to questions like these until such time as we're all wired up with devices that monitor the quantum goings-on in our heads and can reliably correlate those goings-on with which alternative possibilities are open to us.

The third question was whether we act freely routinely or only very occasionally. It would be much better, of course, if we did it routinely; after all, it would seem that this is what we ordinarily assume when we go about our everyday lives. So, how plausible is it that we *do* routinely act freely, on a libertarian view? Well, let's distinguish here between leeway and strong source libertarianism. The Kane-style strong source libertarian might seem to be in a better position than the leeway libertarian, since Kane thinks that we can perfectly well act freely a lot of the time, even if those actions fail to meet the requirements of SFAs, and even if we are not in *any* sense indeterministic initiators of them, so long as they trace back in the right way to SFAs. But, again, we currently have no idea at all whether those character-forming decisions we occasionally make are indeterministically caused or not. (We might be able to tell just by introspection whether we satisfy the condition of *trying* to make each of the alternative decisions; but we cannot tell just by introspection whether or not it is undetermined which decision we'll end up making; more on this in a moment.) Nor, I suggest, do we even know on any given occasion whether there *was* some relevantly character-forming decision in our past history – let alone whether it was indeterministically caused in the way that is required for genuinely buck-stopping SFAs. We might ask Wally whether there was any moment at which he made some particularly character-forming decision in the past that led to his now deciding to hand the wallet in. Wally might well have no idea what the answer to that question is.

What about leeway libertarianism? Well, as we saw in §5.5, it seems that the leeway libertarian is saddled with the problem of luck. Let's grant, for the sake of the argument, that a lot of our decisions really are indeterministically caused – and indeed in such a way that we could, at or around the time of the decision, we could have done otherwise. As we saw, however, if those decisions are indeterministically caused in a way that is *random* – analogous to having a tiny roulette wheel or coin-tossing device in one's head – then even so, we will not thereby act freely, because what we end up doing is not within our control. As we saw, Kane claims to solve the problem of luck by appealing to SFAs – and let's grant, again for the sake of the argument, that he succeeds. So a possible way of trying to save leeway libertarianism from the problem of luck would be simply to add to the leeway libertarian's could-have-done-otherwise requirement (enshrined in (II-Def-Leeway)) the requirement that free decisions comply with Kane's account of SFAs. In other words, could simply replace (II-Def-Leeway) with (II-Free-SS). In that case, our decisions will not, in general, be a matter of luck at all, so long as they meet those requirements.

Well, that might help the leeway libertarian out in the sense that it means that leeway libertarianism could, *in principle,* be true of most agents, most of the time – perhaps there are *possible* scenarios where agents' decisions routinely meet Kane's conditions on SFAs. But – and we don't need to know anything about physics to be able say this – it is incredibly implausible to suppose that *our actual* decisions routinely satisfy Kane's demands on SFAs. Remember, an SFA is a decision about whether or not to *A,* such that the agent is simultaneously trying to decide to *A and* to decide *not* to *A.* Even if we do, indeed, *sometimes* perform SFAs, they are surely not commonplace, everyday phenomena. In the last hour, I decided to make a cup of tea, throw away some mouldy potatoes, and rewrite this section. Clearly, none of these could possibly have been SFAs. I was not simultaneously trying to decide to do *and* trying to decide *not* to do any of these things. (I was *tempted* to watch TV instead of rewriting this section, but I was certainly not *trying* to decide to do that.) So, if the leeway libertarian tries to get around the problem of luck by imposing Kane's requirements on SFAs on *all* our free actions, it will turn out that, in fact, most of what we do is not done freely – even if the relevant decisions are indeterministically caused in such a way as to render us able to do otherwise.

It's worth returning briefly here to our introspective awareness of our own deliberation (see §5.3). It might *seem* to me, when I'm thinking about what to do, that there is more than one option available to me.

After all, if it didn't seem that way, it's not clear why I'd be deliberating in the first place. But does how things seem to me *really* amount to its seeming to me that more than one option is left open *by the past plus the laws*? If not, then whatever account we *do* give of how things seem to me, it's not going to connect in any interesting way with libertarianism. On the other hand, if how things seem to me really *does* amount to its seeming to me that more than one option is left open by the past plus the laws, then we get the connection with libertarianism, but at the cost of having no idea at all whether how things seem is really how they are. It would be a very bold claim indeed to say that we have good reason to think that our own decisions are indeterministically caused solely on the basis of our phenomenology!

While I have been somewhat dismissive of the claim that we have any reason whatsoever to think that any version of libertarianism is actually *true*, however, it's worth asking how the empirical facts stack up when it comes to compatibilism. You might be tempted to think that the compatibilist is in no better a position than the incompatibilist in this regard, since we have no more reason to think that determinism is true than we do to think that actual agents are (sometimes) indeterministic initiators of their actions.

You may have noticed, however, that the compatibilist theories discussed in Chapter 2 not only don't require the falsity of determinism – they wouldn't be compatibilist theories if they did – they also don't require the *truth* of determinism. As I said in §1.3, until around the middle of the twentieth century, most philosophers simply assumed that determinism is true. (This being so, there is an old term, 'soft determinism', denoting the combination of *determinism* and the thesis that agents at least sometimes act freely – and, by and large, pretty much all compatibilists were, in fact, soft determinists. 'Soft determinism' contrasted with 'hard determinism' on the one hand – incompatibilism plus determinism – and libertarianism on the other, where libertarianism was generally conceived as a dualist version of the agent-causal view.) Nowadays, philosophers in general – and compatibilists in particular – normally *don't* assume that determinism is true.

It therefore would not be fair to claim that compatibilist theories are hostage to the empirical facts in anything like the way that libertarian theories are. Compatibilist theories are, of course, hostage to empirical facts: it's an empirical fact about me whether or not I am currently acting under any freedom-undermining pathological compulsion, whether the structure of my will is in order, and (if you insist on thinking this is relevant) whether or not I have not had a wholesale overnight psychology-replacement operation courtesy of a band of evil alien neuroscientists. But, by and large (though not, of course, infallibly), we are normally entitled to be pretty confident that the relevant compatibilist requirements (unlike incompatibilist requirements, I've argued) are satisfied.

On the other hand, we cannot, as I have just said, be confident that determinism is true – or that, if indeterminism is true, it is somehow confined to the quantum realm in a way that doesn't render any relevant macroscopic or psychological processes indeterministic, too. This being so, we compatibilists should therefore be a little cautious about trying to undermine incompatibilism by pushing the problem of luck. For of course it might, for all we know, turn out that quite a lot of what we do *is* undetermined by the past plus the laws. So, if we think that this would undermine free will, then we'll have to admit that we are *not* after all entitled to be confident that we routinely act freely.

5.8   Pessimism

Pessimism (as I'm defining it here) comes in two varieties: weaker and stronger. The stronger variety is the view that free will is *impossible*, at least for beings even remotely like *us*. Galen Strawson (1994) motivates this variety of pessimism by what he calls the 'Basic Argument', which aims to show that agents can only be morally responsible if they are what Dennett calls 'self-made selves'. Since it would be completely impossible for human beings to be self-made selves, moral responsibility is impossible – at least for beings like us. The weaker variety of pessimism doesn't take free will to be *impossible* for finite, flesh-and-blood beings like us; this kind of pessimist simply thinks that it is extremely *implausible* to suppose that beings like us possess free will. One way to motivate this weaker variety of pessimism comes from Pereboom (2001), and in essence it involves pooling some argumentative resources we've already gathered from this chapter and Chapter 4. I'll look at Strawson's and Pereboom's arguments in turn.

Let's start, then, with the Basic Argument, which is an infinite regress argument. Recall the motivation for source incompatibilism: in order to be 'ultimately responsible' for our actions, the buck must stop with us, as opposed to flowing right through us and back to our parents, our grandparents, and so on, *ad infinitum*. The source incompatibilist holds that the right kind of indeterminism – Kane's self-forming actions, say – can stop the buck. The proponent of the Basic Argument disagrees: *even if* a given decision is a SFA (or meets whatever other conditions the source libertarian postulates), and assuming that Kane is right that the problem of luck can be solved, SFAs do not (*pace* Kane) deliver 'ultimate' responsibility.

Why not? Well – so runs the argument – in order to be *ultimately* (or, as Strawson sometimes puts it, 'truly') morally responsible for a given action, you must have performed that action for a reason. And – to quote Strawson – 'when one acts for a reason, what one does is a function of how one is, mentally speaking' (1994, 6). To put it another way, what *counts* as a reason to do (or not to do) something is a function of the kind of character you have, your beliefs and desires, and so on. Some people are moved by whether or not the contemplated action will harm the environment; others aren't. For Carly, the fact that she has an overdue gas bill counts as a good reason to steal your car; for other people with an overdue gas bill, it doesn't. For Wally, the fact that the owner of the wallet would probably very much like to have it back again is a good reason to hand it in to the police station; others are unmoved by this kind of consideration. But in order to be *ultimately* responsible for your action, you must surely be ultimately responsible for your having the reasons you had for acting in the way you did; that is to say, you must be ultimately responsible for having the character you have (that is to say, for being the way you are, mentally speaking). But you can only be ultimately responsible for *that* if, in turn, you consciously *chose* to be that way – and did so in the light of *reasons* for being that way. But then *those* reasons – reasons for choosing the character you now have – must themselves have been a function of how you were, mentally speaking, at the time of your choice. And to be ultimately responsible for *that*, again you must have chosen to be that way. And so it goes on, and on, without end. So in order to be ultimately morally responsible for any action, I would have to have made infinitely many prior choices – which, of course, is impossible. (Maybe God could do it, but God is most certainly not a being anything like *us*.)

We might put the matter in terms of self-forming actions, SFAs, as follows. Recall Mila, the would-be assassin we met in §5.4. There she is, with the PM in view, having her crisis of conscience and (we may suppose) satisfying all the criteria for SFAs: she's trying both to decide to shoot and to decide not to shoot, and her decision is genuinely undetermined by the past plus the laws. For Kane, that's enough to make Mila ultimately responsible for shooting the PM. According to the Basic Argument, however, it isn't. For how is it that Mila came to have the kind of character such that she had just the reasons she had for shooting the PM? Remember, Mila's reasons for shooting include the large amount of money she's being offered and the fact that she really hates the PM. But the fact that those *are* reasons for Mila is itself due to relevant features of her character. After all, plenty of people wouldn't commit murder, no matter how much money they were offered; and plenty of people don't develop a murderous hatred of politicians, even if the politician in question is indirectly responsible for, say, the death of a loved one.

The pertinent question, then, is whether the character from which Mila's reasons flow was itself merely determined by her upbringing, her genetic inheritance, and other details. If so, then, *pace* Kane, she lacks ultimate responsibility for shooting the PM. To have ultimate responsibility, she would have had to choose, at some earlier point, to be the kind of person she is – the kind of person who, in that situation, acts for just those reasons. Well, let's suppose there *was* such a choice; let's even suppose it was another SFA. But now we run into the same question: How is it that Mila *then* came to have the kind of character that confronted her with *that* choice, and led (without determining, if it was a SFA) to her making the choice she did? Was it determined by her upbringing and other traits, or does it, in turn, trace back to yet another SFA? But Mila has only been alive and capable of making character-forming decisions for so long; there must have been a *first* SFA that Mila performed, since clearly she can't have performed infinitely many of them in her finite lifetime. So she cannot have been ultimately responsible for *that* SFA, since it sprang from reasons which, by hypothesis, were not of her own choosing.

What should we make of the Basic Argument? Well, it certainly looks valid, if we accept the premise that 'ultimate' responsibility for an action in turn requires ultimate responsibility for the having the reasons in the light of which one decides to perform it. And so the argument certainly seems to spell trouble for the source libertarian. Remember, the source libertarian's starting point is the thought that determinism prevents agents from being the 'ultimate' source of their actions because the inexorable chain of causes and effects passes right through the agent and – back in time – out the other side. What Strawson's argument suggests is that *inexorability* – that is, determinism – wasn't really the problem in the first place. Even if we add indeterministic choice points – SFAs – into our story, the fact that an agent faces just the choice points they do is itself something that they are not ultimately responsible for. So, if we want agents to really be the *ultimate* source of their action, it looks as though adding a dose of indeterminism – perhaps in the guise of SFAs – doesn't really solve the problem that it was supposed to solve.

One response to the Basic Argument would be to concede the conclusion that nobody is ever *ultimately* morally responsible for anything, but to deny that moral responsibility *simpliciter requires* ultimate moral responsibility. (Note that this line of response isn't available to the source libertarian, since the motivation for source libertarianism is, precisely, the alleged need for ultimate responsibility. So, the source libertarian needs to argue, in the face of the Basic Argument, that her alleged buck-stopper is *enough* of a buck-stopper to deliver ultimate responsibility.)

Here's an analogy: Suppose that the chain of causes and effects – whether deterministic or not – can be traced back *ad infinitum*, so that there is no 'first' or 'ultimate' cause of anything. The causes of any given event in turn are caused by preceding events, which are themselves caused by preceding events, without end. But it doesn't follow from the lack of *ultimate* causes that there are no such things as *causes*: just because there is no ultimate cause of, say, the banging door I just heard, that doesn't in the least undermine the claim that the banging door was *caused* – by a gust of wind, perhaps, or someone pushing it a bit too hard. Similarly, we might say, for moral responsibility: perhaps we can be morally responsible for our actions – be appropriate objects of praise and blame, reward and punishment, gratitude and resentment – even if we accept that we are not *ultimately* morally responsible for them.

Dennett pursues something like this line of thought. Dennett concedes that 'a completely self-made self, one hundred per cent responsible for its own character, [is] an impossibility' (1984, 156). But – *contra* Strawson – Dennett thinks that this in no way undermines the claim that normal human adults really are (often) morally responsible for what they do. What is needed, Dennett says, is 'to find a way of making a responsible self out of initially non-responsible choices, so that there is a gradual acquisition of responsibility by the individual' (1984, 84).

Dennett thinks we can indeed find a way of doing just this, while the Strawsonian pessimist thinks that the trick cannot, in principle, be turned. In essence, the difference here depends upon what we think we mean by 'responsibility'. Strawson clearly thinks the notion of 'ulti-mate' or 'true' moral responsibility just *is* our ordinary, common-sense notion of moral responsibility: the kind of moral responsibility that we naturally ascribe to someone when we resent their unkind behaviour or punish their criminal activity or praise their selflessness. But that is precisely what the line of thought just described denies. For Dennett, our ordinary notion of moral responsibility is the notion of a feature that we normal human beings gradually acquire over time as we grow up: it simply is *not* the notion of 'ultimate' responsibility. The question of who is right about this is, of course, a difficult one to answer; I'll return briefly to it in §7.5.

Let's turn to the weaker variety of pessimism. Pereboom's argument for the view (he calls it 'hard incompatibilism') runs roughly as follows. First, Pereboom argues that determinism and free will are incompatible. This will come as no surprise to you, given that you've already come across his 'four-case argument' for incompatibilism in §4.3. Given the fact that this argument is a sourcehood argument, you should also be unsurprised that Pereboom thinks that the only way for an agent to decide freely and morally responsibly is for her decision to be *ultimately* produced by a source over which she has control. But, Pereboom thinks, the only way that condition can be satisfied is if the agent *agent-causes* her action. If the action is undetermined by the past plus the laws, but the agent *doesn't* agent-cause her action, then her performing the action is merely a matter of luck, and hence she is not morally responsible for it. (Pereboom in fact runs an indeterministic manipulation argument here: an action that is indeterministically produced but not agent-caused – even an SFA – is no different in any relevant respect to one that is produced by a 'randomizing manipulator' (2001, 52).) Finally, while an act that is agent-caused *does* satisfy the 'ultimate control' condition (and Pereboom argues that the Basic Argument fails against an appropriately specified agent-causal view (2001, 65–68)), that is only because the agent-causal view 'builds into the agent, as a primitive power, the capacity to be a source of action that is required for moral responsibility' (2002, 478). And, while the agent-causal view is 'coherent as far as we can tell', unfortunately, 'given evidence from our best scientific theories, it is not credible that we are in fact agent-causes. We are therefore left with the view that we do not have free will of the kind required for moral responsibility' (*ibid.*).

I shall not discuss Pereboom's argument for hard incompatibilism here, since in essence (though not necessarily in the detail) it simply marshals the combined resources of various arguments we're already familiar with. However, it is worth thinking a little bit about what he thinks the *consequences* of his argument are. Recall the discussion of reactive attitudes in §2.4. P.F. Strawson holds that no fancy abstract argument posed by a philosopher – and Pereboom's is such an argument – could possibly undermine freedom of the will, since without freedom of the will *all* of our reactive attitudes would be unwarranted, and this is a possibility that it would be irrational – not to mention psychologically impossible – for us to take seriously.

Pereboom disagrees with the claim that repudiating freedom of the will would require regarding all of the reactive attitudes as unwarranted. While '[a]ccepting [hard incompatibilism] demands giving up our ordinary view of ourselves as blameworthy for immoral actions and praiseworthy for those that are morally exemplary' (2002, 479), the consequences of this are not nearly as undesirable as Strawson thinks; indeed, there are some positive up-sides to embracing the view. One consequence (I won't discuss whether or not this is a positive benefit of the view) is that we should endorse a non-retributivist theory of punishment, since clearly it would be wrong to seek retribution against someone who is not blameworthy. (It's crucial to Pereboom's account that actions can be right or wrong even if we are not morally responsible for performing them.)

When it comes to reactive attitudes in particular – the cornerstone of Strawson's view – Pereboom thinks that enough of them are compatible with hard incompatibilism, or have aspects that are compatible with it, to deliver most of what we care about. Some have to go – indignation is one – but some don't. For example, it's perfectly consistent with hard incompatibilism that I might forgive a friend for doing me a wrong, in the sense that I decide to stop regarding the bad behaviour as a reason for terminating or changing the nature of our friendship. The only aspect of forgiveness we have to give up on is 'the willingness to disregard deserved blame or punishment' (2002, 485), since, of course, there *is* no deserved blame or punishment on Pereboom's view.

One might, of course, dispute Pereboom's claim about the reactive attitudes. You might, for example, suspect that we cannot 'chop up' an attitude such as forgiveness into different components, keeping some and discarding others. For example, you might take the view that *merely* deciding not to terminate a friendship on the basis of a friend's bad behaviour isn't a *component* or *aspect* of forgiveness; it just isn't, in and of itself, *forgiveness* at all. In other words, you might want to argue that it's an *essential* feature of forgiveness that it includes disregarding *deserved* blame or punishment. In that case, while Pereboom may be right that hard incompatibilism leaves most of the important *practical* aspects of our day-to-day dealings with others intact, it is not true to say that there is really anything left of our *reactive attitudes* themselves. On the other hand, if Pereboom *is* right, that does rather seem to undermine P.F. Strawson's argument for compatibilism.

5.9   Conclusion

We've seen in this chapter that incompatibilists come in many different shapes and sizes. When it comes to the question whether any of us *actually* ever act freely, their answers range from 'definitely not' (Galen

Strawson), through 'almost certainly not' (Pereboom), to a straightforward 'yes' (libertarians). And incompatibilists differ on the question of *why* determinism is incompatible with acting freely. For Strawson, determinism is really beside the point: indeterministic agents cannot act freely either (unless of course they are 'self-made selves'). For other incompatibilists, determinism deprives agents of the ability to act freely either because deterministic agents lack 'elbow room' or the ability to do otherwise (leeway incompatibilism) or because they fail to be ultimate *sources* of their actions (source incompatibilism).

One point I have been stressing in this chapter, however, is that an incompatibilist *theory* of free will needs to do more than simply explain why deterministic agents (allegedly) *lack* free will; it needs to explain what the conditions are under which *in*deterministic agents *have* it. That is, it needs to provide *sufficient*, and not merely *necessary*, conditions for acting freely. I have tried, through the admittedly somewhat inelegant mechanism of (II-Def) and (II-Free), to spell out what such sufficient conditions might look like for different kinds of incompatibilist.

My own view, as was already clear before this chapter began, is that incompatibilism in general – and hence any incompatibilist *theory* – lacks adequate motivation, because there are perfectly acceptable compatibilist responses available to the main arguments for incompatibilism, namely, the arguments surveyed in Chapters 3 and 4. And things are about to get worse for the incompatibilist (or so I think), because in the next chapter I turn to Frankfurt's 'nefarious neurosurgeon' case – a thought experiment that casts serious doubt on the claim that acting freely requires the kinds of alternative possibilities that are ruled out by determinism.

6
Frankfurt's Nefarious Neurosurgeon

6.1 Introduction

The compatibilist responses to the Consequence Argument (CA) canvassed in Chapter 3 fall into two broad categories. First, there are those who argue that there is a sense in which agents are able to do other than what they actually do that is compatible with the truth of determinism, and that it is this kind of ability to do otherwise – and not the kind presupposed by CA – that is required for acting freely. Second, there are those who argue that the ability to do otherwise is simply irrelevant to whether one acts freely and therefore morally responsibly.

Harry Frankfurt's famous paper, 'Alternate Possibilities and Moral Responsibility' (1969), follows the second path, but with a twist – and a highly controversial twist it is, as we shall see. As we saw in §3.3, Dennett's response to CA is, in effect, to claim that there is nothing even *prima facie* problematic in taking psychologically normal deterministic agents to be morally responsible for what they do. After all, we hold people responsible for what they do *all the time*, and most of us do it without bothering to even consider whether their actions might be determined by the past plus the laws. Frankfurt takes a rather different tack. His basic idea is: OK, let's start with an agent (he's called Jones) who satisfies whatever conditions you think are required for acting freely. And let's assume that he has at least *one* alternative possibility open to him, in whatever sense of 'alternative possibility' or 'could have done otherwise' you like: in fact, he decides to A, but he might not have made that decision. And now, let's rob Jones of that alternative possibility, simply by stipulating that there's someone else (Black) waiting in the wings who will *make* Jones decide to A if Jones doesn't do it all by himself. But Jones *does* decide to A all by himself – Black never needs to intervene. Frankfurt's central thought is that 'stripping away' Jones's alternative possibility in this manner *makes no difference* to Jones's culpability for his decision – and, hence, no difference to the fact that he decides freely. Hence, alternative possibilities can't be required for acting freely.

After describing the case in more detail (§6.2) and explaining the moral that Frankfurt himself draws from it (§6.3), in §§6.3–6.9 I survey some of the responses to Frankfurt's argument that incompatibilists have come up with. This includes a discussion of 'weak source incompatibilism' and 'weak agent causalism' – positions briefly described in §§5.4 and 5.6. Along the way, we'll see that the dialectical situation with respect to Frankfurt's argument is rather complex. This is because, being an argument against the principle that acting freely requires the ability to do otherwise, it is simultaneously an argument *in defence of* compatibilism (since it purports to undermine a key premise in CA) and an argument *against* incompatibilism (since, as we saw in Chapter 5, the connection between acting freely and the ability to do otherwise is enshrined in various positive incompatibilist theories of free will). In §6.10, I briefly sum up where I think Frankfurt's argument leaves us.

Before getting to Frankfurt's famous case, let's start with an older and simpler one: John Locke's man in a locked room. Locke says:

> ... suppose a man be carried, whilst fast asleep, into a room where is a person he longs to see and speak with; and be there locked fast in, beyond his power to get out: he awakes, and is glad to find himself in so desirable company, which he stays willingly in, i.e. prefers his stay to going away. I ask, is not this stay voluntary? I think nobody will doubt it: and yet, being locked fast in, it is evident he is not at liberty not to stay, he has not freedom to be gone. (1690, Book II, Chapter XXI, §10)

Consider this passage in the context of the claim that acting freely requires the ability to do otherwise. Locke is arguing, in effect, that this claim is false: the man freely remains in the locked room even though he cannot leave. (He is not *free to leave*, but it doesn't follow that he doesn't freely remain.) To put it another way, the man's alternative possibility – leaving the room – has been stripped away, but that doesn't make any difference to whether he freely remains; he freely remains whether the door is locked or unlocked.

Unfortunately, this case is not going to cut much ice with the incompatibilist, who will doubtless reply that while Locke may be right that the man freely remains, this would *only* be because he freely *decides* or *intends* to remain in the room – and in order to do *that* freely, he must have been able to *decide* to leave the room. In other words, Locke's argument shows, at best, that the following principle is false:

(P1) *S* freely does *A* only if *S* could have done otherwise *than A,*

where *A* is an overt action (or omission), such as remaining in the room or making a cup of tea. It does *not* show that the following principle is false:

(P2) *S* freely does *A* only if *S* could have done otherwise *than decide to A,*

where, again, *A* is an overt action or omission. So, the idea here would be that one's actions can 'inherit' their freedom from the free decisions that give rise to them. And, of course (P2), on the understanding of 'could have done otherwise' at work in CA, is just as incompatible with determinism as is (P1).

Now, Locke himself clearly has no truck with (P2). The passage quoted above continues: 'So that liberty is not an idea belonging to volition, or preferring; but to the person having the power of doing, or forbearing to do, according as the mind shall choose or direct'. In other words, Locke thinks the question of freedom should be confined to our overt actions, and we simply should not ask about whether the 'will' is free. This view was later echoed by Hume who, as we saw in §2.2, says: 'By liberty ... we can only mean *a power of acting or not acting, according to the determinations of the will;* that is, if we choose to remain at rest, we may; if we choose to move, we also may' (1748, §8).

Locke's and Hume's views here are very close to the conditional analysis of 'could have done otherwise' discussed in §3.2. Interestingly, Locke himself anticipates something similar to the vicious regress problem identified in §3.2:

> Concerning a man's liberty, there ... is raised this further question, *Whether a man be free to will?* which I think is what is meant, when it is disputed whether the will be free. (1690, Book II, Chapter XXI, §22)
>
> ... to make a man free after this manner, by making the action of willing to depend on his will, there must be another antecedent will, to determine the acts of this will, and another to determine that, and so *in infinitum*: for wherever one stops, the actions of the last will cannot be free. (1690, Book II, Chapter XXI, §23)

It is for this reason that he holds that 'the question is not proper, whether the will be free, but whether a man be free' (1690, Book II, Chapter XXI, §21): It is only by restricting the question of freedom to our *overt* (non-mental) actions that we can avoid the vicious regress.

Be that as it may, compatibilists – and Frankfurt in particular – do not follow Locke down this road (which is why defenders of the conditional analysis get themselves into trouble; Locke saw that one coming and headed it off at the pass). Instead, Frankfurt wants to show that even (P2) is false, and he does this by internalising the 'locked room' case, so that it is alternatives to the *decision*, and not merely the overt action (in Locke's case, leaving the room), that are cut off.

6.2   The Frankfurt case

Here, then, is a quick summary of Frankfurt's 'nefarious neurosurgeon' thought experiment (1969, 835–6). (I have taken some liberties with the formulation, but the basic gist is the same.) Black, the nefarious neurosurgeon (or 'counterfactual intervener', as he is sometimes called), wants Jones to kill Smith: Black wants Smith dead, and he knows Jones is seriously considering killing him, and, of course, Black would rather someone else do it than do it himself, so that he doesn't run the risk of being sent to prison. Unfortunately, *making* Jones kill Smith is tricky: Black cannot blackmail him or force him at gunpoint to do it, since such activities will still be likely to result in a lengthy prison term.

Fortunately for Black, this thought experiment is set at some unspecified time in the future when neuroscience is much more advanced, and he is a skilled neurosurgeon. Unbeknownst to Jones, Black implants a special remote-control device in Jones's brain, which enables Black to intervene in Jones's deliberation: Black can press a button and *make* Jones decide to kill Smith. Realising that if he pushes the button and is subsequently discovered he will, again, be subject to a lengthy prison term, Black decides on the following course of action. He will wait until Jones is *about* to make up his mind. If, at that point, Black figures out that Jones is about to decide to kill Smith, Black will do nothing: he will sit back and let events take their natural course, and Smith (assuming Jones has a good murder plan) will end up dead. However, if Jones is about to decide *not* to kill Smith, Black will press the button and force Jones to decide to kill Smith.

How does Black figure out whether or not Jones is about to decide to kill Smith? Well, perhaps Black has been observing Jones for a long time and is extremely good at predicting his decisions on the basis of inadvertent facial movements. For example, maybe whenever Jones is about to decide to do something bad, his face twitches; but whenever he's about to decide to refrain from doing something bad, there is no twitch. So, Black waits to see whether there is a twitch, and, if doesn't see a twitch at the relevant time, he presses the button. Or we can imagine that the device has a second function: It monitors neurological activity and relays this information to Black, so that Black can track Jones's thoughts. (If you're not sure about whether it's really, in principle, possible to track people's thoughts by tracking their neurological activity, no matter: what's important is that Black is tracking whatever causal processes are going on in Jones's head that are relevant to his deliberation and decision about whether to kill Smith.)

Now, as things turn out, Jones does decide on his own – without Black's intervention – to kill Smith: Black sees that he is about to make that decision (perhaps by observing the twitch, or perhaps by checking the read-out of Jones's neurological activity) and does not press the button, and Jones duly decides to, and does, kill Smith. The question is: Is Jones morally responsible for killing Smith? Frankfurt thinks that the answer is clearly 'Yes'. After all, if Black hadn't been on the scene, Jones unquestionably would have been morally responsible for killing Smith; and everything in Jones's *actual* deliberation, including the decision itself, happened exactly as it would have happened had Black not been around. (We are assuming that in the Black-free version of the case, Jones satisfies whatever requirements you think are needed for him to be morally responsible.) The only difference was the presence of the device – but all the device *actually* did was quietly monitor Jones's neurological activity. It wasn't involved *at all* in the process that led up to the decision, or in the decision itself.

But, of course (or so says Frankfurt, at any rate), Jones *could not have done otherwise* than decide to kill Smith, since, had he been on the verge of making a different decision, Black would have intervened and forced Jones to decide to kill Smith anyway. Thus, the nefarious neurosurgeon case is a counter-example to (P2) above: Since Jones was morally responsible for killing Smith, he must have killed Smith freely (since moral responsibility requires acting freely). So, he killed Smith freely and yet was unable to make a different decision to the one he actually made.

6.3   Frankfurt's analysis of the case

Before we get on to the implications that Frankfurt's argument has (if sound) for CA – and for incompatibilism – it's worth briefly rehearsing where Frankfurt thinks the nefarious neurosurgeon case leaves us. His declared target is what he calls the 'Principle of Alternate Possibilities' ('PAP' for short):

> (PAP) A person is morally responsible for what he has done only if he could have done otherwise. (1969, 829)

(PAP) is, in effect, the moral responsibility equivalent of principle (P1) above. And, since moral responsibility requires freedom of action, if (PAP) is false, then (P1) must be false too. But, as should be clear by now, in fact Frankfurt's argument (if sound) establishes the falsity not only of (P1) but of (P2) as well: Jones morally responsibly – and hence freely – kills Smith despite being unable *not* to decide to kill him.

Frankfurt's main intention is not only to show that (PAP) is false, but also to show that we should replace it with a related principle, which I'll call the 'Principle of Unforced Action' (PUA):

> (PUA) *S* is morally responsible for *A* only if it is not the case that: *S* did *A only because* she could not have done otherwise.

What's the difference between (PAP) and (PUA)? Well, consider the difference between an unwilling prisoner – let's call her Pri – and Locke's man in the locked room who has no desire to leave (let's call him Will). Changing Locke's case somewhat, suppose that, in each case, there's someone outside the room calling for help. Pri wants to go and help, but she can't, and she knows it: There's nothing she can do. Will, by contrast, is quite content to stay where he is, despite being able to hear the call for help. Even if he knows the door is locked, that fact is of no consequence to him: he has absolutely no desire to go outside and investigate.

Intuitively, Will is blameworthy for remaining in the room, while Pri is not. Why is this? (PUA) provides an answer (although of course there may be other answers one might give). The *only* reason why Pri remains in her cell and doesn't go to the person's aid is that she *can't*: there is nothing else she can do but stay. Pri thus fails to satisfy (PUA) and, for that reason, is not blameworthy. As it happens, Pri also fails to satisfy (PAP). But that, Frankfurt thinks, is irrelevant to her lack of moral responsibility (When I say that she fails to satisfy (PUA), I mean that she fails to satisfy the necessary condition on moral responsibility – the bit after the 'only if' – that (PAU) proposes. The same goes for other cases where I say that an agent does or does not satisfy a given principle.)

By contrast, it is *not* the case that Will *only* remains because he could not have done otherwise. On the contrary: if we want to know why he remains, we don't need to mention the locked door at all. He wants to stay in the room, he has no desire to go and help, and so he stays. Will, like Pri, fails to satisfy (PAP), but, again, that's not relevant. Will *does* satisfy (PUA) (and, we may assume, all the other conditions that moral responsibility requires). Hence, Will *is* morally responsible – and hence blameworthy – for remaining in the room. It is the difference in whether or not they satisfy (PUA) that explains the difference in moral responsibility between Pri and Will.

Now consider the nefarious neurosurgeon case. In that case, does Jones decide to kill Smith *only because* he could not do otherwise? Frankfurt says no: If we were to explain why Jones decided to kill Smith, we would not have to so much as mention Black, any more than we would have to mention the locked door in the case of Will. (Remember: Everything that goes on in Jones's head – or at least everything that has an effect on his actual decision – happens *exactly* the same as it would have done in the absence of the device.) So, Jones, like Will, is morally responsible because, while he fails to satisfy (PAP), it is (PUA) and not (PAP) that places a constraint on moral responsibility, and Jones does satisfy (PUA).

We are now, finally, in a position to return to CA. Does Frankfurt's argument, if sound, scupper it? The short answer is 'Yes'. Assuming that moral responsibility itself requires that one act freely, Frankfurt's counter-example to (PAP) also constitutes a counter-example to (P1): If Jones is morally responsible despite lacking the ability to do otherwise, then he also acts freely despite lacking that ability. And CA has (P1) as a premise.

There is a more satisfying – if slightly longer – answer, however. As we have just seen, Frankfurt is not claiming that alternative possibilities play no role whatsoever in our judgements about freedom and responsibility. On the contrary: (PUA), like (PAP), is an alternative-possibilities requirement on moral responsibility, and hence on freedom (of whatever kind that is required by moral responsibility). But it is only when the agent acts as they do *only because* they could not have done otherwise that the lack of alternative possibilities deprives them of their freedom. Crucially, Frankfurt holds that determinism, just by itself, fails to satisfy this condition. In other words, assuming determinism, it is *not* the case that normal human adults in normal situations behave as they do *only because* they could not have done otherwise. Such agents satisfy (PUA), and hence (assuming they meet any other compatibilist requirements on moral responsibility, too) they are morally responsible for their behaviour.

Why is this? Well, Frankfurt admittedly is not entirely clear on this point, and what he says is open to interpretation. On one interpretation, the reason is that when we explain an ordinary, common-or-garden act, such as my making a cup of tea or Wally's handing in the wallet he finds on the street to the police station, we simply do not need to appeal in our explanation to the fact that the act was *determined*. After all, compare the case where Wally *is* fully determined by his character, circumstances and deliberation (and whatever other features of the situation are relevant) to hand in the wallet to the case where he is *not* fully determined by exactly those features to do it. Presumably, we would give exactly the same explanation in each case: we would mention the circumstances, his character and his particular beliefs and desires at the time. Would adding – in the former case where he is determined – the fact that he was, in fact, determined to hand it in contribute anything extra to our explanation? Arguably not. After all, the fact that he was determined to hand it in was not, itself, a *cause* of his doing so; the causes were the particular events and circumstances that led to his action. It just so happens that those causes *determined* that he would do it; but that fact is not, in itself, an additional cause of the action, so it would not play any role in the explanation.

On a second interpretation, when Frankfurt says that a person is not morally responsible if he performed the act *only because* he could not have done otherwise, he means that (as he puts it) 'when he did what he did it was not because that was what he really wanted to do' (1969, 838). This is a rather different claim: on this way of looking at things, acting only because you couldn't have done otherwise is a matter of failing to do *what you really want*. What might this amount to? Well, some cases are straightforward. Pri does not 'really want' to remain in her cell; on the contrary, she really wants to go and help. So, Frankfurt's account seems to deal with ordinary cases where freedom of *action* is absent – those cases where one is not able to do what one *wants* to do.

Matters are less clear, however, when we consider cases such as the arachnophobe or the addict or the victim of coercion. Presumably, the addict *wants* his next hit – he is responding to a desire – and the arachnophobe presumably very much wants not to pick up the big hairy spider. And presumably even the bank teller who is being forced at gunpoint to open the safe *wants* to do so, in that she wants not to get shot and this is the best way of avoiding it. So, these *seem* to be cases where agents *are* 'doing what they really want', and hence – on this understanding of (PUA) – satisfy (PUA) and hence are morally responsible for their behaviour.

This might seem to be a problem for Frankfurt, since it looks as though (PUA), thus interpreted, delivers the wrong answer in these kinds of case. However, things look decidedly better if we invoke Frankfurt's own hierarchical account of freedom of the will (§2.5), and claim that 'really' wanting something is not merely a matter of wanting it – or even wanting it *a lot*. Rather, it is a matter of 'identifying decisively' with one's (first-order) desire: a matter, that is, of having the will one wants to have. And one might argue that this condition is not met in these cases. The addict does not *want* to want the drug, so he does not 'really want' it (unless he is a 'willing addict', in which case he may well be acting of his own free will – see Frankfurt 1971, 24–5). Similarly, the arachnophobe doesn't *want* to have an aversion to picking up spiders: she wants to be moved to action by a desire to pick the spider up, and she is not (either because she lacks that desire altogether, or because she has it but cannot make it her will). And perhaps (though this may be more controversial) the coerced bank teller, too, is in a situation where she cannot wholeheartedly identify with her desire to open the safe; after all, she also wants *not* to open the safe – she doesn't want the bank robber to escape with the money – and we may suppose that she would ideally like to be acting on the basis of *that* desire. It's just that she has been placed, though no fault of her own, in a situation where that is not a serious option for her. So, perhaps she is doing something she does not 'really want' to do as well. Thus, if we understand acting as one does 'only because' one could not do otherwise as a matter of failing to do 'what one really wants', *and* we understand the latter as a matter of failing to act in accordance with one's second-order volitions, it seems as though we get the right answers after all.

The overall point here, though, is this. Frankfurt has done two things. First, he has provided what seems, at least on the face of it, to be a clear counter-example to (PAP): Jones is, apparently, morally responsible for deciding to kill – and hence for actually killing – Smith, despite his lack of alternative possibilities. And, second, Frankfurt has suggested an alternative principle – the principle that one lacks responsibility if one did what one did *only* because one could not have done otherwise – that is, allegedly, entirely compatible with determinism. Indeed, we might think of the truth of this principle as explaining why one might, at first sight, find (PAP) – and hence incompatibilism – plausible: there is *something* right, Frankfurt thinks, with the claim that there is some sort of connection between the absence of alternative possibilities and lack of moral responsibility. It's just that, when we think things through, we'll see that the connection is that enshrined in his own alternative principle, (PUA), and not in (PAP). Hence, moral responsibility – and so acting freely – is compatible with determinism.

6.4   Incompatibilist responses to Frankfurt

As we'll see, incompatibilists have not held back from trying to avert the threat that the nefarious neurosurgeon case poses to (PAP). Before we proceed to looking at some incompatibilist responses, some preliminary points are in order.

First, as we've already seen, talk of whether or not (PAP) is true is rather loose, in that the real issue isn't whether or not Jones could have done otherwise than *kill Smith*; it's whether he could have done otherwise than *decide* to kill Smith. Indeed, we might think of Jones's moral responsibility for *killing* Smith as a kind of 'derived' moral responsibility that the killing inherits from his moral responsibility for *deciding* to kill Smith – something for which Jones is (allegedly) *directly* morally responsible. If we think of the nefarious neurosurgeon case in that light, we can think of (PAP) as a thesis concerning *direct* moral responsibility, where (PAP) implies – and Frankfurt denies – that Jones is morally responsible for *deciding* to kill Smith only if he could have done otherwise than make that decision.

Second, we need to remind ourselves what all this talk of (PAP) has to do with free will. Remember that the disputed premise in CA is not (PAP) – an alternative-possibilities requirement on moral responsibility – but (P1), an alternative-possibilities requirement on acting freely. However, granting the assumption that (direct) moral responsibility for action *A* requires doing *A* freely, a counter-example to (PAP) is *a fortiori* a counter-example to (P1): if someone can be (directly) morally responsible for *A* while being unable to do otherwise, then they can also do *A* *freely* while being unable to do otherwise, since if they are directly morally responsible for *A*, it follows that *A* is done freely. To put it another way: given our assumption that acting freely is required for (direct) moral responsibility, (P1) entails (PAP). Hence, if (PAP) is false, (P1) must be false, too.

Finally, an important caveat is in order. It relates to the question of what the purpose of Frankfurt's argument is: whom, exactly, is he trying to convince? This is a murky issue because (PAP) – and hence its close relative (P1) – plays a kind of dual role in the free will debate. On the one hand – and this is the role I have been focusing on – (P1) is a premise of CA. So, to show that (P1) is false (by showing that (PAP) is false) constitutes a defence of compatibilism, since if (P1) is false, CA is unsound and hence fails to establish incompatibilism.

On the other hand, and of course relatedly, (P1) is a fundamental tenet of leeway incompatibilism (§5.3). Leeway incompatibilists think that freedom and determinism are incompatible precisely *because* they think that acting freely requires the ability to do otherwise. So, undermining (PAP) is *also* a way of undermining leeway incompatibilism. Moreover, strong source incompatibilists like Kane (§5.4) would seem to be in trouble too. While Kane-style strong source incompatibilists don't require of *every* freely performed action that the agent could have done otherwise at the time of decision, they do require that actions where the agent lacks alternative possibilities trace back to previous, character-forming decisions: 'self-forming actions', or SFAs, as Kane calls them. And SFAs are just as susceptible to nefarious-neurosurgeon-type case as other decisions are; indeed, the Black/Jones/Smith case would seem to be as good a candidate for an SFA as any. So, in principle, our nefarious neurosurgeon could be waiting in the wings any time an SFA is in the offing, thereby depriving our unlucky agent of the alternative possibilities that SFAs would seem to require and hence rendering him morally unaccountable for *all* of his actions. So, again, to undermine (PAP), and hence (P1), is also to undermine strong source incompatibilism. (You may remember I briefly introduced 'weak source incompatibilism' in §5.4 and 'weak agent causalism' in §5.6, and promised to discuss them further in this chapter. That's coming up, in §6.7. Frankfurt's argument is *not* generally taken to undermine either of these positions, as we'll see. But until then, I'm going to ignore them.)

Given this dual role that it has in the debate, then, Frankfurt's argument is simultaneously a defence of compatibilism *and* an attack on incompatibilism. And, as will soon become clear, the viability of Frankfurt's argument would seem to depend – at least in the light of some of the defences of it described below – on which of these dialectical purposes one has in mind. In particular – though this is probably wildly overgeneralising – incompatibilists tend to read the argument as an attack on their position (which, of course, it is), whereas compatibilists tend to read it as a defence of compatibilism (which it also is); and this seems to make a difference to the question of where the burden of proof lies. This is a fine distinction, but I hope its significance will become clear soon enough.

6.5   The dilemma defence

AQ8   Here's a worry about the way Frankfurt sets up his thought experiment. On the one hand, the case requires that Black can *predict* what Jones is going to decide, just before he makes the decision: Black has to judge, on the basis of the presence or absence of the twitch or the read-out from the remote control device or whatever, whether or not Jones is *about* to decide to kill Smith.

Let's call the time at which Black has to either press the button or not (the time when Jones is about to decide) t_1, and the time of Jones's actual decision t_2; and let D be Jones's decision to kill Smith, and T be the sign – whatever it is – that occurs at or just before t_1 and informs Black that Jones is about to do D (and hence prompts Black not to press the button). Now, here's the problem: If Black really is able to predict at t_1 whether or not Jones is going to do D at t_2, surely that means that Jones's mental or neurological state at t_1 must *determine* that he does D at t_2: given that T happens, it must be *guaranteed* that D will follow. But in that case, Jones's state at t_1 must, *just by itself* – that is, independently of the presence of Black – *determine* his decision D. So, the case *presupposes* that (PAP) is false at the outset (assuming we construe the ability to do otherwise in such a way that it is incompatible with determinism) and so cannot *show* that (PAP) is false.

Why is this? Well, we are supposed to judge that Jones is *morally responsible* for D (and hence for actually killing Smith). And we are supposed to judge this on the grounds that everything going on in Jones's head is such that he *would* be morally responsible if Black were not on the scene at all, so that adding Black to the picture – given that he doesn't intervene – doesn't, in fact, causally contribute either to Jones's deliberation or to his actual decision. So, let's imagine *that* hypothetical case, with Black out of the picture. At t_1, Jones's state of mind – call it N – must be such that it is guaranteed to result in D at t_2 – that is, N must be a deterministic cause of D: the state of the Universe at t_1 – including, of course, the state of Jones's mind – together with the laws of nature entails that D will happen.

Why must this be so? Because in the case where Black *is* in the picture (but doesn't intervene), Black is, in effect, indirectly observing N (via the read-out or the twitch T) and is *able to predict* that D will follow. If N plus the other relevant facts – facts that *exclude* Black's potential intervention – didn't *entail* that D would happen but left D with some chance of *not* happening, Black might well get his prediction wrong. That is, it is entirely possible that Black *predicts* that N will result in D without any intervention by him, he consequently decides *not* to press the button, but then N *doesn't* result in D after all, and Jones *fails* to decide to kill Smith.

So, if (as Frankfurt's argument assumes) the *only* difference between the case where Black is in the picture (and not actually interfering) and the case where he isn't is, precisely, whether or not Black is in the picture, then, in *both* cases, N must be a deterministic cause of D. (Otherwise, in the case where Black *is* in the picture, he might get his prediction wrong.) But in that case, it is true in *both* cases that Jones is unable, at t_1, to do otherwise than make decision D. But Frankfurt's argument assumes that Jones is morally responsible for D in the Black-free version of the case. And the only way this could be so, given all of the above, is if deciding freely *doesn't* require that the decision is undetermined by the past plus the laws right up until the moment of decision.

In other words, we will only judge that Jones is morally responsible for D in the case where Black is out of the picture (and so in the case where he *is* in the picture but doesn't intervene) if (PAP) is false – or, to be more precise, if the following principle, which entails (PAP), is false (incidentally, this should remind you of the discussion about the motivation for leeway incompatibilism in §5.3):

(PAP1) S is morally responsible for A (where A is a decision) only if S could have done otherwise than A right up until the time at which A occurs.

The problem for Frankfurt's argument is therefore that it begs the question against the leeway incompatibilist. A leeway incompatibilist will judge that Jones is not morally responsible *even in the case where Black is out of the picture*, since Jones, in that case, could not, at t_1, have done otherwise than do D at t_2. Hence, they will also judge – contrary to what the nefarious neurosurgeon case requires if it is to be a counter-example to (PAP) – that Jones is not morally responsible in the actual case, where Black is present. (Similarly, Frankfurt's argument will beg the question against Kane's strong source incompatibilism if we assume that Jones's decision is a SFA.)

This problem is often put in the form of a dilemma – hence 'dilemma defence'. Suppose we assume that N really does causally determine D – just by itself, that is, independently of the presence of Black. Then, as we've just seen, the Frankfurt case begs the question against the incompatibilist: the claim that Jones is morally responsible presupposes that (PAP1) is false, since if (PAP1) were true, Jones would not even be morally responsible if Black weren't on the scene. Hence, the case is not a counter-example to (PAP1) as applied to Jones's decision, since Jones is not morally responsible for that decision.

Suppose, on the other hand, we assume that N *doesn't* causally determine D – again, that's N just by itself, independently of the presence of

Black. Then Black's presence doesn't make it the case that D *is* causally determined. Why? Because whether or not Black intervenes depends upon whether or not Jones displays sign T, which is itself a result of N. But it's entirely compatible with the laws plus all the facts that obtain at t_1 – the time at which Black fails to observe sign T and therefore decides not to press the button – that Jones steps back from the brink and decides, at t_2, not to kill Smith after all. Hence, Jones *could have done otherwise* – he could still refrain from deciding to kill Smith. So, the case is no counter-example to (PAP), as applied to Jones's decision, since, while Jones is morally responsible for his decision, he could have done otherwise. Either way, then – whether N does or does not determine D – the Frankfurt case is not a counter-example to (PAP).

Is this a good objection to Frankfurt's argument? If it is, then clearly what's needed to revive the argument is a new case that avoids the first horn of the dilemma – that is, a case that has the counterfactual intervener (Black) somehow ensure that Jones decides to kill Smith, but without Jones's own mental processes determining his decision. Whether that can be done has been a topic of intense debate; see, for example, Mele and Robb 1998, Kane 2006, Pereboom 2006.

On the other hand, you might be thinking by now that there is something curious about the dialectic of the dilemma defence, at least if we consider Frankfurt's argument in the context of the Consequence Argument for incompatibilism. This is where the distinction rehearsed in the §6.4 becomes important. Recall that one of the premises of CA is the claim that acting (including deciding) freely requires the ability to do otherwise – an ability that is incompatible with determinism (given CA's understanding of 'could have done otherwise'). If we read Frankfurt's argument as a defence of compatibilism against CA, and against that premise of the argument in particular – which I take it was Frankfurt's intention – then it is not so clear that our counter-example to that premise needs to meet the standards demanded by the dilemma defence.

Recall the first horn of the dilemma: If Jones is determined by N to make decision D, then the incompatibilist will insist that he isn't morally responsible for D (and, indeed, doesn't do D freely) *independently* of whether Black happens to be lurking in the background, ready to press his button. Hence (according to the dilemma defence), on this horn of the dilemma, Frankfurt's case begs the question against the incompatibilist, since it *assumes* that moral responsibility doesn't require the ability to do otherwise.

If your interest is in defending compatibilism, however, you might be inclined to reply: *So what?* We can grant that if we think of the nefarious neurosurgeon case as an *attack* on incompatibilism, then it fails for just the reason given by the dilemma defence. But if we think of it as a *defence of compatibilism* against CA, why should we care if we beg the question against the incompatibilist? After all, the question we are addressing here is whether CA constitutes a *good argument for* incompatibilism. So, let's agree that the incompatibilist – or at least the kind who has *already* assumed that (PAP1) is true – is going to be unmoved by Frankfurt's argument because of the dilemma defence. But then, what business do they have being an incompatibilist in the first place? What, exactly, is their *argument* for that position? If the incompatibilist's answer to that question is: 'The Consequence Argument', then it looks like it is the incompatibilist, and not Frankfurt, who is begging the question. After all, it is the very claim that acting freely (and, hence, morally responsibly) requires the ability to do otherwise, and hence the soundness of CA, that Frankfurt is calling into question. True, the dilemma-defender will not accept Frankfurt's argument (as it stands – though perhaps there is a way of fixing up the counter-example so that they must accept it). But in invoking the dilemma defence, the incompatibilist has *already* committed himself to a principle – (PAP1) – which, without CA to justify it, is simply an unargued assumption that the compatibilist should see no need to accept. So, insofar as we read Frankfurt's argument as a defence of compatibilism against CA, it works just fine. (See Haji and McKenna 2004 for a detailed discussion of the dialectic of the dilemma defence.)

This really is quite an important point, I think. If the dilemma defence is the best that the incompatibilist can do in the face of Frankfurt's argument (and this is a big 'if', admittedly, as the next few sections will show), then she would appear to have *no grounds whatsoever* for believing (PAP1), and hence no grounds for rejecting Dennett's response to CA. (Remember Luther's 'Here I stand' (§3.3): Dennett simply denies that any principle in the ballpark of (PAP1) is true.)

Of course, there are other, sourcehood-based arguments for incompatibilism, such as those discussed in Chapter 4, and those arguments do *not* explicitly appeal to any principle in the ballpark of (PAP1). So, perhaps the dialectical moral we should draw here is that Frankfurt's argument shows *leeway* incompatibilism, but not *source* incompatibilism, to be unmotivated. I'll come back to this line of thought in §6.7.

6.6   The flicker defence

The flicker defence of (PAP) (see e.g. Wyma 1997 and Otsuka 1998) has played a major role in the recent debate about free will. Remember

Locke's story about the man who (allegedly) freely remains in the locked room. The standard incompatibilist response to that story is to say: Yes, the man *does* freely remain in the room, but *only* because he freely *decides* to remain in the room; and one reason why he freely *decides* to remain is that he could have *decided* otherwise.

As we've seen, the Frankfurt case is, in effect, a kind of internalised version of the locked room case: Frankfurt's equivalent of the locked door is Black's potential intervention to force Jones to decide to kill Smith – an internal mental act of Jones's, and not something external, such as a locked door. In essence, the flicker-defender attempts to make a response to Frankfurt that is similar to the incompatibilist response to the locked room case that I just described. That is, flicker-defenders agree with Frankfurt that Jones is morally responsible for killing Smith (if certain additional conditions, about to be explained, are met), and they also agree that Jones cannot do otherwise than decide to kill Smith. However, they claim that what *is* required for Jones to be morally responsible is that there is *some* alternative possibility open to Jones – not the possibility of *deciding* otherwise, but some *other* alternative possibility – such that Jones's deciding to kill Smith inherits its morally-responsible status from the existence of this *other* alternative possibility. And *this* alternative-possibilities requirement is entirely consistent with all of the details of the case that Frankfurt describes.

What might this other alternative possibility be? Well, remember that Black is waiting to see whether or not the neurological sign N occurs. Some versions of the case have Jones blushing (perhaps Jones always blushes when he is about to decide to do something really bad), so that rather than monitoring his neurological activity, Black merely waits to see whether Jones blushes. If he doesn't blush, Black will intervene; if he does, he won't. And this gives us an obvious candidate for an alternative possibility, namely failure to give the neurological sign N, or, in the blushing version, failure to blush: nothing in the case requires us to think that Jones could not have failed to do *that*.

Unfortunately, however, there is a problem with claiming that this kind of alternative possibility is what renders Jones's decision one for which he is morally responsible, namely that it is hard to see how the mere possibility of not blushing (or not being in the neurological state N) could *ground* Jones's moral responsibility for his decision. The stakes are high here: either Jones is going to end up being blameworthy for doing something absolutely despicable, or else he's completely off the hook, morally speaking. That's a very big difference. Do we really want to say that which of these situations is the case depends entirely on *whether*

Jones might not have blushed? The problem here is one concerning what Fischer (1999a) calls 'robustness': the flicker-defender needs to find not merely some alternative possibility or other, but an alternative possibility that is sufficiently *robust* to ground Jones's moral responsibility for his decision. (See also Fischer 2006a; Pereboom 2001, 18–28.)

Robustness seems like a plausible condition on any alternative possibilities that the flicker-defender might propose because, remember, the flicker defence is a defence of incompatibilism. So, the flicker-defender is committed to thinking that if there are *no* alternative possibilities whatsoever on the table, Jones is *not* morally responsible. So the existence of whatever alternative possibility the flicker-defender proposes must explain why Jones *is* morally responsible if that alternative possibility is present, when (according to the incompatibilist) he is *not* morally responsible if it is absent.

To make the point vivid, we might imagine variants on the Frankfurt case where there *are* alternative possibilities, but ones that seem to be *obviously* irrelevant to Jones's moral responsibility. For example, we might imagine that there was some chance that, just before the moment of Black's potential intervention, Jones would be struck by lightning and killed instantly. That's an alternative possibility; moreover, if it had happened, Jones wouldn't have decided to kill Smith. But clearly it isn't one that's relevant to Jones's moral responsibility. Assuming that there are no other alternative possibilities on the table, it would be extremely implausible to say that Jones's moral responsibility for his decision is *due* to the fact that he might have been struck by lightning. Similarly – to borrow from Michael McKenna – we might imagine that Jones could have 'sung a little ditty and done a cutesy jig like Shirley Temple, finishing off with a set of jazz hands; or begun citing nursery rhymes; or made an attempt to eat his fist; or any of a number of equally ludicrous and irrelevant things' (2006, 213). Again, the availability of such possibilities would seem to be entirely irrelevant to Jones's moral responsibility.

How is the flicker-defender to respond to Fischer's challenge? Well, one way they might try to proceed is to think not about alternatives to the blush (or N) itself – the sign on the basis of which Black will or will not intervene – but rather about earlier mental *actions* that Jones might have performed but didn't, or did perform but might not have done. For example, imagine that at some point during his deliberation, prior to the moment of Black's potential intervention, Jones deliberately resolved not to think about the suffering that murdering Smith would cause to Smith's family. Call that act B. It's consistent with the details of the Frankfurt case that Jones was able, at that point, *not* to make that resolution: he could have refrained from doing *B* (though, of course, if he *had* refrained from doing *B*, Black would have pressed the button, and Jones still would have decided to kill Smith.) And *that* – refraining from doing *B* – seems like the kind of alternative possibility that *could* ground Jones's moral responsibility for deciding to kill Smith. After all, a virtuous person would not deliberately resolve to ignore the harm that they might cause. So, perhaps Jones freely, and culpably, performs *B* (by virtue, by incompatibilist lights, by having been able to do otherwise), and *hence* freely and culpably decides to kill Smith.

There is a problem here, however (Fischer 2006a, 37). While we now have what looks like a robust alternative possibility on the table, we can also simply shift the goalposts and revise the Frankfurt case, moving the time at which Black makes *his* decision about whether or not to intervene to the moment when Jones is about to do *B* (a moment at which, we may suppose, he gives off some *other* sign that this is what he is about to do).

This poses a rather nasty dilemma for the flicker-defender, which we can put in terms of Fischer's notion of 'regulative control' briefly explained in §2.2 above. The incompatibilist, remember, holds that regulative control is required for acting freely. (Well, that's the leeway incompatibilist, strictly speaking. On Kane's strong source incompatibilist view, regulative control is required for certain kinds of action – namely SFAs – that constitute the ultimate *sources* of our freedom.) Now, is the 'flicker of freedom' postulated by the flicker-defender an instance of regulative control or not? If it is, then it meets the incompatibilist's standards for freedom, and so it looks like it will be a robust alternative: it will ground Jones's moral responsibility as required. But then we can simply make the goalpost-shifting move just described: any mental *action* of Jones's that he is in control of (in the regulative sense) is one that Black can, in principle, predict and intervene on, thereby removing Jones's regulative control over it and therefore his moral responsibility (by incompatibilist lights) for deciding to kill Smith. On the other hand, if the 'flicker' is *not* an instance of regulative control – such as a blush – then it fails to meet the incompatibilist's own standards for free action, and so it would seem to fail to be robust enough to ground moral responsibility.

Whether or not flicker-defenders can avoid this dilemma is a matter for dispute. However, I'll just make one observation about Fischer's challenge. One way to read the flicker defence is as follows: By the flicker-defender's lights, the Frankfurt case is underspecified, because we are not told which alternative possibilities are open to Jones as he proceeds with his deliberation. One natural assumption would be that he has various 'choice points' – places where he has full regulative control over some mental act. Perhaps, for example, he consciously resolves not to think about Smith's grieving family (*A*). Then he (*B*) runs through the various ways in which his plan for avoiding detection might go wrong and land him in prison, and (*C*) deliberately reminds himself of how likely it is that that plan will work. Then (*D*) he reminds himself of the terrible wrong that Smith has done him. And so on, until he finally decides to kill Smith. Of course, had he failed to perform any of those mental acts, he would have blushed (or whatever), just prior to his final decision, thus prompting Black to press the button. *Given* the assumption, we can, in principle, grant that Jones is indeed morally responsible for his decision, without giving up the idea that alternative possibilities – and robust ones at that – are required for moral responsibility.

Now, it is true that we can now simply shift the goalposts and recast the Frankfurt case as one where Black has the ability to intervene just before any one of the choice points just listed. Indeed, we might imagine a kind of iterated case where Black knows what all the choice points are and knows what sign Jones will unwittingly give when he is about to go one way or the other at *each* such point. (Mele and Robb consider a case like this in their 1998 and dub such cases 'global Frankfurt-style cases'.) *Now* the details of the case are *not* underspecified: we have been told clearly and explicitly that for every choice point – in the above example, *A, B, C* and *D* – Jones lacks the ability to do anything other than what he actually does. Is the flicker-defender rationally required to say that in this, fully-specified version of the case, where it is stipulated that Jones lack any robust alternatives at all, Jones is *still* morally responsible for his decision? (Mele and Robb think this *is* the right thing to say in global Frankfurt-style cases; see the next section for more on this line of thought. Laura Ekstrom (2002, §2), however, disagrees.) It's not obvious that she is. After all, recall the distinction made earlier concerning the aim of Frankfurt's argument. If you're an incompatibilist, and your concern is to rescue the idea that acting freely requires alternative possibilities of some (specifiable) kind, this doesn't commit you to thinking that Jones *must* be morally responsible for deciding to kill Smith, *however* we fill in the details concerning Jones's deliberation. And in particular – and rather obviously, really – it doesn't commit you to thinking that Jones will be morally responsible even if we explicitly rule out *all* of the robust alternative possibilities that, in the underspecified version of the case, we might naturally assume to be present.

On the other hand, things look slightly different if we think of Frankfurt's argument as a defence of compatibilism. The point that Frankfurt wants us to agree with is that the *mere* stripping away of alternative possibilities, effected by the fact that Black is standing by ready to intervene, makes no difference to Jones's culpability – and it makes no difference because it has no effect on the process of deliberation that Jones *actually* follows. Black does not, in fact, *do* anything at all, so everything internal to Jones's deliberation is exactly the way it would be were Black not on the scene. If Frankfurt's argument manages to convince you of *that* (which, of course, it will not if you are already a committed leeway or strong source incompatibilist), then you won't be moved to change your mind about Jones's culpability by the iterated version of the case just described, where Black is ready to step in at *all* the choice points in Jones's deliberation – since, of course, Jones's deliberation *still* proceeds in exactly the way it would have done had Black been absent. So, as a defence of compatibilism, Frankfurt's argument succeeds.

Rather curiously, then, we seem to be left with the conclusion that an incompatibilist flicker-defender who is prepared to change her mind about Jones's culpability in the iterated version of the case can carry on upholding an alternative-possibilities requirement on acting freely (*viz*, there must be *some* mental act during one's process of deliberation such that one could have done otherwise than *that*). On the other hand, someone who, on the basis of the Frankfurt case, comes to agree with Frankfurt that it is the aetiology of the decision that is relevant to freedom, and not the presence of any alternative possibilities, can perfectly legitimately deny (PAP) – and, indeed, *any* alleged alternative-possibilities requirement on acting freely – on that basis. Frankfurt's argument both does and doesn't work – or rather, it works for someone who isn't *already* committed to there being an alternative-possibilities requirement on acting freely, and not for someone who is.

6.7   Weak source incompatibilism and weak agent-causalism

It's finally time to get back to 'weak source incompatibilism' (henceforth 'WSI'), first discussed briefly in §5.4, and weak agent-causalism (§5.6) – henceforth 'WAC'. As I said in Chapter 5, these positions only really make any sense once we have Frankfurt's argument on the table; and now it *is* on the table. So, let's see how the views are supposed to work and whether they are plausible.

Remember what WSI consists in: the claim is that an agent acts freely if and only if they satisfy (i) the standard compatibilist conditions on acting freely *and* (ii) the following principle:

> (CH) An action is free in the sense required for moral responsibility only if it is not produced by a deterministic process that traces back to causal factors beyond the agent's control. (Pereboom 2006, 185)

And to get weak agent-causalism, WAC, we just need to add one further condition, namely that the act in question must be agent-caused. But it's important to note that the extra, agent-causal condition is not a requirement that is independent of (CH). On the contrary: an agent can *only* agent-cause her action by virtue of the fact that the action is not produced by a deterministic process that traces back to causal factors beyond her control. In other words, satisfaction of (CH) is what renders an agent capable of being an agent-cause of her action: if the action failed to satisfy (CH), she would automatically fail to satisfy the agent-causal condition.

One way to put the moral that Frankfurt himself thinks we should draw from the nefarious neurosurgeon case is as follows. What matters to Jones's moral responsibility for killing Smith is *what was going on in his mind* when he was deliberating about what to do. As it is sometimes put, Jones's (and, indeed, anyone's) moral responsibility for a given decision depends *only* on features of the 'actual sequence' – the actual process of deliberation – that the agent goes through before making the decision. Grant that Jones *would have been* morally responsible had Black not been present. What *actually* goes on in Jones's mind is exactly the same, in all relevant respects as what *would* have been going on had Black not been present. (That is, the *actual sequence* is exactly the same as the sequence that would have come about had Black not been present.) Hence, according to Frankfurt, in the *actual* case where Black *is* present (and not intervening), Jones is morally responsible for killing Smith.

The weak source incompatibilist and the weak agent-causalist – unlike their 'strong' cousins – actually *agree* with Frankfurt about the 'actual sequence' part – that is, they agree that Jones's (and, indeed, anyone's) moral responsibility for a given decision depends *only* on features of the actual process of deliberation that the agent goes through. Nonetheless, they claim that Jones – with or without the presence of Black – is *only* morally responsible for killing Smith if he satisfies (CH). (We're assuming, remember, that the standard *compatibilist* conditions on acting freely are satisfied.)

How is this possible? Well, suppose that in the absence of Black, Jones *would* satisfy (CH): His decision would *not* be produced by a deterministic process that traces back to causal factors beyond his control, because the process that led to the decision would be indeterministic. Now, let's add Black to the story. What changes? Well, Black's presence, let's suppose, robs Jones of all *robust* alternative possibilities. But – so the claim goes – it does *not* stop Jones from satisfying (CH). With Black added, it is determined by the past plus the laws that Jones will decide to kill Smith, since the past plus the laws entail that *either* Jones will decide without any help from Black, or else Black will intervene – and, either way, Jones decides to kill Smith. But Jones' decision is not *produced* by a deterministic process that traces back to causal factors beyond the agent's control. The process that actually *produces* Jones's decision – what is going on in Jones's mind as he deliberates – is *not* a deterministic process. After all, if it *were* a deterministic process, Jones would not satisfy (CH) in the Black-free version of the case, and we've ruled that out by hypothesis. So, Jones – despite Black's presence – satisfies (CH). Hence, according to the weak source incompatibilist, Jones is morally responsible; and, according to the weak agent-causalist, Jones is morally responsible, *provided* that he also agent-causes his decision – something that can only be the case if (CH) is satisfied.

It's worth contrasting this response with the flicker defence discussed in the previous section. Fischer's objection to the flicker defence is that Jones has no *robust* alternative possibilities available to him – the kinds of possibility that might plausibly explain why Jones *is* morally responsible, when, in the absence of those possibilities (e.g. if the actual process that led to his decision were deterministic), he would *not* be morally responsible. To put the point slightly less carefully, but perhaps more helpfully, there no mental action at all over which Jones has regulative control – the kind of control that requires the ability to do otherwise. By contrast, neither the weak source incompatibilist nor the weak agent causalist requires any robust alternative possibilities: all they require is that (CH) holds (and, in addition – weak agent-causalist version – that Jones agent-causes his decision).

Why can WSI and WAC get away with this, when the flicker defence can't? The answer lies in the source/leeway distinction. What gets the flicker defence off the ground is the thought that acting freely requires regulative control – the kind of control that requires one to be able to *do* otherwise. This is clearly a leeway requirement on acting freely. Of course, Jones lacks regulative control *over his decision*, but – so the flicker defence goes – that doesn't matter, so long as he has regulative control over some *prior* mental act in his deliberative process. And Fischer's objection is that we can cook the case up in such a way that there is no such prior mental act. WSI and WAC, by contrast, simply don't require regulative control for acting freely: their positions are motivated not by the thought that acting freely requires the ability to do otherwise (a thought which, given the Consequence Argument, motivates leeway incompatibilism), but the thought that the agent needs to be the *source* of her action, in a way that is allegedly ruled out by determinism. But sourcehood, in the relevant sense, only requires the truth of (CH) (plus – WAC version – agent causation); hence, Fischer's objection to the flicker defence simply doesn't apply to WSI or WAC.

We can put the point in terms of the notion of an 'indeterministic initiator', introduced in §5.2. Incompatibilists all agree that if an agent is to *A* freely, they have to be an indeterministic initiator of some action, somewhere along the line – but they differ with respect to what *kind* of indeterministic initiator the agent needs to be. That is, they fill out our 'definition-schema', (II-Def), in different ways. The flicker defence, in effect, requires the agent to be an indeterministic initiator in the sense that, somewhere in his process of deliberation, he could have done otherwise – not otherwise than *A*, but otherwise than some causal ancestor of *A*. WSI and WAC, by contrast, only require the agent to be an indeterministic initiator in the sense that *the deliberative process is not deterministic* (though WAC requires, in addition, that she agent-cause her decision). Whether or not whatever alternative possibilities that arise in the course of the indeterministic deliberative process constitute *robust* alternatives, that is, things the agent could have *done*, such that their ability to do them explains why they are morally responsible for their decision, is simply irrelevant: their moral responsibility is fully explained by features of the actual sequence itself. In other words, we have:

(II-Def-WSI) *S* an *indeterministic initiator* of action *A* if and only if the process of deliberation that leads to *A* is not deterministic.

(II-Def-WAC) *S* an *indeterministic initiator* of action *A* if and only if the process of deliberation that leads to *A* is not deterministic, and *S* agent-causes *A*.

Does either WSI or WAC constitute an acceptable incompatibilist response to Frankfurt's argument? Well, for starters, that depends on what kind of incompatibilist you want to be. If you're moved by the Consequence Argument, neither WSI nor WAC is for you – since both positions happily concede something you're committed to denying, namely that in principle an agent who can never do otherwise than what she actually does may yet routinely act freely. (Imagine an agent, Sam, who has a counterfactual intervener following her around *all the time*, but who fortunately never has to intervene because, as it happens, Sam always does what the intervener wants her to do.)

Of course, that's hardly a surprise, since both WSI and WAC are versions of source incompatibilism. Recall that the motivation for source incompatibilism is supposed to be the idea that determinism precludes agents from being the 'sources' of their actions; or, to put it in terms of buck-stopping, only indeterminism of the right kind can allow agents to stop the buck from flowing right through them and out the other side. So, does either WSI or WAC provide the (allegedly) required buck-stopper?

Let's start with WSI. Indeterministic initiation, of the very weak kind required by (II-Def-WSI), seems not to deliver a buck-stopper, any more than the satisfaction of compatibilist conditions on acting freely delivers just by itself. Consider again the 'global' version of the Frankfurt case: Black is ready to intervene at every one of Jones's 'choice points', so that Jones has no robust alternative possibilities open to him whatsoever. According to WSI, Jones is still morally responsible – but he wouldn't be if his process of deliberation were deterministic. What is supposed to justify this difference in moral responsibility is the thought that Jones, by virtue of being an indeterministic initiator of the very weak kind required by WSI, is the 'source' of his action in a way that Jones's deterministic counterpart is not. But I can see no reason to think that Jones (the indeterministic version) manages to *stop the buck* while his counterpart does not.

The point here is not that there is anything *incoherent* about WSI; there isn't, so far as I can tell. The point is rather that, as a positive view about what acting freely requires, it is completely unmotivated. To put it in terms familiar from the manipulation arguments of Chapter 4, there is no relevant difference – the kind of difference that could plausibly explain a difference in moral responsibility – between Jones, supposing that he satisfies (II-Def-WSI), and his deterministic counterpart, who makes exactly the same decision, goes through exactly the same moves in his deliberative process, but is such that each stage in that process is fully determined.

Does WAC fare any better? It certainly seems to be on firmer ground, because of course WAC supplements (CH) with the requirement that the agent agent-cause her action, and agent causes look like promising buck-stoppers – after all, one might reasonably think that the whole *point* of positing agent causation is to provide the buck-stopper that, according to source incompatibilists, is ruled out by determinism.

The problem for WAC, it seems to me, is that the role of indeterminism in the weak agent-causalist's story has become so attenuated that it's unclear why we need it *at all* in order to secure agent causation (assuming, of course, that the notion of agent causation makes sense in the first place). Recall Thomas Reid's view, mentioned in §5.6, that we human beings are not subject to necessity, but rather have 'active powers'. Reid himself conceives of 'active powers' as requiring that one be able to do something *or not to do it* – that is, as requiring the ability to do otherwise. (In §5.6, I called this kind of view 'strong' agent-causalism.) WAC rejects that conception of agent causation in favour of the view that agent causation merely requires the absence of determinism in the actual sequence that leads to one's decision. But, while the defender of WAC sees a huge gulf between a deterministic agent on the one hand and an indeterministic initiator (in the sense of someone who satisfies (CH)) on the other – a gulf big enough to make it the case that the latter, but not the former, can, in principle, agent-cause her actions – I see only a tiny sliver of a difference. In short, I can't see why a deterministic version of Jones is precluded from agent-causing his decision, while Jones in the global version of the Frankfurt case is not; that is, why the former must merely be caused to act as he does by his beliefs and desires, while the second is capable, at least in principle, of being such that *he* causes himself to act.

As with WSI, the point here is not that there is anything *incoherent* about WAC (although I have my doubts about the very idea of agent causation, irrespective of whether or not it requires indeterminism). The point is, rather, that there seems to be no positive motivation for the claim that agent causation requires mere indeterminism. I can make some sense of the motivation for the idea that agent causation requires the power to perform or refrain from performing some act – that is, for 'strong' agent-causalism. I can't make a lot of sense of the motivation for the idea that agent causation *only* requires indeterminism in the deliberative process.

If I'm right about WSI and WAC (and I might not be; I'm taking a punt here), then what seems to follow is that regulative control, or the ability to do otherwise, lies at the heart of *any* remotely plausible incompatibilist theory of free will. Acting freely, on any sensible incompatibilist theory, *does* require robust alternative possibilities, because only robust alternative possibilities can plausibly be thought to underpin buck-stopping. Perhaps they don't need to be alternative possibilities to the act in question itself; that's the thought that lies behind the flicker defence. It is also the thought that lies behind Kane's strong source incompatibilism: deterministically-caused decisions can, on Kane's view, perfectly well be free, so long as they trace back to SFAs. (Though, of course, since we can pull a Frankfurt on SFAs, Kane needs to find a way of rebutting Frankfurt's argument just as much as the leeway incompatibilist does. The same is true, for that matter, of 'strong' agent-causal theories of free will.)

I said in §5.4 that Kane's view is generally conceived as a 'mixed' or 'impure' view because he is taken to be a source incompatibilist about actions that are causally downstream of SFAs and a leeway incompatibilist about SFAs themselves. I myself don't find that a very helpful way to carve up the territory. While it's true that Kane requires of SFAs the ability to do otherwise, he is clearly a source incompatibilist in the sense that what is important about SFAs is that they are buck-stoppers. So for Kane, I take it, what's important for free will is not leeway or elbow room in and of itself; after all, he rejects the leeway incompatibilist's claim (as I've defined leeway incompatibilism) that acting freely requires the ability to do otherwise at or near the time of action. Rather, what's important for free will is the fact that leeway is required, somewhere in an action's causal history, *in order* for the buck to stop with the agent.

6.8   The *W*-defence

The 'W' in '*W*-defence' stands for 'What should he have done?' and is due to David Widerker (2006). The basic idea is that we should simply resist Frankfurt's claim that Jones is morally responsible for killing Smith. The *W*-defence can thus reasonably claim to being the most straightforward defence of incompatibilism against Frankfurt's argument. We don't need to worry about robust alternative possibilities or anything of that sort; we just need to stand true to our incompatibilist principles (if we have them) and flat-out let Jones off the hook.

Why should we let him off? Well, Widerker says, (a) you are only blameworthy for something if it would have been morally reasonable to expect you to not to have done it. (Widerker calls this the 'Principle of Alternative Expectations'.) Since (b) it is *not* morally reasonable to expect Jones to have refrained from killing Smith – since this is not something he *could* have done – it follows that Jones is not, in fact, blameworthy for killing (or deciding to kill) Smith. As Widerker puts it (the case here is one where Jones breaks a promise rather than kills Smith):

...since you, Frankfurt, wish to hold (Jones) blameworthy for his decision to break his promise, tell me *what, in your opinion, should he have done instead?* Now, you cannot claim that he should not have decided to break the promise, since this was something that was not in Jones's power to do. Hence, I do not see how you can hold Jones blameworthy for his decision to break the promise. (2006, 63)

Is Widerker's response convincing? One reason to think not is that the principle it appeals to, the Principle of Alternative Expectations, applies only to *blameworthy* actions. But, of course, moral responsibility is sometimes a matter of praiseworthiness. It's just an artefact of the Frankfurt case as it happens to be set up that Jones is potentially blameworthy for his decision; we could just as easily cook up a case where he is potentially praiseworthy instead. Imagine that Jones is deliberating about whether or not to rescue a puppy, and Black – not so nefarious now – is standing by, ready to press the button if Jones is on the verge of deciding not to go ahead. The *W*-defence simply doesn't say anything about whether or not Jones is praiseworthy in this case. Of course, one might try to come up with a praiseworthy variant on the Principle of Alternative Expectations, but it's unclear that any such principle will be at all plausible.

This may remind you of Wolf's account of 'asymmetrical freedom', briefly discussed in §3.3. Wolf requires alternative possibilities for blameworthy actions because, she thinks, the agent must be such that they could have done otherwise *had there been good and sufficient reasons to do so* – which, of course, there generally will be when the act in question is morally wrong. That principle is pretty close to the principle Widerker appeals to. But note that Wolf thinks that this means that morally *good* actions do *not* require the ability to do otherwise; and that does seem to suggest that there may be no alternative-possibilities condition on praiseworthy actions available for the *W*-defender to appeal to.

Of course, if Widerker's sole concern was to show that alternative possibilities are required for blameworthiness, then this would not be an objection to his position. But I think it's safe to assume that that isn't his sole concern; and in any case, even if it is, someone who wants to justify an alternative-possibilities requirement on moral responsibility *tout court* cannot appeal to the *W*-defence as it stands.

As with the flicker defence, the *W*-defence is most naturally read as a defence *of incompatibilism* and not a direct attack on Frankfurt's argument against (PAP) considered as a defence of compatibilism. For of course, even if the *W*-defence can be supplemented in the way I just said it requires, the *compatibilist* need not be remotely moved by it. As Frankfurt himself says: 'What should Jones have done instead of what he did? He should have behaved virtuously. In deciding of his own free will to break his promise, he violated the requirements of morality. Instead of doing that, he should have refrained from violating those requirements' (2006, 343).

6.9   Could Jones really not have done otherwise?

The final kind of response to the Frankfurt case that we'll consider simply flat-out denies that Jones could not have done otherwise than decide to kill Smith. Here is the basic idea (due to Maria Alvarez 2009; see also Larvor 2010; Di Nucci 2011).

First, we need to ask what it means to say that someone 'could have done otherwise'. Does it mean that there is some possible *action* that they could have performed but didn't? When we think about decisions, it's easy to think that the answer has to be 'Yes': after all, if you are deciding between A and B, and you end up deciding on A, then it looks like there will always be an alternative possibility that itself constitutes a mental action, *viz*, your deciding on B instead. But when we think of other kinds of action, both mental and non-mental, things become less clear. I scratched my nose just now. I could (let's suppose) have done otherwise. Need my 'doing otherwise' have been an *action*? It would have been the action of not-scratching-my-nose, perhaps, or maybe instead it would have been whatever other action I would have performed if I hadn't scratched my nose – continuing to type, say. But we need not say this. We can simply say that I could have 'done' otherwise simply by *refraining* from scratching my nose. Similarly, I formed the intention to scratch my nose just before I scratched it. Surely, the mere fact (assuming it is a fact) that I could have *refrained* from forming that intention is enough to make it the case that I could have done otherwise – never mind whether my so refraining would itself have counted as an action. So, perhaps we want to say that one way of being able to do otherwise than decide to A, when it comes to a decision, is simply being able to *refrain* from deciding to A. (In that case, we should not – as I have often done up to now – characterise the ability to do otherwise than decide to A as the ability to *decide* otherwise, since that presupposes that the ability to do otherwise *does* consist in making some *other* decision.)

That's the first piece of background we need. Here's the second. A decision is a mental *action*. And for something to count as an action, it has to be something the agent *does*, and not merely something that *happens to* the agent. To use an example of Alvarez's: 'Suppose that an earthquake makes Jim's limbs move in the way in which they move whenever he dances the samba. The fact that his limbs moved so is not enough to conclude that Jim danced the samba, nor to conclude that Jim moved his limbs, for the earthquake caused Jim's limbs to move, but it did not cause Jim to move his limbs' (2009, 65–6).

Now, with this distinction in play, let's consider Jones's situation, and, in particular, what would have happened if Black had seen the sign that would have prompted him to intervene. The Frankfurt case depends upon the claim that Black *would have made Jones decide* to kill Smith. But surely this case is just like the samba case. Surely, Black's manipulating Jones's brain activity would not count as *Jones deciding* to kill Smith, any more than the earthquake's causing Jim's bodily movements counts as Jim's *dancing the samba*.

If that is right, then the thing that would have happened had Jones not decided all on his own to kill Smith would *not* have been Jones deciding to kill Smith: it would not have been an *action* of Jones's at all, any more than the earthquake-induced movement of Jim's limbs is an action. In that case, it is not true that *whatever happened*, Jones would have decided to kill Smith. For it turns out that, had he not been about to decide to kill Smith on his own, thereby causing Black to intervene, what would have happened would *not* have been Jones's deciding to kill Smith.

Now let's put that thought together with the first point about the ability to do otherwise than *A* being a matter of being able to refrain from doing *A*, as opposed to being a matter of being able to *do* something else – that is, perform some *other* action. Now we can ask the question: Could Jones have done otherwise than decide to kill Smith? Alvarez's answer is: Yes, he could. There is no other *action* he could have performed, thanks to Black's presence: he could not, in particular, have decided *not* to kill Smith. Nonetheless, he could have *refrained* from deciding to kill Smith. And this is so because Black could have intervened; and if he *had* intervened, Jones would not have decided to kill Smith. (Remember Jim and the samba.) To put it another way, it was up to Jones whether or not to decide to kill Smith: he could have decided to do it, or he could have refrained from making that decision. Of course, Jones himself is unaware of exactly what this refraining would amount to. From Jones's point of view – not knowing that Black is lurking in the shadows – it might seem that his options are: decide to kill Smith, or decide *not* to kill Smith – and this latter is certainly *one* way of refraining from deciding to kill Smith. In fact, however, the refraining would happen in a completely different way, via Black's manipulation of Jones's brain. But that manipulation still counts as Jones refraining from deciding to kill Smith. Hence, it is indeed up to Jones whether he decides or refrains from deciding to kill Smith: He *could have done otherwise*.

If this line of thought is right, then it turns out that the Frankfurt case poses no threat whatsoever to the Principle of Alternate Possibilities, for it is not even a *prima facie* counter-example to the principle. The case is only a counter-example if it describes a situation in which Jones could not have done otherwise; and that criterion is not met. (The success of Alvarez's response, of course, depends on our not being able to cook up a *new* case where, on the alternative course of events that Black might have initiated, Jones *does* genuinely decide to kill Smith.)

It's worth briefly comparing Alvarez's response to Frankfurt to the flicker defence. Both responses trade on the thought that there is a morally relevant difference between the actual case, where Jones decides on his own to kill Smith (and hence is morally responsible), and the 'alternative pathway' (as it's sometimes called) where Black intervenes and so Jones doesn't decide on his own (and so clearly *isn't* morally responsible). The flicker-defender locates the difference in the fact that, on the alternative pathway, Jones's decision is deterministically caused by Black's intervention, while Alvarez locates it in the fact that on the alternative pathway, Jones doesn't *decide* to kill Smith at all.

6.10   Conclusion

The vast literature that has been spawned by Frankfurt's original paper is, as should by now be very clear, a bit of a minefield. Here, for what it's worth, is my take on it. Let's assume, for starters, that some version or other of the Frankfurt case gets around Alvarez's worry, so that we do have a genuine case on the table where Jones is (allegedly) morally responsible for his decision even though he could not have done otherwise – indeed, let's imagine that he has no robust alternative possibilities open to him whatsoever. I think Frankfurt is absolutely right that Jones is culpable, that the 'stripping away' of alternative possibilities makes no difference to his culpability, and that what is important for culpability – indeed, for deciding and acting freely – is the nature of the actual deliberative process that leads to one's decision. And it doesn't matter if that process is in fact deterministic, because deterministic deliberation is *not* such that one does what one does *only because* one could not have done otherwise. I'm completely, and I think entirely legitimately, unmoved by all of the defences of (PAP) and its ilk that have been discussed in this chapter. But then, I'm a compatibilist.

How do things look from an incompatibilist perspective? Well, on the one hand, nothing in Frankfurt's argument conclusively demonstrates that incompatibilism is false. For example, the argument doesn't *show* that the incompatibilist who holds that Jones simply isn't blameworthy is mistaken. After all, the argument simply presupposes that Jones is morally responsible; there's nothing *incoherent* about denying that assumption, even if the committed compatibilist – and perhaps the floating voter as well – will find the claim that the question of Jones's culpability rests on the entirely passive presence of Black deeply implausible.

On the other hand, Frankfurt's argument *does* (or so I think) raise serious doubts about the *justification* for incompatibilism. The argument (I claim) shows the Consequence Argument to rest on a premise, (PAP), that itself lacks justification. This being so, it would seem that leeway incompatibilism is unmotivated, since the justification for leeway incompatibilism is supposed to be, precisely, CA.

So, I think the conclusion we should draw is that only source incompatibilism is left in the running: the kind of incompatibilism that is (allegedly) justified by the thought that determinism is incompatible with agents being the source of their actions in some sense that is required for acting freely and morally responsibly. My speculative suggestion in §6.7 – based on an admittedly sketchy argument to the effect that 'weak' versions of source incompatibilism, WSI and WAC, are unmotivated – was that any remotely credible version of source incompatibilism must hold that an agent As freely only if there is some relevant *robust* alternative possibility available to them, somewhere in the causal history of the action: the kind of alternative possibility, that is, that might plausibly be thought to serve as a buck-stopper.

If that's right, then the *strong* source incompatibilist can in principle appeal to one of the defences suggested in this chapter without begging the question against Frankfurt, because she has reasons, independent of CA, for holding that the ability to do otherwise is required for acting freely.

It is worth stressing, however, that a defence against Frankfurt really is needed. It is sometimes said that Frankfurt's argument cuts no ice against the source incompatibilist. I think that's wrong. It cuts no ice against WSI because according to WSI (and, for that matter, WAC) all that is required is that the actual sequence leading to the decision is indeterministic. But I think WSI is an implausible position in any case because it fails to meet the incompatibilist's own buck-stopping requirement. *Strong* source incompatibilism, by contrast, requires robust alternative possibilities, and so Frankfurt's argument poses a challenge that needs to be met.

7
Other Issues

7.1 Introduction

Freedom of the will is a huge topic both historically and in contemporary philosophy. I've aimed in this book to cover what seem to be the positions and arguments that are most discussed by contemporary metaphysicians, but I've had to leave plenty out along the way in the interest of brevity. In this chapter, I provide a brief and partial survey of some issues that I have hitherto ignored or skirted around. In §7.2, I discuss free will and foreknowledge; and in §7.3, I explain the apparent threat to freedom of the will posed by recent research in neuroscience. In §7.4, I consider what role our intuitions about the various thought experiments described in this book ought to have in the debate about free will and why; and I consider whether, and to what extent, 'experimental philosophy' might be useful in this regard. Finally, in §7.5, I consider the question of what 'morally responsible' really means, and indeed whether this is a question that needs to be decisively answered if we are to make progress in our thinking about free will.

7.2 Free will and foreknowledge

One long-standing question in the philosophy of religion is whether the fact that God (who is omniscient) *knows* – and knows infallibly – what you will do renders you unfree. For example, suppose that God knows that you will have toast for breakfast tomorrow. Then it seems to follow straight off that you cannot do otherwise than have toast for breakfast. After all, if it were *possible* for you to do otherwise, then it seems that it would be possible for God to be wrong about your breakfast choice. But God, being omniscient, cannot be wrong about that.

Note that the argument does not presuppose determinism. If God is omniscient, then God knows what is going to happen *even if* what is going to happen is not determined by the past plus the laws. The best *we mere human beings* can aspire to (and, in fact, even this is almost certainly beyond us, even in principle) is knowing about the past plus the laws: our only way of reliably predicting what's going to happen in the future is to base it on an *inference* from the state of the world (or a small part of it) together with (what we hope is) knowledge of the laws of nature. But God is not temporally restricted in this way: his knowledge of the future is not based on such an inference. He just *knows* what's going to happen. So the problem of divine foreknowledge isn't just a problem if determinism is true; it's a problem either way.

Various solutions to the problem have been proposed (see Zagzebski 2002 for a survey). One view that has been alleged to solve the problem is the view that there is simply no fact of the matter about what will happen in the future: facts about what will happen only become genuine facts at the point at which the events in question actually happen, that is, become *present* (see e.g. Rhoda, Boyd and Belt 2006). On this view, then, God *cannot* know that I will have toast for breakfast tomorrow, since there is not yet any fact of the matter about what I'll have, and hence there is nothing, yet, for God *to* know. And this is supposed to be compatible with God's omniscience, because for God to be omniscient is for God to know everything that *can be known*. After all, it would seem that to expect any more than this would be to expect God to be able to know things that are unknowable – and not even God can pull off something that is *impossible*!

Another solution (see Plantinga 1986) – sometimes called the 'Ockhamist' solution, after William of Ockham (sometimes spelled 'Occam') – is to argue that God's foreknowledge is in fact compatible with the ability to do otherwise. The force of the argument from divine foreknowledge comes from the thought that we lack the power to render God's infallible predictions false. But we might argue that, while we lack *that* power – nobody can make it the case that God falsely believes anything – we still have a power over *what God believes*. So, for example, grant that I do have toast for breakfast tomorrow, and hence that God knows that I'll do that. This, it is claimed, is nonetheless compatible with my being able to have cereal instead. For, were I to have cereal instead, God – being omniscient – would, of course, *not* believe that I will have toast; he would instead believe that I will have cereal. To put things in terms of possible worlds (see §3.4): in the *actual* world – let's suppose – I have toast for breakfast tomorrow, and so God believes (indeed knows) that this is what I'll do. But in the closest possible world(s) where I have cereal, God believes (and again, knows) that I'll do *that*. The fact that, were I to have cereal, God would believe (and indeed know) something different to what he actually knows does not render me unable to have cereal rather than toast.

This line of thought bears some similarity to Lewis's local miracle compatibilism, discussed in §3.4. On Lewis's view, I am able to do something (have cereal for breakfast, for example) such that, were I to do it, an actual law of nature would *not* be a law of nature. But this ability does not consist in some sort of magical power over the laws. Similarly, the above reply to the argument from divine foreknowledge claims that I am able to do something (have cereal) such that, were I to do it, God would not know something that he actually knows. But, analogously, this ability does not constitute some sort of magical power over God's state of knowledge. In particular, it doesn't constitute the power to make God fail to be omniscient. Instead, it's just the power to affect what he believes.

Of course, a somewhat more straightforward response to the problem would be to deny the existence of God. But even with God out of the picture, the problem of foreknowledge still plays a role in the free will debate. This is largely because *determinism* seems to raise the possibility of foreknowledge. After all, while we actual human beings are currently a very long way off being able to predict human behaviour with any great level of reliability, armed with our rather patchy knowledge of the relevant laws of nature plus facts about people's psychological states and/or the states of their brains and/or their local environment, these are the kinds of thing that seem *in principle* to be the kinds of things we human beings, and certainly less-than-omniscient deities, *could* know; and if we (or such deities) *did* know them, then if determinism is true, we (they) would be able to predict with certainty how people would behave.

We've already an argument that exploits this connection between determinism and predictability: Mele's zygote argument (§4.5). Diana is just such a less-than-omniscient deity: she is not *omniscient*, but she knows the laws of nature and all the relevant facts about the world prior to Ernie's conception, and hence – assuming determinism – she knows what Ernie will do thirty years hence. Diana would not be able to do that if some facts about Ernie and/or his environment were not determined by the laws plus the past. (I noted in §4.5 that Mele includes the caveat that Humeanism about laws is false. This is precisely because he thinks that if Humeanism were true, Diana would *not* be in a position to know the laws of nature, and so, again, would not be able to predict Ernie's behaviour with certainty. The question about the relationship between Humeanism and the possibility of anyone – God aside – being able to know any laws of nature is an interesting one; see Bird 2008.) Were we to try to run a version of the zygote argument where Diana is omniscient, so can know what Ernie will do without having to infer it from the laws plus the past, we would essentially be back in the territory of the argument from divine foreknowledge, and as such, the argument would not be an argument against compatibilism *specifically*, since Diana would just as well be able to reliably predict what Ernie would do even if determinism were false.

Saul Smilansky offers a different argument against compatibilism, again based on the connection between determinism and the possibility of foreknowledge. Smilanksy argues that compatibilists must – implausibly – accept the moral defensibility of prepunishment, since, if we *knew* that someone were going to commit a crime, what could possibly be wrong with punishing them before the crime has even been committed? (See Smilansky 2007; Beebee 2008.)

Other arguments that draw on the connection between determinism and foreknowledge focus not on the possibility that *other* people (or minor deities) could predict what we are going to do, but on the possibility that we *ourselves* could know this. We touched on one in §1.3: Ginet's (1962) argument for 'contra-causal' free will. If our decisions were caused, Ginet thinks, it would be possible in principle to know in advance what one were going to decide, before one decided it. But it is impossible to decide to do something if you already know what it is you're going to decide. Hence, decisions cannot be caused. Now, as I said in §1.3, Ginet's argument is only even *prima facie* sound if we assume that all causation is necessarily deterministic causation, which (arguably) it isn't. But we can recast the argument as an argument against the claim that decisions can be *deterministically* caused by recasting the first premise as: 'If our decisions were deterministically caused, it would be possible in principle to know in advance what one was going to decide, before one decided it'. Again, then, we have the thought that determinism rules out acting freely *because* determinism entails the possibility of foreknowledge. (Richard La Croix (1976) presents an interesting version of Ginet's argument, by arguing that God himself – being omniscient – cannot decide freely because he always knows in advance what he's going to decide. See also Kapitan 1984.)

My own view, for what it's worth, is that the mere fact that *in principle* we could, if determinism is true, figure out what we, or other people, are going to do by knowing the relevant laws and facts about the past is no *more* of a problem than is the fact that we could *in principle* build a time machine, zip into the future, and find out what we (or other people) are going to do. And *that* problem is no more of a problem for compatibilists than it is for incompatibilists. On the other hand, that doesn't mean there isn't a problem about the possibility of foreknowledge; only that it isn't a problem that uniquely confronts the compatibilist. There is clearly something right about the thought that we cannot coherently both know what we're going to decide *and* still *decide*; after all, we can only *deliberate* about which of two or more alternatives to perform if we regard it as an open question which of them we'll end up doing. Resolving this problem is not a straightforward matter. (But see Sorensen 1984; Bok 1998, Chapter 2.)

7.3 Free will and neuroscience

One reason why the problem of foreknowledge (in the case of determinism rather than theism) might not seem very pressing is that we seem to be an awfully long way away from actually being able to predict people's behaviour very reliably. Of course, we can predict people's behaviour to *some* extent. Indeed, David Hume (1748, §8) pointed out that human behaviour is manifestly eminently predictable, and that we rely on that predictability all the time; and he used this fact to argue that nobody *really* thinks that human actions are not subject to necessity (or, as we might put it, are not causally determined). I would never walk down the street if I seriously thought there was some chance that a random stranger would attack me with an axe; nor would I get on a bus if I didn't wholeheartedly believe that the driver would take the bus where it is supposed to go.

On the other hand, that kind of predictability is not 100 per cent reliable, and so it's not at all clear that Hume is entitled to claim that we generally rely on the assumption that human actions are deterministically caused. Random axe attacks are not completely unheard of, and it's not *certain* that your bus driver will follow the approved route. Generally speaking, bus drivers follow the approved route because that's their job, and they don't want to get the sack. That people don't want to get the sack and will therefore generally behave in such as way as to avoid it is a pretty reliable psychological generalisation, but maybe on *this* occasion the driver has just been served with notice of redundancy and plans to get her own back by dumping all the passengers in the middle of nowhere. Of course, this hardly ever happens, so it's safe to assume that it won't. But its being safe to *assume* something is surely a lot less demanding than being *certain* of it.

Some developments in neuroscience over the last 25 years or so, however, have been claimed to make the predictability of human decisions a reality rather than a mere distant possibility – and not just predictability of the kinds of action we're *already* pretty good at predicting (that the bus driver will turn left at the lights, say), but of kinds of action that we would *not* normally be able to predict. Moreover, such predictions are being made on the basis not of knowing someone's *psychological* states and figuring out what people with those sorts of beliefs and desires typically do – which is how we normally predict people's behaviour – but on the basis of knowledge of information about the states of their *brains*. And some neuroscientists have claimed that this predictability on the basis of brain states is a serious threat to freedom of the will.

The classic experiment here is Benjamin Libet's. Here's a very brief summary. The experimental subjects were wired up to a machine that takes electrical readings from the scalp, and placed in front of a big clock face with a fast-moving hand. The experimenters asked each subject to flex their wrist from time to time – whenever they wanted, and not at some pre-arranged moment – and to note where the hand on the clock was when they first became aware of the urge to do so. What the experimenters found was that there was a spike in electrical activity – known as 'readiness potential' – on average 550 ms (just over half a second) before the participants began to move their wrists, and 350 ms before they claimed to have felt the urge to flex. In his provocatively titled paper, 'Do We Have Free Will?' (1999), Libet concludes that the 'initiation of the freely voluntary act appears to begin in the brain unconsciously, well before the person consciously knows he wants to act!' (1999, 51). In other words – to put it in deliberately contentious terms – your brain 'decides' that you're going to flex your wrist, and you only become consciously aware of this 'decision' a little later on.

Libet then asks: 'Is there, then, any role for conscious will in the performance of a voluntary act?' (*ibid*.). Libet thinks there may be. A different experiment seems to indicate that there is a brief window of opportunity of about 100 ms, in between the onset of the readiness potential and the moment of no return (the point when your muscles are all ready to go, and there's nothing you can do about it), 'in which the conscious function might affect the final outcome of the volitional process' (*ibid*.) That is, the 'conscious will' may yet be able to perform a 'vetoing' function. Again putting it in deliberately contentious terms, once your brain has 'decided' that you're going to flex your wrist, *you* (that is, your conscious will) have a brief opportunity to overrule the decision. *'Conscious-will could thus affect the outcome* of the volitional process', Libet says, 'even though the latter was initiated by unconscious cerebral processes. Conscious-will might block or veto the process, so that no act occurs' (1999, 51–2). He considers the possibility that this veto process might itself have unconscious origins in the brain, but claims that if this were so it would be 'unacceptable' to hold that the individual is making a 'genuine choice' or that the process 'could still be viewed as a free will process' (1999, 52).

What are we to make of Libet's claim that freedom of the will is, at best, limited to one's ability to veto brain processes that are initiated unconsciously, and, at worst (if the veto process is itself initiated unconsciously), absent all together? Well, Libet is assuming that any process that originates unconsciously in the brain *cannot* be a process that in any way amounts to something that the agent does *freely*. Is this a plausible claim? If not, then the fact (if it is a fact – and let's assume it is) that conscious urges to act are reliably preceded by unconscious brain processes (as measured by the onset of the readiness potential) – interesting though it undoubtedly is – will not give us even *prima facie* grounds for thinking that our actions (or decisions or the acquisition of intentions or whatever) are never freely performed. I'll leave the question of whether Libet is right as an exercise for the reader (though see e.g. Mele 2006, 2008b and 2009 for detailed discussion of Libet's experiments and the conclusions he draws). If you've read the rest of this book, I am hoping you will be able to figure out a satisfactory answer for yourself.

7.4   Free will, intuitions and experimental philosophy

You may have noticed that the debate about free will relies very heavily on appeals to what we do or do not find intuitively plausible – or, to put it another way, on appeals to our *intuitions*. One standard mode of argument is to ask the reader to consult her intuitions – about Carly or Wally or Jones or Plum or Ernie or one of the many other characters who make their appearance in this book and elsewhere in the literature – and then to try to show that those intuitions are not endorsed by a particular theoretical position. Thus, for example, Ernie's lack of moral responsibility for doing something he was intended by Diana, who created him, to perform is alleged by Mele to be in tension with compatibilism; and Jones's responsibility for killing Smith is alleged by Frankfurt to be incompatible with the claim that acting freely requires the ability to do otherwise. And the moral is then taken to be that we should renounce the theoretical position, thus allowing us to maintain the intuitively plausible view about Ernie, or Jones or whoever, that we started out with.

As we've seen in various places, this kind of argumentative strategy is not without its problems. One problem is that not everybody shares the same intuitions. Consider Frankfurt's denial that manipulation cases show that there must be historical conditions on moral responsibility (§4.4). Frankfurt takes it to be intuitively plausible that, as he puts it, the 'fact that someone is a pig warrants treating him like a pig' – no matter how he came to acquire his unpleasant character. Thus, from Frankfurt's perspective, history-sensitive compatibilism is completely unmotivated. However, from the perspective of those compatibilists who have different intuitions about manipulation cases, history-sensitive compatibilism *is* motivated, because it accords with *their* intuitions.

A second problem is that not everyone agrees that our initial intuitions need to be borne out by our theoretical commitments in the first place. When a philosopher is said to 'bite the bullet', this normally means that they are accepting a consequence of their theory that they themselves regard as intuitively implausible, and are doing so for the sake of maintaining that theory. And some philosophers do explicitly engage in bullet-biting. So, how are we to distinguish between when it is and isn't OK to bite the bullet? Or should we insist that bullet-biting is *never* an acceptable strategy?

Certainly there may be cases where our initial intuitions have to berevoked because they turn out, on reflection, to be in tension *with one other*. Pereboom's four-case argument, for example, aims to show that compatibilist intuitions cannot *all* be accommodated by a compatibilist theory of free will, since, while – according to the compatibilist – intuitively Plum-1 is not responsible while Plum-4 *is* responsible, there are no *grounds* for drawing any such distinction between them. If Pereboom is right, then the compatibilist *has* to give up on one of the claims that they take to be intuitively plausible. (Pereboom thinks they should give up on the intuition that Plum-4 is responsible, thereby abandoning compatibilism. McKenna, who runs the four-case argument in reverse, holds that it is the intuition that Plum-1 is *not* responsible that should be revoked.) Clearly, in cases where our intuitions are collectively unstable or in tension with one another, something has to give – but, as the dispute between Pereboom and McKenna shows, there are then going to be disagreements about *which* of our collectively unstable intuitions we should revoke.

One general question that all this raises is: Why are intuitions supposed to be so important in the first place? Why does our initial, untutored, intuitive view about a particular thought-experiment deserve to be accorded any respect at all? Given the central role that intuitions play in philosophical arguments (and not just in the area of free will), this is a surprisingly difficult question to answer. One kind of answer stresses an analogy between philosophical and scientific theorising. Both philosophy (or some of it) and the sciences aim to come up with general hypotheses about the nature of reality – whether it is how chemicals react with one another, what the relationship is between an object's force, mass and acceleration, or what the circumstances are in which people act freely. Scientific theories are, of course, hostage to observable facts about the world: If your theory says that the interaction of chemicals A and B will produce results C, and it turns out that results C do not, in fact, obtain when A and B interact, then – assuming that we have ruled out experimental error (perhaps the samples were contaminated or the measuring equipment was faulty) – our initial hypothesis must be false.

Philosophical theories, by and large, cannot be empirically tested in this way. Suppose, for example, our theory entails that a normal deterministic agent performing action A in normal circumstances does A freely. And here's a potential instance of that generalization: I, a normal, deterministic agent, just decided freely to make a cup of tea. If we wanted to use this case to test the generalization, we'd have to establish independently (a) whether I really am (or was, just now) a normal, deterministic agent, and (b) whether I just acted freely. Perhaps in principle, (a) is empirically testable: in principle, empirical investigation might reveal that I was, in fact, an indeterministic initiator of my action, or that I am suffering from a serious psychiatric disorder, or am being manipulated by evil neuroscientists. But (b) is not: no amount of empirical investigation of my brain or my psychology or anything else will tell us, *independently*, whether I really did just decide freely to make a cup of tea. That is something we can only *infer* from our best theory of the conditions required for acting freely, and so cannot be established independently and hence used as a *test* of whether our best theory is correct.

Hence, we need to rely on intuitions: intuitions, so this line of thought goes, are the philosopher's equivalent of empirical data. Intuitions (for example, the intuition that I – a normal human being who may well be fully deterministic – just decided freely to make a cup of tea) are the evidence against which our philosophical theories are tested, just as empirical data constitute the evidence against which scientific theories are tested. (See, for example, Sosa 2007; Paul 2010.)

Of course, one problem with this approach is that we now need to know what to do when different people's intuitions conflict. If we get a conflict in *empirical* evidence – for example, if one group of experimenters in chemistry gets one result and another group gets a different result – that is grounds for revisiting the experiments: something, somewhere must have gone wrong in one of them. (The microscope was faulty, or whatever.) Eventually – or so we hope – everyone will come to agree on what the facts really are, and hence on whether or not the theory that is being tested has been confirmed or refuted. Philosophical intuitions do not appear to be like that at all: there are no microscopes that might be faulty, and no test tubes that might not have been cleaned properly. Are we then to say that some people's intuitions are right and others' are wrong, and if so, on what grounds might we make these claims? The answer to that question is far from clear (though, as we'll see in a moment, perhaps some headway can be made on it).

A second approach, taken by Lewis, is to take it to be a *methodological* principle that we should preserve our 'common-sense' theory of the world (or the 'folk theory', as it's sometimes called) as far as possible in constructing our philosophical theories: 'It is far beyond our power', Lewis says, 'to weave a brand new fabric of adequate theory *ex nihilo*, so we must perforce conserve the one we've got. A worthwhile theory must be credible, and a credible theory must be conservative. It cannot gain, and it cannot deserve, credence if it disagrees with too much of common sense' (1986c, 134). On this kind of view, our untutored philosophical intuitions are not analogous to scientific *observations*; rather, they are the consequences of our pre-existing common-sense *theory* about the world. (This theory, we may suppose, is normally only implicit. You don't find out what the common-sense theory of freedom, or the mind, or knowledge, or whatever is by asking people to describe it; ask someone who hasn't thought about philosophy before to tell you what the necessary and sufficient conditions for knowledge are, and you're liable to get a blank look. On the other hand, if you describe various scenarios to someone and ask them whether, in each of those scenarios, *S* knows that *p*, you can *infer* what their implicit theory of knowledge is from their answers.)

Lewis takes it that 'common sense is a settled body of theory' (*ibid.*) – so it seems that, by definition, cases where different people's intuitions conflict are cases where there *is* no settled common-sense theory – no implicit theory that *we*, collectively, subscribe to – and hence, in effect, nothing that needs to be preserved. But that seems like an unsatisfactory situation, too, at least in areas of philosophy, such as the free will debate, where intuitions seem to diverge in a widespread and persistent way. For if we are to ignore *all* intuitions in cases of divergence, it seems that we lack any constraints on our philosophical theorising, and so we really have nothing in which to anchor our theories. If we couldn't legitimately appeal to intuitions at all in the free will debate, or could only appeal to them very rarely (that is, just in those rare cases where we mostly agree with each other), it's unclear that we'd be able to make any serious progress at all: as Lewis says, it is 'far beyond our power to weave a brand new fabric of adequate theory *ex nihilo*'.

One way in which philosophers have recently sought to make some headway when it comes to intuitions is to engage in what has become known as *experimental philosophy*. Experimental philosophers do not resort to microscopes or test tubes – they don't need laboratories. Rather, their job, as far as experimentation is concerned, is to solicit the intuitions of ordinary, untutored people with no background philosophical theories to taint their intuitive reactions to thought experiments. And the area of free will and moral responsibility is one in which experimental philosophers have been very active.

How might soliciting the intuitions of 'the folk' (as in 'folk theory') help us in constructing and testing philosophical theories? Well, let's start with the Lewisian conception of the role of folk theory. Clearly, if our philosophical theorising is to be constrained by folk theory, we'd better have a good idea of what the folk actually think. Philosophers are strongly predisposed to assume that *their* intuitions accord with everyone else's: we tend to say, 'intuitively, such-and-such', which is pretty much like saying 'according to *my* intuitions, such-and-such; and I fully expect you to agree with me'. But there is no particular reason to think that other philosophers generally *will* agree with us, especially when we consider that the philosophers who engage in constructing thought experiments generally already have a fixed view about the issue under discussion. This being so, it is really quite likely that their intuitions are 'theory-laden': infected by the theoretical commitments they already have. And, of course, the mere fact that philosophers frequently disagree with each other about what is and is not intuitively plausible gives us grounds for thinking that we should not automatically expect philosophers' intuitions to coincide with those of the folk. So, if we really want to know what the 'folk theory' says, the best we can do, surely, is to ask the folk.

Similarly, if we think of the role of intuitions as analogous to that of empirical evidence in the sciences, consulting the folk is a good idea. For – or at least, so we might hope – perhaps philosophers' disagreement about what constitutes the most intuitively plausible view to take about Ernie or Jones or whomever is explained by the differing theoretical commitments they bring to the table. So, if we ask people who don't have any pre-existing theoretical commitments, perhaps they won't exhibit the same level of disagreement. Of course, that hope might turn out to be in vain: perhaps the folk disagree amongst themselves, even given their theoretically untainted viewpoint. That, it seems, would spell potential trouble for both of the approaches to intuitions just considered.

As it turns out, different experimental philosophy studies have come to different conclusions when attempting to investigate whether people intuitively think that (for example) deterministic agents are morally responsible for what they do. Some studies have elicited compatibilist intuitions from the majority of participants, while others have found incompatibilism to be the majority view. How can this be, and what conclusions should we draw? Well, in a scientific context, the natural explanation of differing experimental results in the same apparent circumstances is that the experimental circumstances differ in some hitherto unnoticed way. According to Shaun Nichols and Joshua Knobe (2007), this is exactly what has happened in studies of intuitions when it comes to moral responsibility.

Studies in experimental philosophy generally involve presenting people with a thought experiment – a short description of a possible scenario – and then asking them a question about it. So, for example, this might involve describing the universe in deterministic terms and then asking whether a particular person (Joe, say) who performs a particular act (robbing a bank, say) is morally responsible for doing so. Nichols and Knobe argue that people's intuitions are normally dependent on whether the question asked is an abstract or concrete one. In particular, if the experimenter sets up a fully deterministic scenario – so that it's clear that agents' actions in the scenario are determined by the laws plus the past – and then just asks the abstract question, 'Is it possible for people in this scenario to be morally responsible for their actions?', the answer tends to be 'No'. That is, the experimenters tend to get incompatibilist answers. (In Nichols and Knobe's version, 86 per cent said 'No'.) On the other hand, if the deterministic scenario is set up in exactly the same way, but people are asked whether a particular person who commits a particularly heinous act is morally responsible (in Nichols and Knobe's case, whether Bill is morally responsible for killing his wife and children so that he can run off with his secretary), the answer tends to be 'Yes' – that is, they get *compatibilist* answers (72 per cent said 'Yes' in Nichols and Knobe's study).

Suppose that Nichols and Knobe are right. What follows? Well, they hypothesise that the explanation for the difference in responses is *affect*. Presented with a scenario where a specific agent behaves badly (killing his wife and children, for example), an emotional response is triggered, and this emotional response causes them to judge the agent to be morally responsible. By contrast, presented with an abstract question ('are people in deterministic universes morally responsible for their behaviour?'), no such emotional response is triggered.

Supposing that Nichols and Knobe are right about *this*. Again, we can ask what follows. Specifically, should we conclude that the effect of affect is a *distorting* one? (Nichols and Knobe call this view the 'performance error model', and they argue that it is most likely to be the correct model.) On this hypothesis, people's *real* view is incompatibilism, but this judgement can be distorted by their emotional reactions to concrete cases involving bad behaviour. Alternatively, we might conclude that it is *failure* to engage people's emotional responses that produces a distorting effect. (Nichols and Knobe call this view the 'affective competence model'.) Some *prima facie* evidence for this view comes from studies of people who have difficulty with emotional processing, whose results seem to show that 'when we strip away the capacity for affective reactions, it seems that we are not left with a person who can apply the fundamental criteria of morality in an especially impartial or unbiased fashion. Instead, we seem to be left with someone who has trouble understanding what morality is all about' (2007, 673). So, we might conclude that it is the abstract questions that are producing the distortion by suppressing the kinds of emotional responses that underpin competence in making moral judgements.

The question of the proper role of intuitions in philosophical theorising – and how (if at all) we can go about figuring out what the 'right' intuitions are – is therefore a very difficult one to answer. Given the prominent role of intuitive reactions to possible cases in the free will debate, this may engender a sceptical attitude toward the whole enterprise. I myself think that would be something of an overreaction (obviously, otherwise I wouldn't have bothered writing this book). After all, one thing I hope you have gleaned from this book is that, while intuitions may be a less than fully secure starting point for one's philosophical theorising, they certainly aren't the whole story. The debate about free will isn't simply a matter of 'intuition-bashing', with, for example, compatibilists and incompatibilists simply asserting their positions and hoping that if they thump the table hard enough their opponents will agree with them. On the contrary: the debate contains a good deal of sophisticated and subtle argument, and a wide range of quite detailed theories. If all I'd done were to present a large number of scenarios and ask you what your intuitive reactions to them were, it would have been a very boring book indeed.

7.5   What *is* moral responsibility anyway?

As we've seen, it's a vain hope to suppose that we might secure consensus when it comes to intuitive judgments about some of the thought experiments that play a key role in the free will debate. In addition – and this is an issue touched on in §2.3 – sometimes it's hard not to get the feeling that at least some of the participants in the debate about free will are simply talking past each other. Take, for example, the radically different views taken by Galen Strawson and Dennett. Strawson holds that nobody is ever 'ultimately' morally responsible for anything unless she is (as Dennett puts it) 'a completely self-made self, one hundred per cent responsible for (her) own character' (1984, 156) – something that Dennett and Strawson agree to be impossible. Strawson's conclusion is that moral responsibility is impossible; Dennett's, in effect, is that moral responsibility does not require 'ultimate' responsibility. This debate at least partly boils down to the question of what we *mean* when we say that someone is morally responsible. Does being morally responsible entail being *ultimately* responsible or not?

We might approach this question in (at least) four different ways. First, we might take it that 'moral responsibility', as an expression of English that is routinely used by ordinary people, has a unique meaning, and we might take a view about what that meaning *is*. This, I think, is what is *in fact* going on in the dispute between Dennett and Galen Strawson's dispute about whether moral responsibility requires ultimate responsibility: Strawson holds that the ordinary notion of moral responsibility enshrined in Western culture (and others) just *is* the notion of ultimate responsibility. Dennett disagrees: we just *do* go around holding ourselves and others morally responsible for what we do, without being in the slightest bit interested in whether we are self-made selves. And that just *shows* that, according to the ordinary notion of moral responsibility, moral responsibility doesn't require ultimate responsibility.

If we conceive of the issue in this way, it is, of course, not obvious who's right. One way we might try to resolve the dispute would be to do some experimental philosophy, as discussed in the previous section. Unfortunately, as we've seen, the untutored intuitions of people with no philosophical axe to grind don't seem to deliver a clear result on this score, and indeed seem to be easily swayed by the kind of question we ask (e.g. by whether we trigger people's emotional reactions).

Even if we *could* decisively answer the question of what, in the mouths of ordinary language-users, the words 'morally responsible' mean, however, it would still, in principle, be open to us to argue for a 'revisionary' account of moral responsibility, on the grounds that the ordinary concept of moral responsibility is defective in some way (see Vargas 2005). For example, if we agree with Galen Strawson that the ordinary concept of moral responsibility just *is* the concept of *ultimate* responsibility, we might try to argue that this concept has its roots in a theistic conception of human beings, so that if we abandon that theistic conception, our concept of moral responsibility ought to be revised accordingly. Thus, Galen Strawson says that 'true moral responsibility is of such a kind that, if we have it, then it *makes sense*, at least, to suppose that it could be just to punish some of us with (eternal) torment in hell and reward others with (eternal) bliss in heaven' (1998, 9). But from an atheist viewpoint, for example, it is completely unclear why we should conceive of 'true moral responsibility' in those terms. According to this second line of thought, then, the right question to ask is not what our *actual* concept of moral responsibility is, but what it *ought* to be in order to best satisfy our needs, given the kind of world we actually inhabit.

A third way of approaching the question about the meaning of 'moral responsibility' is to accept that the term is simply *ambiguous*. Some authors have argued that 'moral responsibility' just isn't a unitary concept: there are different senses of 'morally responsible'. This certainly goes some way towards explaining why we can feel ambivalent about some of the cases we are presented with when we engage with the literature on freedom of the will. Gary Watson (1996), for example, distinguishes between the 'accountability' aspect of the concept of responsibility – which is closely allied to the idea that moral responsibility amounts to the appropriateness of adopting reactive attitudes towards the agent in question (§2.4) – and the 'self-disclosure' aspect, which is tied to the idea that the agent's action is 'attributable' to the agent: it is, as Fischer puts it, '"really an agent's" or "the agent's own" in some appropriate sense' (1999b, 96). The diagnostic potential of Watson's view can be seen when we consider cases such as Carly, our born-and-bred car thief from Chapter 1. We might try to explain our ambivalence in the face of the question of whether Carly is morally responsible for stealing your car by holding that she satisfies the attributability condition – her action really is her *own* action – while denying that she is really *accountable* for it, in the sense of being blameworthy. (This, of course, is debatable. Plenty of compatibilists will hold that Carly is straightforwardly blameworthy for stealing your car.) See Eshleman 2009; Fischer 1999b, §I for more on the idea that 'moral responsibility' is not a unitary concept.

A fourth approach to the question would be simply to abandon the project of attempting to argue about what 'our' concept of moral responsibility is or ought to be, or whether it is ambiguous. Instead, we can grant that there are different senses of 'morally responsible' – indeed, different senses of 'free' – at work in the philosophical literature. And we can ask which *kinds* of moral responsibility (or freedom), variously defined, are the kinds of moral responsibility (or freedom) that (a) we are likely to *actually* have, and (b) we would ideally *like* to have – where our answers to (a) and (b) may well be different. Imagine, for example, that our answer to (a) is: We lack libertarian free will but typically possess the kind of moral responsibility delivered by satisfaction of the standard compatibilist conditions on acting freely. Would that be a *problem*? If things were to turn out that way, what exactly would we be missing out on, and would it be such a great loss?

Take, for example, Pereboom's 'hard incompatibilist' position (§5.8). Pereboom thinks that beings like us lack free will and moral responsibility, and hence are never praiseworthy or blameworthy for anything; nonetheless, *contra* P. F. Strawson, our lives have meaning, and many of the reactive attitudes are still at least partially appropriate. If we think of Pereboom as articulating one *kind* of moral responsibility – the kind that corresponds to the meaning of 'moral responsibility' as *he* uses that expression, and a kind that we don't have – we can sensibly ask what it is that we're missing out on, and whether we've lost anything that we really care about (or ought to care about).

On this way of seeing the matter, we can't answer the question 'What are we missing out on?' just by saying, 'Of course we're missing out on something if Pereboom is right: we're living in a world in which nobody is praiseworthy or blameworthy for anything! That's surely not the kind of world we'd ideally want to live in'. And we can't do that, because if Pereboom means something different by 'moral responsibility' than, say, Dennett does, then he must also mean something different by 'praiseworthy' and 'blameworthy'. (After all, you're praiseworthy for something just if you're morally responsible for doing something good, and blameworthy if you're morally responsible for doing something bad.) So, the question is whether we would be missing out on anything worth caring about if nobody were praiseworthy or blameworthy *in Pereboom's sense*, and not whether we would be missing out on anything worth caring about if nobody were praiseworthy or blameworthy *in (say) Dennett's sense*.

I think most compatibilists would simply deny that a world in which we have Pereboom's kind of morally responsibility would really be any better, in any respect we really have any reason to care about, to the world we actually live in. It just wouldn't make any important *difference* to us if we were agent-causes of our actions of a kind that is required for free will and moral responsibility in Pereboom's sense of those terms. At any rate, that's the view I'm inclined to take of the matter.

7.6 Conclusion

If you've managed to get this far, you now really know quite a lot about the contemporary debate about free will. More importantly, I hope you are now armed with the resources to decide – provisionally, of course! – what *you* think. Is free will compatible with determinism, and, if not, which kind of incompatibilist view is right? More importantly – or so I think – is it plausible to think that *we* actual human beings routinely act freely? And, if not, what consequences does that have for our responses to, and relationships with, other people, and for our conception of ourselves? My own (again, provisional) general view is, I think, clear enough; but, of course, you most certainly should not take my word for anything. One of the great joys of philosophy is that you don't have to take *anybody's* word for anything. Of course, that also poses a major challenge: When so much is up for dispute, it's hard to know where to start. Overall, however, I think it's more of a blessing than a curse. I hope you agree.

Bibliography

Alvarez, M. 2009. 'Actions, Thought-experiments and the Principle of Alternate Possibilities', *Australasian Journal of Philosophy*, 87: 61–81.

Armstrong, D.M. 1980. *Nominalism and Realism, vol. I: Universals and Scientific Realism*. Cambridge: Cambridge University Press.

—— 1983. *What is a Law of Nature?* Cambridge: Cambridge University Press.

Aune, B. 1967. 'Hypotheticals and "Can": Another Look', *Analysis*, 27: 191–5.

Balaguer, M. 2010. *Free Will as an Open Scientific Problem*. Cambridge, MA: MIT Press.

Beebee, H. 2000. 'The Non-Governing Conception of Laws of Nature', *Philosophy and Phenomenological Research*, 56: 571–94. Reprinted in J.W. Carroll (ed.), *Readings in Laws of Nature* (Pittsburgh: Pittsburgh University Press, 2004).

—— 2003. 'Local Miracle Compatibilism', *Noûs*, 37: 258–77.

—— 2008. 'Smilansky's Alleged Refutation of Compatibilism', *Analysis*, 68: 258–60.

—— and A.R. Mele. 2002. 'Humean Compatiblism', *Mind*, 111: 201–23.

Berofsky, B. 1987. *Freedom From Necessity*. London: Routledge & Kegan Paul.

Bird, A. 2008. 'The Epistemological Argument against Lewis's Regularity View of Laws, *Philosophical Studies*, 138: 73–89.

Bok, H. 1998. *Freedom and Responsibility*. Princeton: Princeton University Press.

Clarke, R. 1993. 'Toward a Credible Agent-Causal Account of Free Will', *Noûs*, 27: 191–203.

—— 1996. 'Agent Causation and Event Causation in the Production of Free Action', *Philosophical Topics*, 24: 19–48.

Demetriou, K. 2010. 'The Soft-Line Solution to Pereboom's Four-Case Argument', *Australasian Journal of Philosophy*, 88: 595–617.

Dennett, D. 1973. 'Mechanism and Responsibility', in T. Honderich (ed.), *Essays on Freedom of Action*, London: Routledge & Kegan Paul. Reprinted in Watson 1983.

—— 1984. *Elbow Room*. Cambridge, MA: Bradford Books.

Descartes, R. 1641. *Meditations on First Philosophy,* in J. Cottingham, R. Stoothoff and D. Murdoch (trans.), *Descartes: Selected Philosophical Writings*. Cambridge: Cambridge University Press, 1988.

Di Nucci, E. 2011. 'Frankfurt Counterexample Defended', *Analysis*, 71: 102–4.

Ekstrom, L. 2002. 'Libertarianism and Frankfurt-style Cases', in Kane 2002, 309–22.

Eshleman, A. 2009. 'Moral Responsibility', in E. N. Zalta (ed.), *The Stanford Encyclopedia of Philosophy (Winter 2009 Edition)*, http://plato.stanford.edu/archives/win2009/entries/moral-responsibility/.

Fara, M. 2008. 'Masked Abilities and Compatibilism, *Mind*, 117: 843–65.

Fischer, J.M. 1994. *The Metaphysics of Free Will*. Malden, MA: Blackwell.

—— 1999. 'Responsibility and Self-expression', *The Journal of Ethics*, 3: 277–97. Reprinted in Fischer 2006b.

—— 1999a. 'Recent Work on Moral Responsibility', *Ethics,* 110: 93–139.

—— 2006a. 'Responsibility and Alternative Possibilities', in Widerker and McKenna 2006, 27–52.

—— 2006b. *My Way: Essays on Moral Responsibility.* New York: Oxford University Press.

—— 2011. 'The Zygote Argument Remixed', *Analysis,* 71: 267–72.

—— 2012. 'Responsibility and Autonomy: The Problem of Mission Creep', *Philosophical Issues,* 22: 165–84.

—— and M. Ravizza. 1998. *Responsibility and Control.* Cambridge: Cambridge University Press.

Foster, J. 2004. *The Divine Lawmaker: Lectures on Induction, Laws of Nature, and the Existence of God.* Oxford: Oxford University Press.

Frankfurt, H. 1969. 'Alternate Possibilities and Moral Responsibility', *The Journal of Philosophy,* 66: 829–39.

—— 1971. 'Freedom of the Will and the Concept of a Person', *The Journal of Philosophy,* 68: 5–20.

—— 1988. 'Identification and Wholeheartedness', in his *The Importance of What We Care About,* Cambridge: Cambridge University Press.

—— 1999. 'Responses', *The Journal of Ethics,* 3: 367–72.

—— 2002. 'Reply to John Martin Fischer', in S. Buss and L. Overton (eds), *Contours of Agency: Essays on Themes from Harry Frankfurt.* Cambridge, MA: MIT Press.

—— 2006. 'Some Thoughts Concerning PAP', in Widerker and McKenna 2006, 339–45.

Ginet, C. 1962. 'Can the Will be Caused?', *The Philosophical Review,* 71: 49–55.

Graham, P.A. 2008. 'A Defense of Local Miracle Compatibilism', *Philosophical Studies,* 140: 65–82.

Haji, I. and M. McKenna. 2004. 'Dialectical Delicacies in the Debate about Freedom and Alternative Possibilities', *The Journal of Philosophy,* 101: 299–314.

Hume, D. 1748. *An Enquiry Concerning Human Understanding,* ed. T.L. Beauchamp. New York: Oxford University Press, 2000.

Kane, R. 1999. 'Responsibility, Luck, and Chance: Reflections on Free Will and Indeterminism', *The Journal of Philosophy,* 96: 217–40.

—— (ed.) 2002. *The Oxford Handbook of Free Will.* New York: Oxford University Press.

—— 2006. 'Responsibility, Indeterminism and Frankfurt-style Cases: Reply to Mele and Robb', in Widerker and McKenna 2006, 91–106.

Kapitan, T. 1984. 'Can God Make Up His Mind?', *International Journal for Philosophy of Religion,* 15: 37–47.

—— 2000. 'Autonomy and Manipulation', *Philosophical Perspectives,* 14: 81–104.

Kearns, S. 2012. 'Aborting the Zygote Argument', *Philosophical Studies,* 160: 379–89.

La Croix, R. 1976. 'Omniprescience and Divine Determinism', *Religious Studies,* 12: 365–81.

Larvor, B. 2010. 'Frankfurt Counter-example Defused', *Analysis,* 70: 506–8.

Lehrer, K. 1968. 'Cans without Ifs', *Analysis,* 29: 29–32.

Lewis, D.K. 1973. *Counterfactuals.* Cambridge, MA: Harvard University Press.

—— 1979. 'Counterfactual Dependence and Time's Arrow', *Noûs,* 13: 455–76. (Reprinted in his 1986a.)

—— 1981. 'Are We Free to Break the Laws?' *Theoria,* 47: 113–21. (Reprinted in his 1986a.)

____ 1986a. *Philosophical Papers*, vol. II. New York: Oxford University Press.

____ 1986b. 'Postscripts to "A Subjectivist's Guide to Objective Chance"' in his 1986a, 114–32.

____ 1986c. *On the Plurality of Worlds*. Malden, MA: Blackwell.

Libet, B. 1999. 'Do We Have Free Will?' *Journal of Consciousness Studies*, 6: 47–57.

Locke, J. 1690. *An Essay Concerning Human Understanding*. Penn State Electronic Classics Series. http://www2.hn.psu.edu/faculty/jmanis/locke/humanund.pdf

Markosian, N. 1999. 'A Compatibilist Version of the Theory of Agent Causation', *Pacific Philosophical Quarterly*, 80: 257–77.

McKenna, M. 2006. 'Robustness, Control, and the Demand for Morally Significant Alternatives: Frankfurt Examples with Oodles and Oodles of Alternatives', in Widerker and McKenna, 201–17.

____ 2008. 'A Hard-Line Reply to Pereboom's Four-Case Manipulation Argument', *Philosophy and Phenomenological Research*, 77: 142–59.

____ 2009. 'Compatibilism', in E.N. Zalta (ed.), *The Stanford Encyclopedia of Philosophy* (Winter 2009 Edition), http://plato.stanford.edu/archives/win2009/entries/compatibilism.

Mele, A.R. 1995. *Autonomous Agents*. Oxford: Oxford University Press.

____ 2005. 'A Critique of Pereboom's "Four-Case Argument" for Incompatibilism', *Analysis*, 65: 75–80.

____ 2006. *Free Will and Luck*. New York: Oxford University Press.

____ 2008a. 'Manipulation, Compatibilism, and Moral Responsibility', *Journal of Ethics*, 12: 263–86.

____ 2008b. 'Free Will and Science', *American Philosophical Quarterly*, 45: 107–30.

____ 2009. *Effective Intentions: The Power of Conscious Will*. New York: Oxford University Press.

____ and D. Robb. 1998. 'Rescuing Frankfurt-style Cases', *The Philosophical Review*, 107: 97–112.

Mill, J.S. 1875. *A System of Logic*. London: Longmans.

Moore, G.E. 1912. *Ethics*, ed. W. H. Shaw. Oxford: Oxford University Press, 2005.

Nahmias, E., S. Morris, T. Nadelhoffer and J. Turner. 2004. 'The Phenomenology of Free Will', *Journal of Consciousness Studies*, 11: 162–79.

Nichols, S. and J. Knobe. 2007. 'Moral Responsibility and Determinism: The Cognitive Science of Folk Intuitions', *Noûs*, 41: 663–85.

Nozick, R. 1981. *Philosophical Explanations*. Cambridge, MA: Harvard University Press.

Oakley, S. 2006. 'Defending Local Miracle Compatibilism', *Philosophical Studies*, 130: 337–49.

O'Connor, T. 1995. 'Agent Causation', in T. O'Connor (ed.), *Agents, Causes, and Events*. New York: Oxford University Press.

____ 1996. 'Why Agent Causation?', *Philosophical Topics*, 24: 143–58.

____ 2002. 'Agent-Causal Theories of Freedom', in Kane 2002, 317–28.

Otsuka, M. 1998. 'Incompatibilism and the Avoidability of Blame', *Ethics*, 108: 685–701.

Paul, L.A. 2010. 'A New Role for Experimental Work in Metaphysics', *Review of Philosophy and Psychology*, 1: 461–76.

Pereboom, D. 2001. *Living Without Free Will*. Cambridge: Cambridge University Press.

—— 2002. 'Living Without Free Will: The Case for Hard Incompatibilism', in Kane 2002, 477–88.

—— 2006. 'Source Incompatibilism and Alternative Possibilities', in Widerker and McKenna 2006, 185–99.

Plantinga, A. 1986. 'On Ockham's Way Out', *Faith and Philosophy*, 3: 235–69.

Ramsey, F.P. 1978. 'Universals of Law and Fact' in his *Foundations*, ed. D.H. Mellor. London: Routledge & Kegan Paul, 128–32.

Reid, T. 1788. *Essays on the Active Powers of Man*, ed. K. Haakonssen and J. Harris. Edinburgh: Edinburgh University Press, 2010.

Rhoda, A.R., G.A. Boyd and T.G. Belt. 2006. 'Open Theism, Omniscience, and the Nature of the Future', *Faith and Philosophy*, 23: 432–59.

Searle, J. 1984. *Minds, Brains, and Science*. Cambridge, MA: Harvard University Press.

Smilansky, S. 2007. 'Determinism and Prepunishment: The Radical Nature of Compatibilism', *Analysis*, 67: 347–49.

Smith, M. 1997. 'A Theory of Freedom and Responsibility', in G. Cullity and B. Gaut, (eds), *Ethics and Practical Reason*. Oxford: Clarendon Press.

Sorensen, R. 1984. 'Uncaused Decisions and Pre-Decisional Blindspots', *Philosophical Studies*, 45: 51–6.

Sosa, E. 2007. 'Experimental Philosophy and Philosophical Intuition', *Philosophical Studies*, 132: 99–107.

Steward, H. 2012. *A Metaphysics for Freedom*. Oxford: Oxford University Press.

Strawson, G. 1994. 'The Impossibility of Moral Responsibility', *Philosophical Studies*, 75: 5–24.

Strawson, P.F. 1962. 'Freedom and Resentment', *Proceedings of the British Academy*, 48: 1–25. Reprinted in Watson 1983 (page references are to Watson).

van Inwagen, P. 1975. 'The Incompatibility of Free Will and Determinism', *Philosophical Studies*, 27: 185–99. (Reprinted in Watson 1983.)

Vargas, M. 'The Revisionist's Guide to Responsibility', *Philosophical Studies*, 125: 399–429.

Watson, G. 1975. 'Free Agency', *The Journal of Philosophy*, 72: 205–20. Reprinted in Watson (ed.) 1983.

—— (ed.) 1983. *Free Will*. New York: Oxford University Press.

—— 1996. 'Two Faces of Responsibility', *Philosophical Topics*, 24: 227–48.

Widerker, D. 2006. 'Blameworthiness and Frankfurt's Argument against the Principle of Alternate Possibilities', in Widerker and McKenna 2006, 53–73.

—— and M. McKenna (eds). 2006. *Moral Responsibility and Alternative Possibilities*. Aldershot: Ashgate.

Wilson, G. and S. Shpall. 2012. 'Action', in E. N. Zalta (ed.), *The Stanford Encyclopedia of Philosophy (Summer 2012 Edition)*, http://plato.stanford.edu/archives/sum2012/entries/action/.

Wolf, S. 1980. 'Asymmetrical Freedom', *The Journal of Philosophy*, 77: 151–66.

Wyma, K.D. 1997. 'Moral Responsibility and Leeway for Action', *American Philosophical Quarterly*, 34: 57–70.

Zagzebski, L.T. 2002. 'Recent Work on Divine Foreknowledge and Free Will', in Kane 2002, 45–64.

Index

Printed and bound by CPI Group (UK) Ltd, Croydon, CR0 4YY